# Steinway

From Glory to Controversy

The Family, the Business, The Piano

# Steinway

From Glory to Controversy

The Family, The Business,
The Piano

by
Susan Goldenberg

Mosaic Press
Oakville, ON. - Buffalo, N.Y.

**Canadian Cataloguing in Publication Data**

Goldenberg, Susan, 1944-
 Steinway from glory to controversy : the family, the business, the piano

Includes bibliographical references and index.
ISBN 0-88962-607-3

1. Steinway family.   2. Steinway & Sons - History.
3. Piano makers - New York (State) - New York - History.
4. Piano - History.   I. Title.

ML424.S76G65   1996            786.2'197471            C96-930829-9

No part of this book may be reproduced or transmitted in any form, by any means, electronic or mechanical, including photocopying and recording information storage and retrieval systems, without permission in writing from the publisher, except by a reviewer who may quote brief passages in a review.

Published by MOSAIC PRESS, P.O. Box 1032, Oakville, Ontario, L6J 5E9, Canada. Offices and warehouse at 1252 Speers Road, Units #1&2, Oakville, Ontario, L6L 5N9, Canada and Mosaic Press, 85 River Rock Drive, Suite 202, Buffalo, N.Y., 14207, USA.

Mosaic Press acknowledges the assistance of the Canada Council, the Ontario Arts Council, the Ontario Ministry of Culture, Tourism and Recreation and the Dept. of Canadian Heritage, Government of Canada, for their support of our publishing programme.

Copyright © Susan Goldenberg, 1996

Lyric excerpts of "I Love A Piano" by Irving Berlin
    © Copyright 1915 by Irving Berlin
    © Copyright Renewed. International Copyright Secured
    Used by Permission. All Rights Reserved

Cover and book design by Susan Parker
Printed and bound in Canada
ISBN   0-88962-607-3

**In Canada:**
MOSAIC PRESS, 1252 Speers Road, Units #1&2, Oakville, Ontario, L6L 5N9, Canada. P.O. Box 1032, Oakville, Ontario, L6J 5E9
**In the United States:**
MOSAIC PRESS, 85 River Rock Drive, Suite 202, Buffalo, N.Y., 14207
**In the UK and Western Europe:**
DRAKE INTERNATIONAL SERVICES, Market House, Market Place, Deddington, Oxford. OX15 OSF

*Other Books by the Author*

Troubled Skies: Crisis, Competition & Control in Canada's Airline Industry

Global Pursuit: Canadian Business Strategies for Winning in the Borderless World

Hands Across The Ocean: Managing Joint Ventures (With a spotlight on China and Japan)

Trading: Inside the World's Leading Stock Exchanges

The Thomson Empire

Canadian Pacific: A Portrait of Power

Men of Property: The Canadian Developers Who Are Buying America

*Dedication*

To My Parents

# Contents

| | |
|---|---|
| Acknowledgments | viii |
| Family Tree | ix |
| Prelude | x |
| Chapter I<br>Henry Engelhard and Sons | 15 |
| Chapter II<br>William | 35 |
| Chapter III<br>William: The Last Twenty Years | 49 |
| Chapter IV<br>The Nephews | 77 |
| Chapter V<br>Theodore Edwin: The Early Years | 93 |
| Chapter VI<br>Theodore Edwin: The Later Years | 119 |
| Chapter VII<br>Henry | 135 |
| Chapter VIII<br>The CBS Years | 155 |
| Chapter IX<br>The Owners After CBS | 191 |
| Bibliography | 223 |
| Endnotes | 229 |
| Index | 243 |

## Acknowledgments

The book primarily is based on interviews I did and, to some extent, on what archives there are on the Steinway family and firm plus others on historical related events. The interviews were done across the United States as well as in England, Germany (including a visit to the birthplace of the founder), Japan, and Canada. They were with: the Steinway family; family friends; succeeding purchasers; management and factory workers; executives appointed during the CBS ownership period; retired employees; piano dealers; tuners; performers; celebrity owners; competitive manufacturers; symphony and concert hall directors; record producers; nightclub operators; schools of music; and advertising agencies. I am exceedingly grateful for the interviews and wish to express my deep appreciation for them.

S.G.

# THE STEINWAYS
(This table includes only those members mentioned in the history)

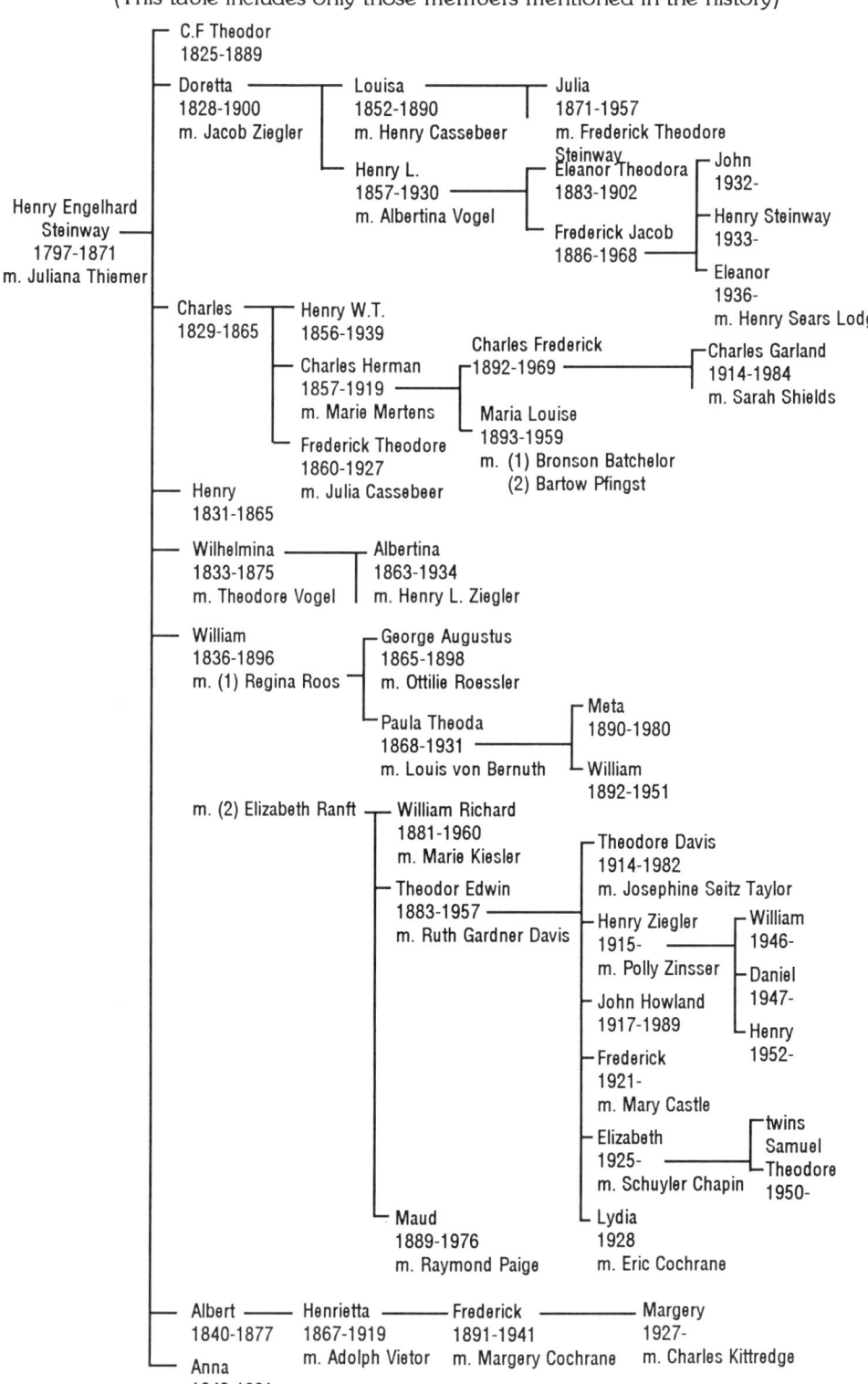

# *Prelude*

Few names have been so revered by the public for excellence, glamour, and social status as the Steinway piano. But Steinway & Sons, established in 1853, no longer is a god on a pedestal. It has slipped from glory to controversy over the quality of its piano, as it increasingly relies on mechanization rather than hand craftsmanship as in the past. Some well-known performers in its roster of "Steinway artists" publicly criticized its pianos. One - André Watts - went so far as to switch to the Yamaha concert piano, but recently resumed playing Steinways, although not as a "Steinway artist" - an endorser of the piano.

There also has been considerable controversy over three changes in ownership over the past two decades after more than a century of family ownership. The third change occurred in 1995. Since 1972, when the family - in a move that some members bitterly opposed - sold the business, Steinway has been owned by people with no background in pianomaking. Furthermore, since 1987, the heads of its United States factory have lacked experience in pianomaking.

Broadcasting giant CBS owned Steinway from 1972 to 1985 when it sold it to Boston brothers Jack Birmingham, a trial lawyer, and Robert, a former mail-order marketer. In turn, they sold it in April 1995 to the Selmer Company of Elkhart, Indiana, a major manufacturer of brass, woodwind, stringed, and percussion instruments, established in 1900. President Bill Clinton owns one of its saxophones.[1]

Since 1993, Selmer's voting stock has been controlled by Kyle Kirkland and Dana Messina, two California-based entrepreneurs who were only thirty-one at the time of purchase. They also have investments in a food, a textile, a paper, and a beer company.

Even though fewer than three percent of the pianos sold in the United States are Steinways, and Steinway has under 1 percent of the worldwide market,[2] the company wields an influence vastly disproportionate to its size. It remains an historical icon because it created the modern piano and because many renowned people have played its pianos. Franz Liszt, Richard Wagner, Sergei Rachmaninoff, Ignacy Paderewski, Josef Hofmann, Anton Rubinstein, Artur Rubinstein, Vladimir Horowitz, and Myra Hess were "Steinway artists." Ninety percent of today's concert artists insist on playing a Steinway on stage and in recordings.[3]

In addition, although its revenue of around $100 million is only one-sixth that of the U.S. piano industry leader, Yamaha Corporation of America, Steinway & Sons accounts for half the profitability in the industry, according to Dana Messina, one of the current controlling shareholders.[4] "Nothing competes against Steinway in its class of piano," he maintains. "In dollar volume, Yamaha sells more, but for every dollar Yamaha makes in revenue, it makes less profit." However, that is only a partial explanation: the differential also is due to Steinway pianos costing considerably more than competitors'.

Although the controversy swirling around Steinway became acute in recent years, it actually began to slip from glory around the time of its centennial in 1953. From the 1950s through the early 1970s, when the Steinways still owned and ran the business, there was controversy over poor factory organization, order backlogs, and the family's unwillingness to spend on the upgrading of its Long Island, New York, and Hamburg, Germany plants. Instead, the family wanted the money mainly for itself in the form of dividends.

From 1972 until 1985, when CBS owned Steinway, there was continued controversy about the inefficient layout of the Long Island factory (each stage of production tended to be distant from the next) and about the poor construction and appearance of the pianos. Although CBS invested substantially to improve the factories and pianos, the thirteen years it owned Steinway were marred by management acrimony. During those turbulent years, there were four presidents; in the company's previous 119 years, there were only six.

After CBS sold Steinway in 1985 to the Birminghams, the controversy intensified. Whereas the presidents installed by CBS all had backgrounds in piano manufacturing, the Birminghams had no experience in the music industry. Moreover, the management turmoil continued as the Birminghams replaced the last CBS-appointed president, a highly respected piano manufacturing veteran, plus the Long Island factory manager who had worked at Steinway for more than twenty years. Like the Birminghams, the new president and factory manager they appointed had no background in pianomaking. Also, during their ten-year ownership, three concert and artist managers - the liaison with performers - departed. By contrast, in the preceding fifty years, there were only two C and A manager changeovers.

But most significantly, the controversy over the quality of the pianos deepened, arising largely from the Birminghams' introduction of increased mechanization. They maintained these changes made production more consistent, but critics countered that the result was a severe decline in quality. Selmer is continuing the Birminghams' manufacturing methods.

The changes undermined the more than a century Steinway had spent carving out a special niche for itself as an almost sacred place of master craftsmen steeped in the heritage and love of pianomaking. Experienced as the newcomers are in manufacturing and engineering, the question is whether today's high-tech, coldly mathematical manufacturing methods are suitable for a company that prided itself on its emphasis on instilling the best of the human soul in pianomaking.

Additionally, the Birminghams departed dramatically from Steinway & Sons' credo never to sully the company's illustrious name by also making cheaper pianos. In January 1992, Steinway dealers started carrying the *Boston* line of inexpensive upright and grand pianos designed by Steinway engineers, but made by Kawai, a Japanese manufacturer of mid-priced pianos. Ironically, in 1987, the Birminghams had terminated a major dealer, a former Steinway executive, for also promoting the concert and artist program of Yamaha, Japan's largest piano manufacturer, whose pianos he carried as well as Steinways. Other manufacturers do not insist on exclusivity regarding concert and artist activities. The dealer sued Steinway on anti-trust grounds, but lost. The climate was ripe for Steinway's victory in view of increasing anti-Japanese economic sentiment.

The escalating controversy about Steinway & Sons is a sad departure from the glory long associated with the Steinway name. Due to the firm's outpouring of inventions, primarily between 1859 and 1875, no longer did people think the only good piano was an imported one from Europe. Instead, thanks to Steinway, the United States became the world's piano capital and American firms exported to Europe. Steinway & Sons was in the lead with 70 percent of foreign orders.

Steinway also was the first major U.S. pianomaker to form a manufacturing subsidiary in Europe as well as to open retail stores there. The factory, located in Hamburg, began operations in 1880, shortly after the company solidified its position as the largest of the seventy U.S. piano manufacturers, forty-five of which had sprung up since Steinway's establishment. The first overseas store - in London - was opened in 1875, five years before the Hamburg factory. A Hamburg outlet was added in 1904 and one in Berlin in 1909.

Besides virtually reinventing the piano, Steinway & Sons introduced to America the European practice of presenting milestone pianos to famous people, correctly reasoning that Mr. and Mrs. Average Public would want to own the same brand of piano as the rich and well known. The first recipient was Czar Alexander of Russia, to whom the 25,000th Steinway was shipped in 1872.

At one time or another, the rulers of England, Russia, Spain, Germany, Sweden, Norway, Belgium, Italy, Portugal, Persia, and Turkey owned a Steinway. The main piano at the White House is a Steinway. Eleanor Roosevelt had one of George Gershwin's Steinways at her New York City residence; it was given to her by Gershwin's mother after his death.[5]

At the other end of the spectrum, the Playboy Clubs during their heyday owned close to forty Steinways. The club's custom was for its bunnies to lay down their trays at 1:00 a.m., take off their high heel shoes, and climb onto the piano lid, which was reinforced with steel braces, to perform the Twist. Next, female guests were invited to join them; this practice was discontinued after a drunken woman refused to remove her spike heels, ruining the top of a piano.[6]

Steinway also was the first pianomaker to advertise regularly. The advertisements served to convince the American public that the piano was the best way to demonstrate social standing, woo a young lady, add polish to children's education, and provide home entertainment during an age when movies, radio, and television did not yet exist. Soon American novelists had their social-climbing or sweet young heroines play the piano just as Thackeray's Becky Sharp did in *Vanity Fair* and Dickens's Agnes Wickfield in *David Copperfield.*

Further, Steinway & Sons is unique among the world's pianomakers in its establishment of a company town. Located in New York on Long Island, the four hundred-acre community, called Steinway Village, was developed in the 1870s and had a population of seven thousand by 1890. It contained a satellite factory to the company's then main plant in Manhattan plus housing, a school, churches, library, park, post office, and streetcar line.

Today Steinway Village has been absorbed into Long Island City, but vestiges of the Steinway influence remain in addition to the factory, which became, and remains today, the company's principal location. Thirty-ninth Street also is known as Steinway Street. The library continues to bear the Steinway name and unrelated businesses, such as the Steinway Deli and Steinway Auto Parts, have borrowed it. Many of the original workers' houses still line the streets near the factory.

For many years, the Steinways owned America's premier concert and lecture hall. It, too, bore the family's name. The imposing $250,000, four-story, white marble Steinway Hall was erected in 1866 just thirteen years after Steinway & Sons was founded. Located at 109 East Fourteenth Street, it was conveniently near the Fifth Avenue Renaissance palazzi and French châteaux of the Astors, Vanderbilts, and other wealthy families who patronized the arts. Steinway Hall reigned supreme in the music world for a quarter century until the more lavish Carnegie Hall eclipsed it.

The Steinways did not confine themselves to building pianos. For years they scouted Europe for young virtuoso pianists for whom they arranged concert tours throughout the United States - and provided the Steinways on which they played. Thanks to the Steinways, Americans were introduced to such geniuses as Anton Rubinstein and Ignacy Paderewski when both were near the threshold of their fame.

Steinway is also distinctive in its longevity as a family business. Surveys have reported that only 30 percent of family businesses last for two generations and just half of these remain in the family's hands into the third or fourth generations. Steinway & Sons belongs to this special group. For four generations it was owned and managed by the Steinways. The president, main plant manager, and head of advertising were always members of the family.

There are still many Steinways but only one remains at the business. Henry Steinway was head of the company from 1957 to 1977 and now, eighty-one years old, [as of 1996] serves as a "consultant." After Henry, it will be Steinway & Sons in name only.

# Chapter I
# *Henry Engelhard and Sons*

It all began with a German peasant's illiterate son who did not learn how to differentiate piano notes until he was in his early twenties.

The contrast between the mild appearance and indomitable temperament of Steinway & Sons' founder, Henry Engelhard Steinway (the anglicized version of the German Heinrich Engelhard Steinweg) was striking. Outwardly, the very short Henry was unprepossessing save for his dark bushy moustache, heavy sideburns, and thick eyebrows. Only the firm set of his mouth indicated his determination to attain his lifelong ambition to be pianomaker to the world. This resoluteness led him to give up his prosperous existence in Germany for the slums of New York because like many other Europeans, he was convinced the United States offered greater opportunities.

Born February 15, 1797, in the tiny village of Wolfshagen in the Harz Mountains in central Germany, Henry was the youngest of twelve children. He had a hard childhood. While his father, Heinrich Zacharias, was away much of the time, fighting in the lengthy Napoleonic wars, his mother died. The children fended for themselves by catching fish in the nearby mountain streams and by growing vegetables in a small garden beside their log and stone cottage. It is speculated that the family took its surname, Steinweg, which means *stone way* in English, from the stony path that led up to their home.

Henry was left entirely on his own when his father, who had returned from the wars along with those of his brothers who had survived the battlefield, was fatally struck by lightning during a storm. Homeless and penniless, seventeen-year-old Henry enlisted in the Prussian Army at the time its elderly field marshall, von Blücher, was marching to join the Duke of Wellington for the decisive 1815 battle of Waterloo against Napoleon.

While in the army, Henry entertained his fellow soldiers by strumming a zither, a simple stringed instrument. After his three years' service was over, Henry decided to wed his interest in music with that of cabinetmaking, a popular profession in the Harz Mountains, to which he returned. His goal was to make pianos, which had been invented more than a century earlier, in 1709, by Bartolommeo Cristofori, an Italian, who took care of Prince Ferdinand de Medici's forty harpsichords. Cristofori called his invention *gravicembalo col piano e forte* - harpsichord with soft and loud. In colloquial use, the phrase was shortened to *piano*. The piano quickly gained popularity because it provided a far greater range of dynamic expression than the stringed instruments in favor in the sixteenth and seventeenth centuries, the clavichord and the harpsichord.

With the harpsichord, the strings were plucked by a quill, and the same volume was emitted regardless of how strongly the keys were struck. In the case of the clavichord, the volume could be modulated but unfortunately the sound was almost inaudible. The problem stemmed from the way the instrument was constructed: The *tangent*, a small metal blade embedded in the back of each string, served to both strike and stop the string. Thus, when the clavichordist removed his or her finger from the key, the tone would disappear. Both instruments were easily drowned out by conversation.

Cristofori's aim was to produce an instrument capable of a wide range of responses from soft to loud depending on the force with which it was played. His solution was the development of a keyboard instrument that sounded by means of strings struck by hammers. So that a hammer would not either jam or bounce back and muffle the tone, Cristofori installed an *escapement* mechanism that brought it close to a string, yet enabled it to fall back even if the key was still held down. This permitted *repetition*, the restriking of a note before the key returned to its original position.

By the time Henry Engelhard Steinway became interested in pianomaking, the reputation for excellence had switched to Germany from Italy. In the mid-nineteenth century, German pianomakers were so well regarded that the French and the English sought their help in making the instrument.

But according to the trade guild rules of the day in Germany, becoming a pianomaker involved a tedious process of five years as an apprentice followed by another five as a journeyman before he could set up shop on his own. Henry, seeing no need for such a drawnout process, searched for a way to get started more quickly.

First he went to Goslar, a charming village in the Harz Mountains that had retained its medieval appearance. Located near silver mines,

Goslar was a wealthy community. To his dismay, Henry discovered it was impossible for him to take advantage of Goslar's good fortune because the trade guild restrictions were entrenched there.

Consequently, Henry moved eleven miles west to Seesen where he had heard a cabinetmaker and an organ-builder were willing to teach without a formal indenture. Seesen was an astute second choice. Founded in the year 974 by one of the many German emperors who hailed from that region, it was home to many well-to-do merchants and farmers who could afford pianos. Moreover, Henry had the field to himself as there were no other pianomakers in the region.

The only problem in Seesen was the multitude of fires. Their frequency aroused the suspicion that they were set deliberately whenever the residents felt their homes were too small or dilapidated.

This rumor was given credence by the fact that the townspeople were allowed by the Duke of Braunschweig (Brunswick), the duchy in which Seesen was located, to cut timber in his forests. According to Seesen folklore, once when the town was yet again on fire, a resident shouted, "Oh no, we didn't want it to turn out so badly!" Finally, to prevent such blazes from destroying the whole town, the duke ordered wide spaces to be left between the rows of houses so as to impede flames from leaping row to row.[1]

It was in Seesen that the illiterate Henry was taught how to play the piano by the son of the local cantor, who pasted the notes on the keyboard as an aid.[2] Henry apparently never did learn to write. Any document that required a signature bore only an $X$ and not his name.[3]

Word quickly spread about Henry's skill and his *meisterstück* (masterpiece), an inlaid writing desk with numerous secret compartments, was purchased by Seesen's chief justice. In 1815, on completion of his seven years of training, Henry married Juliana Thiemer, the daughter of Seesen's apothecary. As a wedding gift, he made her his first piano, dubbed the *kitchen piano* by his descendants because he converted the washing area of their kitchen into a workshop where he constructed the instrument.

Soon the house was too small as Henry and Juliana had a large family of eight children and his piano business prospered rapidly. The children were: Christian Friedrich Theodor (born 1825), Doretta (1828), Karl (1829), Heinrich Junior (1831), Wilhelmina (1833), Wilhelm (1836), Albrect (1840), and Anna (1842). Later, Henry anglicized the four younger sons' names to Charles, Henry, William and Albert. Henry bought a two-story house in the center of Seesen and built onto it a large, two-winged factory at the back.

In 1839 Henry won his first gold medal for pianomaking at a contest in Braunschweig at which Theodor demonstrated the instrument. The victory made Henry's already successful business thrive even more and he was eager to expand further.

Once again, his ambitions collided with the bureaucracy, in this instance the prohibitively high territorial tariffs that effectively cut off trade between duchies. As early as 1845, he considered emigrating to America. The idea became more attractive during the 1848 revolutions that engulfed Europe. Henry's second oldest son, Charles, then nineteen and the radical of the family, was an outspoken sympathizer of the cause in Germany for greater democracy through the institution of free elections and open parliamentary debate.

Worried about the economic stranglehold and also about what would befall Charles in the aftermath of the revolutions' collapse, Henry dispatched him to the United States to scout opportunities. Charles became part of the "Forty-Eighters," the thousands of disappointed German liberals who fled across the ocean following the failure of their crusade. They were a gifted group, skilled in science, medicine, silversmithing, engraving and music.

On his arrival in New York, Charles had the good fortune to be hired by Bacon and Raven, the city's largest pianomaker. He sent home glowing reports about how democracy was thriving in America. "Its progressive spirit, its restless striving after improvement and its free institutions recognize the individuality of every man and enable him to make his mark as well as imbue him with that irresistible desire to go ahead and come out first in the race for improvement," he wrote.

Convinced that he would fare even better in the United States, Henry sold his home and, in May 1850, booked passage for himself and his family for the maiden voyage from Hamburg of the steamliner *Helena Sloman*, one of the largest boats of its day. Only the eldest son, Theodor, then twenty-five, remained behind. Luck was with the Steinways in their choice of sailing date: six months later, on the boat's third crossing to New York, it was wrecked by a violent gale. Most of the people aboard were rescued by a nearby ship but ten were swept to their deaths.[4] The Steinways' journey was at an auspicious time both for music and the United States. The nineteenth century was the most outstanding epoch in classical music. In the first half of the century, there were Mendelssohn, Chopin, Schumann, Berlioz, Mussorgsky, Wagner, Liszt, Franck, and Johann Strauss. They were succeeded by Dvořák, Grieg, Saint-Saëns, Richard Strauss, Rachmaninoff, and Prokofiev.

The new richness of the world of music coincided with an era of unprecedented wealth in the United States. Every day fresh fortunes were made as gold, silver, copper, and oil were discovered and railroad construction boomed. Never had America known such a period of unbroken prosperity. It meant hundreds of households could easily afford pianos on which to play the wonderful new melodies.

Henry decided to remain in New York rather than settle elsewhere. With a population of half a million, it was the country's largest city, as well as the hub of the piano industry. A further attraction was that it contained the biggest concentration of Germans outside Germany. The family headed for Kleindeutschland (Little Germany) on the Lower East Side where two-thirds of the city's 75,000 Germans lived.[5]

Their first address was 199 Hester Street, a tenement above a shop. They had one of eight apartments on their floor. It was tiny, with only a two-window living room and a windowless bedroom. The ward in which they lived - the Tenth - was then the world's most crowded slum. The density of population bred so much disease and misery that health officials called the district the "typhus ward" and the "suicide ward."[6]

Although Henry had sufficient savings to start his own firm immediately, he believed he and his sons should first work for different pianomakers so as to absorb what was happening in the industry in America. Soon Henry Junior was writing Theodor: "Papa is making soundboards for a pianomaker named Laucht at six dollars a week. He could make seven if he could speak English. I am working with a pianomaker named Pirson who has invented a crazy instrument - two pianos back to back. He has got much publicity on this. I get seven dollars a week."[7]

William, the second youngest son, who would become Henry Engelhard's successor as the head of Steinway & Sons, worked for the esteemed pianomaker William Nunns & Company, which was noted for its innovations. Formed in 1821 by two ex-Londoners, brothers William and Robert Nunns, the company developed techniques for making hammers and graduating the thickness of the strings from the treble to the bass for greater sonority.

William was fascinated by the vast difference between Germany and the United States in the training of craftsmen. He observed: "In Germany, after having been released from school at age fourteen or fifteen, a boy is apprenticed to a master mechanic for six or seven years. It is true that he receives his board and lodging; but he has to pay a hundred and twenty-five dollars in *lehrgeld* [learning money] to indemnify the boss for the time lost in instructing him or for the defective workmanship in spoiled material which may result from his unskillfulness.

"No American boy would be willing to be placed in the position of an apprentice for six or seven years, although that is the only way in which a business can be acquired thoroughly in all its branches and details. To enact laws telling a lad to remain with an employer and make up in the later years of his apprenticeship the losses he has caused in the first years does not suit American ideas and probably never will."[8]

All of William's brothers and his father ultimately wound up working for Bacon & Raven, but it was William's misfortune to still be at Nunns when the firm went bankrupt early in 1853. His misery was intensified by the loss also of $240, the portion of his three years' wages that Nunns had withheld under the infamous "truck" system of the period. Under this system, employers apportioned part of their workers' salaries to them for groceries and clothes and retained the rest, acting as self-appointed banks but without paying interest and sometimes not even dispersing the principal. Consequently, such companies were often over $100,000 in debt in wages to their workers.

Shortly after William became jobless, the workers at Bacon & Raven, including Henry and his sons, went on strike. To Henry, the timing seemed propitious to start his own business, free of the burden of having to compete at the outset with this former employer. The date he selected for the opening day was March 5, 1853, William's seventeenth birthday. He made Steinway & Sons a partnership because he considered his sons an integral part of the business, forming with him half the initial labor force of ten. Also, as Henry was fifty-six when he launched the company, he had to take into account the fact that his sons would one day be in charge.

Steinway & Sons began in humble premises in a loft at the rear of 85 Varick Street, a building that later was demolished to make way for the Holland Tunnel entrance. It was at this point that Henry anglicized the family surname as well as his first name and those of his sons with him in America.

Steinway & Sons was American but its customs remained largely Teutonic. Most significantly, it was to be purely a masculine preserve. Henry's great-grandson Henry Ziegler Steinway, president from 1955 to 1977, describes this anti-female attitude as "like that of any old-fashioned German outfit. In those days, women were expected to stay at home. That's the way it was."[9]

But while they had no title, Juliana and her two eldest daughters, Doretta and Wilhelmina, wielded considerable power. All business conferences and decisions took place at home, often around the kitchen table as Juliana served dumplings, so that she knew about and had a say in everything. And it was Doretta, a talented pianist, who suggested that she and Wilhelmina, a gifted singer, help sell pianos by offering free lessons to purchasers who needed them, a suggestion her father adopted.

Within six months, the fledgling firm recorded its initial sale on September 16 to a Brooklyn family. Shortly afterward, the first in what would become a long list of celebrity purchases was made. The buyer was inventor and philanthropist Peter Cooper, best known for building the first American steam locomotive. The way the first sale was entered in Steinway's records initiated a dilemma that has hounded buyers of its pianos ever since: how to determine the age of their piano.

The problem stems from the first American Steinway not being designated number one, but instead being given three digits - 483 - because the Steinways already had made 482 pianos in Germany. As the years wore on, the pianos were assigned serial numbers in four, five, and six figures commensurate with the level of production reached. The best way to gauge a Steinway's age is to place the number against landmarks in the company's output: No. 1,000 in 1856, No. 5,000 in 1861, No. 45,000 in 1881, No. 370,000 in 1961, No. 463,000 in 1979, and No. 500,000 in June 1988.

At first, Steinway produced only one piano a week, purchasing the outer case from Pirson, the firm for which Henry Junior had worked on his arrival in New York. As the business thrived, production was expanded to three pianos a week, but it could not keep pace with demand. Steinway was frequently out of stock, a problem that would plague the company and its dealers from generation to generation.

The rapid growth dictated a shift within a year into larger quarters on Walker Street, also in Lower Manhattan. It was a stroke of poetic justice because the building had been the shop of William Nunns, the firm whose bankruptcy had so impoverished William Steinway. As business expanded, the Steinways had to recruit more workers. They found the easiest way was to go to Ellis Island and hire people from the boatloads of immigrants.

By 1860, Steinway & Sons again needed larger quarters. It decided to fulfill its requirement on a big scale both from necessity and out of the desire to surpass its chief competitor, Chickering and Sons, established in 1823 in Boston. In 1853, the year Steinway & Sons was launched, Chickering had constructed on Boston's Tremont Street what was then the largest industrial building in the United States. Not only the factory's size won admiration, but also its many freight elevators and its eleven miles of steam pipes for heating. The Chickerings accurately boasted that their premises had the greatest cubic content of any building in the United States except the Capitol in Washington.

Not to be outdone, Steinway & Sons purchased almost the entire square block between Fourth and Lexington avenues, bounded by Fifty-Second and Forty-third streets, at the suggestion of William, who pointed out that "the Harlem and New Haven railroad tracks pass directly in front so hundreds of thousands of people will become acquainted with the name of Steinway. The factory will be a standing advertisement of incalculable value not to be overlooked." To be near the factory, Henry moved into a house behind it on Lexington Avenue. His sons, Henry Junior and Charles, both now married, bought homes on either side.

The $150,000 manufactory dwarfed Chickering's pride and joy. Chickering's factory frontage was 275 feet, Steinway's 630; Chickering's, five stories, Steinway's six, if, as was done in those days, the basement was counted as a floor. Chickering reveled in showing off its steam pipes; Steinway one-upped it by emphasizing its double iron doors that could block the spread of a fire from one wing to another. More than a century later, when the Seagram Building was erected on the site of the factory, which Steinway & Sons closed in 1909, the construction foreman marveled to John Howland Steinway about the quality of the materials. "I'm amazed that they built a twelve-foot-thick fieldstone and mortar foundation for a building of this height," he told John.[10]

On August 30, 1860, the company proudly held its first press party to celebrate the opening of the factory. William and Charles guided the reporters through every nook and cranny. Then, as the scribe for Frank Leslie's *Illustrated Daily Graphic* coyly put it, they served "a handsome and abundant collation consisting of choice viands and fluids of brands not to be mentioned but with respect."[11]

The Steinways had only to start a project and, it seemed, a war or depression would erupt. The Fourth Avenue factory was completed on the eve of the Civil War; the company town that William started a decade later was in its infancy when a major economic downturn occurred.

In 1858, when the Steinways bought the property for their manufactory, the then relatively unknown Abraham Lincoln was warning about a "house divided." Like many emigrants from Germany, the Steinways sympathized with the Union's cause. Three members of the family enlisted. Charles became paymaster of the Fifth New York Regiment; Albert was a second lieutenant in the same unit. Wilhelmina's husband, Theodore Vogel, who was superintendent of the plant, also joined. Around the time the trio left, Henry and Juliana's youngest child, Anna, died at the age of nineteen. The cause of her death was not recorded.

Keeping the business afloat during the war was a major challenge for William, who by 1860, at the age of twenty-four, was running the business, although he did not become its head until 1865. Like other Northern pianomakers, Steinway & Sons lost nearly all its claims against Southern piano dealers. What to charge for pianos also plagued William, who pegged prices to fluctuations in the price of gold, his favorite economic barometer. As gold constantly soared and dipped, William had to follow suit with his price list. It was at this time that Steinway & Sons, established during a strike, began to experience its own labor difficulties.

The trouble began brewing in 1861 when, as a reaction to the depression that characterized the early months of the Civil War, William cut salaries. When the economy improved in 1862, he raised wages beyond their original level, but his employees were dissatisfied because the increase was not equivalent to the jump that had occurred in the cost of living.

Therefore, in September 1863, they elected to join the one thousand-member New York Pianomakers' Society, which, the next month, demanded that employers pay full wages irrespective of good or bad times and that all firms pay equally, beginning with a 25 percent raise. The union further stipulated that the owners submit their books for inspection every Saturday afternoon "so we may satisfy ourselves that you have strictly carried out our instructions."[12] When the "gentlemen bosses" were asked for their response, William's friend and competitor, Albert Weber, who started his firm two years before Steinway & Sons was established, had a scathing reply. "Gentlemen employees," he said, "your demands are exceedingly moderate. But in your very modesty you have omitted the most important point - that every

Saturday afternoon, when you have looked over the manufacturers' books, the employees shall go a-bowling and the bosses shall be made to set up the tenpins for their workmen."[13]

After both sides calmed down, the owners agreed to hike wages by 15 percent immediately and, provided the volume of business warranted it, to pay a further 10 percent later. Business did improve but the pledge was not honored. In February 1864, Steinway & Sons was one of two firms targeted for a showdown strike, with members at other companies assessed to support the strikers financially. But before the workers could act, the manufacturers responded with a lockout. As business dried up, William, anxious to resume production, urged his colleagues to grant the 10 percent raise to which he, too, had at first been opposed. After a month, the impasse was resolved by the owners taking back the workers in return for their dropping their demand for more money.

As the business situation brightened, the Steinways suffered the double blow of the deaths within twenty days of each other of Henry Junior and Charles in the spring of 1865. Young Henry died of tuberculosis at the age of thirty-four, leaving three young daughters, and Charles two years older, died of typhoid fever, leaving three young sons. Their deaths followed that of Theodore Vogel in 1874 during his service in the Union Army.

The three deaths not only left the family heartbroken, but they also took their toll on the management of Steinway & Sons. Henry Engelhard, sixty-eight in 1865, no longer was active in the business. Appointing William his successor, he decided that his eldest son, Theodor, should come over from Germany and help out.

It was a big step for the loyal Theodor to take. Now thirty-nine years old, he had done very well on his own. In 1859, he had moved his business from Seesen thirty-four miles north to the large community of Braunschweig. When he left for New York, Theodor, now married, regarded it as a permanent move and sold his firm to three of his workmen, Grotrian, Helferrich, and Schulz. He permitted them to include "Successors to Th. Steinweg" in their firm's name.[14] A century later, this gesture would result in a trademark infringement suit.

Theodor and William were a good team. William was urbane and cosmopolitan, skilled at smoothing the ruffled feelings caused by Theodor's irascibility and eqully adept in promoting the revolutionary piano Theodor created. For Theodor was a mechanical genius, responsible for the most important piano inventions ever developed by one person except for Cristofori. Of the fifty-five Steinway & Sons' patents in existence when he died, he had devised forty-five. All told, Steinway pianos now are based on 125 patents. Several more are pending. Thanks to his many innovations, Theodor singlehandedly created a demand for grand pianos of which William previously had complained that "sales are about as scarce as angels' visits."[15]

Theodor arrived in New York at the onset of a period of unparalleled ingenuity that would mold modern America. The new Western Union Company was stringing telegraph wire from coast to coast; the first underwater transatlantic cable was laid; Alexander Graham Bell was developing the telephone; two Milwaukee inventors, Christopher Sholes and Carlos Glidden, were devising the typewriter; and Thomas Edison, having invented the gramophone, was experimenting on how to commercially distribute electricity from generating stations.

Theodor's motto was: "Geselte ist, wer was kann; Meister ist, wer was ersann; Lehrling ist jedermann." (Who knows his trade is a journeyman; a master is he who invents the plan; an apprentice, each and every man.) His genius was to apply the principles of acoustics and physics to the piano to produce the desired singing sound. Theodor had received top grades in acoustics at the Jacobson Institute, Seesen's foremost school. To learn how to maximize the impact of the *attack*, the brief moment when the hammer strikes the string, he had sought advice from his friend, Berlin physicist Hermann von Helmholtz, the most respected acoustics expert of his age. Additionally, Theodor was the world's leading collector of musical instruments, globe-trotting in his hunt. He studied their construction to discover ways to improve the sound of the piano.

To appreciate Theodor's genius, it is necessary to understand the piano's basic construction. The modern piano has six major elements: strings, soundboard, bridge, action, case, and pedals. Early pianos had only two strings as it was thought ample variety of sound would result from the hammers striking the strings at different angles. Today's piano has 232 - three for each note in the treble at the right of the keyboard, two for each in the tenor at the middle, and one for each in the bass at the left. With more than one string for most notes, performers can keep playing even if one snaps. Metal wire, developed in the tenth century for musical instruments, was formerly used for strings. Now the material is high-tensile steel.

Each string is wound around a separate tuning pin located at the keyboard end of the piano. They are called tuning pins because they can be turned to increase or decrease the tension of the strings so as to alter the pitch. At first, the pins were forged from iron; today, they are made of hardened steel. The originals were much smaller than those now used because the string tension was only about one-eighth of what it is today.

Through holes in a frame that extends from front to back, the strings are inserted into a strong wooden block known as the *pinblock* or *wrest plank*. In early pianos, the plank was made from solid timber, usually beech or oak. In modern ones, cross-laminated maple is used. Initially, the frame, too, was made of wood. Later the wood was fortified with metal braces, but forceful pressure still often caused the frame to snap and wrench away the wrest plank. Franz Liszt, for example, was famous for demolishing pianos by his powerful playing. Then, in 1825, an American, Alpheus Babcock, solved the problem by designing a 100 percent cast-iron plate.

Its massiveness made it possible for the piano to withstand far greater tension from the strings and thus produce greater volume. The tension imposed by the strings in modern pianos is enormous - from sixteen tons in the smallest five-foot-one-inch *baby* grand up to twenty-three tons in the nine-foot concert grand.

Starting at metal stud guideposts called *agraffes*, located at the edge of the iron frame, sometimes referred to as the *plate*, the strings run through the agraffes and along the topside of the frame to the far end of the frame where they are looped around *hitchpins*, so named because they serve the same purpose as a hitching post for a horse's reins. The strings are laid out along the plate so that they pass over the *soundboard* and *bridge* that lie underneath. Without these two devices, audiences could not hear a piano because the vibration of the strings in response to the striking of keys causes little audible sound on its own. The bridge acts as the intermediary between the plate and the soundboard.

The strings convey their vibrations to the bridge, which, in turn, transmits them to the soundboard. It then enables the vibrations to be efficiently converted into sound waves, thereby making the piano audible. Strips of wood, called *ribs*, are attached to the underside of the soundboard to increase the amplification.

The *action* consists of the keys, the hammers, and the mechanism that impels the hammers toward the strings when the keys are depressed. All told, the action has six thousand parts, or about half the components in the modern piano. The number of keys has gradually increased from twenty-eight to eighty-eight, giving composers a much broader ranger of choice. Beethoven, for instance, wrote two of his early works, the *Moonlight* and *Pathétique* sonatas, on a sixty-one key instrument, the *Appassionata* on a sixty-eight-key piano, and the *Hammerklavier* on a seventy-three one. (*Klavier* is German for *piano.*)

    The eighty-eight-key piano was developed by the mid-nineteenth century. It has fifty-two white keys for playing whole notes and thirty-six raised black keys for playing sharps and flats. It sometimes is described as a seven and a quarter *octave* instrument (an octave consists of eight white keys but seven different notes, with the last note of one octave serving as the first of the next).

    The largest keyboard today is ninety-seven keys, made by Bösendorfer, a Viennese firm established in 1828 and purchased in 1966 by Indiana-based Kimball International. The extra keys, located at the bass end, provide a very deep sound comparable to a sixteen-foot pipe on an organ.

    It first was made in the late 1800s for composers to transcribe organ pieces. In addition, Bösendorfer produces a ninety-two-key instrument and the regular eighty-eight.

    That the standard piano has eighty-eight keys occasionally slips the memory of even the most accomplished musicians. Many years ago, Vladimir Horowitz, who used the Steinway exclusively since 1926, sent a complimentary message backstage to his close friend Paul Muni who was starring in *Inherit the Wind* on Broadway. "Thank you, but I will never be able to create the excitement you do at the 88," Muni replied. Puzzled at the reference, Horowitz first showed Muni's note to his wife, Wanda. "Is that an automobile?" he asked her. "I don't know, let's ask Sonia," Wanda replied. Sonia, the Horowitzes' daughter, tried to enlighten her parents. "Maybe it's the number of keys on a piano," she suggested. "Do you know how many there are?" "No, I've never counted them," Horowitz answered.[16]

    When Horowitz's RCA record producer, Jack Pfeiffer, told that story to Jascha Heifetz, the noted violinist who could also play the piano, Heifetz interrupted him as he repeated Muni's praise. "What did he mean - is that a car?" Heifetz asked, just like Horowitz.[17] Probably both were thinking of the *Oldsmobile '88.* For a long time, Oldsmobile named its vehicles by numerals; the '88 is derived from the Rocket '88 engine the firm developed in 1948.

    The hammers initially were covered with sponge, tinder, india rubber, deer hide, or leather. Their impact either was too heavy or too light, and they could not be adjusted. These problems were solved in 1820 by a Frenchman, Henri Pape, who discovered that felt made from premium wool provided the necessary flexibility. If the felt is too firm, it causes a harsh tone; to correct this and get a mellower tone, its fibers are loosened with needlepricks. Conversely, if the tone is too mellow and lacks brilliance, filing the felt creates a harder tone.

The innards of the piano are enclosed in a wooden case otherwise known as the *rim*. Actually, there are two rims: the outer or exterior wall and a not quite as high interior rim to which the plate and soundboard are attached. The final major element of the piano is the *pedal*. All pianos have two; some have a third, located in the middle. The pedal at the right (the *loud* or *sustaining* one) permits the strings to vibrate freely no matter what keys are played. That at the left (the *soft* or *una corda*) reduces the volume, and the middle pedal (the *sostenuto*) only affects the crispness of treble notes.

By the time Theodor Steinway arrived in New York, many improvements had been made to Cristofori's invention. One of the most notable had been devised by Theodor's brother, Henry Junior. In 1859, at the age of twenty-eight, Henry created a revolutionary realignment of the piano's *scale* - the strings' vibrating lengths, placement, and the point at which they are struck by the hammers. Until then, piano manufacturers crowded the strings for grands either in a parallel pattern or did some modest cross-stringing to intensify the volume.

What Henry Junior did resulted in the wing shape of the modern piano. He allowed the strings room to vibrate more by placing them in the pattern of a gradually expanding fan with the longer bass strings stretched lightly over the rest. Because the strings gradually lengthen from the treble to the bass, the piano's case was reshaped from a long rectangle into its now-familiar contour.

Henry's rearrangement enabled pianists to produce greater volume with less effort than before. As *The New York Times'* report of his death aptly noted, "Few men ever lived who were better acquainted with the construction of the piano. He reduced its manufacture to a science."[18]

Theodor followed up on Henry's vital contribution with a multitude of changes that covered every other aspect of the piano. When he was finished, he had developed the modern piano as we still know it today. Realizing that the piano would sound much better if two existing ideas, overstringing and the cast-iron plate, were combined, he turned his attention first to the latter. While Babcock's invention had prevented the piano from falling apart, the construction still lacked the sturdiness for it to withstand powerful string tension. Hence, it continued to emit a grating thin, nasal whine.

Theodor solved the problem by using stronger cast-iron alloys and by lining the metal braces of the plate with the wrest plank. Consequently, the plank no longer moved up and down in tandem with the strings. The result was that a Steinway piano had double the tensile strength of previous pianos and thus could withstand far greater pressure from the strings.

Further, instead of leaving the plate flat, as was customary, Theodor created a *cupola* frame. The raised bell-shaped openings promote the unfettered transmission of the sound waves from underneath the frame. Theodor also reshaped the curve of the soundboard to duplicate the tympanic function of the human eardrum. His invention prompted Helmholtz to praise him for the resultant "combination tones and sustained sound that is far more sensitive than in the case of everyday instruments where the sound dies away so rapidly."

To provide greater resonance, Theodor repositioned the bridge from the rear of the piano toward the middle. For the largest grands, he developed the *ring* bridge - two bridges glued together in a loop. This bridge is used by Steinway only on its two biggest grands - the *B* and the concert *D* - because the curve is too big for its smaller instruments. (As *B* and *D* sound alike over the telephone, Steinway refers to the *B* as *boy* and the *D* as *dog* and asks dealers, "Do you want a boy or a dog?")[19]

Having revised the mechanism, Theodor switched his attention to the shaping of the rims. Until then, the rims were made separately and consisted of one layer of wood each, with the inner cut thinner than the outer - a method that some pianomakers continue to follow today. Theodor's innovations were having the outer and inner rims bent as a unit and using several layers of glued-together lengths of wood equivalent to the distance of the piano's perimeter from the bass to the treble.

There are no recorded instances of modern pianos, in which the outer rim is prebent separately and then wrapped around the inner one, having disintegrated when played. But Steinway maintains that Theodor's simultaneous bending process, still used, provides a stronger foundation for the soundboard so that it projects the notes better.

For observers, the rim binding has always been the most fascinating step in the up to nine months it takes to prepare a Steinway for the market.[20] The process commences outdoors in Steinway's lumberyard at its Long Island City and Hamburg plants. Hamburg cuts its own wood from huge tree trunks; the Long Island City plant stockpiles two million feet of precut board, which it fences in and guards by round-the-clock patrols. Because wood is a living material that expands and shrinks, to make a piano its moisture content must be reduced so as to minimize the possibility of changes in dimension. The drying out is begun naturally outside for several months and then completed over a two-week period in 160-degree kilns.

The kiln process is necessary because the sunshine dries only the surface of the wood; the kiln draws out the moisture from inside. Subsequently those portions of the sheets of wood that contain imperfections are sliced out. Approximately 60 percent of the lumber is rejected. However, it is not tossed out; it is put to good use as fuel in a wood-burning boiler.

The wood that survives the selection process is planed for smoothness. The planing also removes any pollution absorbed from the outdoor exposure. Next, still following the process recommended by Theodor, the wood is glued together in long strips. To provide resilience, these strips are laminated together with a maximum of eighteen - nine for the inner rim and nine for the outer - for the concert grand *D*, down to a minimum of twelve for the baby grand *S*. For the *D*, the thickness amounts to three and one-quarter inches, for the *S*, two and one-eighth inches. This stack, which is comparable to a couple of pages, is called a book.

Now for the particularly intriguing stage. Standing around the rim-bending room, like silent, empty hulks awaiting their cargo, are piano-shaped steel presses, matching the different size grands that Steinway makes. New York produces five: the five-foot one-inch *S*; five-foot seven-inch *M*; five-foot ten-and-a-half inch *L*; six-foot ten-and-a-half-inch *B*; and eight-foot eleven- and -three-quarter-inch *D*. Hamburg makes all these plus three that New York discontinued: the five-foot eleven-inch *O*, six-foot two-inch *A*; and seven-foot five-inch *C*. So unsurpassable was Theodor's concept that the presses are duplicates of his original designs. The only concession to the passage of time is that they are replaced every twenty years.

At 9:30 a.m., a team of seven men picks up the *book* of planks for the *D* and carries it over to the waiting press. Starting at the straight bass side, the team bends the rim around the curve and down to the treble. The wood is screwed into place with giant clamps. From start to finish, a period of about twenty minutes, there is almost utter silence. The smaller grands also undergo similar moldings.

What is now a piano rim in the making is left on the press all day. After its removal, it is placed in a 85-degree room for three months for the smaller grands, six for the *D*. At the end of this time, if a crack has shown up, the rim is destroyed, a fate that befalls one in two hundred. The Long Island facility places rims vertically, giving the impression of a long row of cathedrals. In Hamburg, they are laid flat and stacked on top of one another. But the overall drying time is the same.

Having revamped the frame and case, Theodor went on to revolutionize the construction of the piano's keybed. The old system consisted of a wood frame filled in with thin wood panels. Under a strong touch, the panels emitted a drumming noise, and the beds frequently rose from their proper level in response to atmospheric conditions. Theodor replaced the panels with layers of felt, eliminating the drumming sound and allowing the wood to expand and contract without causing the keybeds to change position. In addition, he perfected the *sustaining* pedal so that even though the fingers are lifted from the keys, the tone continues as long as the foot is on the pedal. A patent was taken out in his brother Albert's name for the sostenuto pedal, although Albert's chief responsibility was as William's assistant and Theodor's was to work on the piano.

The tonal effects produced by this pedal immediately caught the fancy of composers. An enthused Liszt wrote, "I am sending you two versions of the *Dance of the Sylphs* and No. 3 of my *Consolation*, the transcription of which I shall gladly perfect by adapting them to fully accommodate your sostenuto pedal."

The change in construction Theodor initiated garnered Steinway & Sons award after award for its pianos at world fairs. In 1867, its grand won first prize at the Paris World Fair and received unsolicited accolades from composers Gioachhino Rossini of Italy and Hector Berlioz of France.

"Your piano is like a nightingale cooing in a thunderstorm," Rossini wrote.[21] "Your piano has beautiful and rare qualities," said Berlioz.[22] Even Liszt, to whom competitor Frank Chickering had presented a free grand, shortly afterward wrote that he preferred a Steinway. "Your new grand is a glorious masterpiece in power, sonority, singing quality, and perfect harmonic effect," he said.[23] Nine years later, in 1876, Steinway attained further glory when its grand won first prize at the American centennial exposition in Philadelphia.

Theodor also dramatically altered the way uprights were made. The first upright was created in 1811 by an Englishman, Robert Wornum. Its appearance was bizarre at the front of the piano. Theodor approached the construction of the upright in a far different manner, encasing the mechanism vertically on the inside of a birch frame, which he affixed to the back of the piano. His concept led to a fuller, more powerful tone similar to that emitted by a grand.

The public's response was enthusiastic. The *New York Tribune* characterized the improvement as "so marked that in many respects it is a new instrument." The paper presciently continued that "it promises to be the favorite of its class." By 1880 two-thirds of all pianos sold in the United States were uprights.

Steinway also was a pioneer in the use of machinery for the preliminary stages of pianomaking. Its Fourth Avenue factory in Manhattan contained 165 planing, sawing, jointing, drilling, and other woodworking machines. William Steinway proudly estimated they replaced the hand labor of at least nine hundred workmen. "They do all the hard work which formerly endangered the health, and even the lives, of the workmen employed in this type of labor," he explained.[24]

While Theodor was redesigning the piano and William was planning the company town of Steinway Village, their father was preoccupied with a project of his own. In 1870, at the age of seventy-three, he commissioned an $80,000 mausoleum with room for two hundred, at Green-Wood Cemetery in Brooklyn. The most elite in New York, the 425-acre cemetery is designed in so labyrinthine a fashion that its paved winding paths have names such as Maple, Orchard, and Chapel Hill so people can find their way around. Over the years, Samuel Morse, Duncan Phyfe, Charles Tiffany, and Horace Greeley have been buried there. Shortly after the mausoleum was completed, Henry died in 1871. Two thousand persons came in a cortège of 861 carriages to his funeral at Steinway Hall at which an organist and a band of nineteen musicians played.[25]

Inasmuch as members of the now-huge Steinway family no longer all live in New York but are scattered across the United States, and also because many prefer cremation, little of the Steinway mausoleum has been filled. Consequently, Henry Engelhard's great-grandson John Howland Steinway described it as "the only half-empty apartment house in Brooklyn."[26]

With Henry's death, William, then thirty-five and already in charge for six years, became the dominant figure at Steinway & Sons.

The outlook for the eighteen-year-old company was auspicious. Its sales topped $2 million and it was the world's foremost pianomaker in terms of size as well as innovations.[27] Each day it produced ten pianos, one per working hour. In one year alone, it made five times as many as Henry Engelhard had made during twenty-five years back in Germany, and with six hundred employees in New York, the company was that city's leading employer.

But insofar as William was concerned, that was just the beginning.

## Chapter II
## *William*

William Steinway was not handsome but his well-cared for moustache, rimless glasses, and barrel chest gave him an air of authority and distinction. Moreover, despite attacks of gout and rheumatism, when he became head of Steinway, he still had the powerful physique that had enabled him in his youth to fight off twenty toughs and to save his brother Henry from drowning after an hour's battle against the surf and undertow at Coney Island.[1] At the end of each year, he made a practice of recording in his Diary his height, weight (which fluctuated between 190 and 210 pounds), and chest measurement (forty-six inches). Concerned about his bodily functions, he regularly recorded his bowel movements, as well.

He was known for his feats of strength. He could write his name on a chalkboard while balancing a fifty-pound bowling ball with his little finger looped through the ball's opening. He also was able to pick up with one hand a quarter keg of beer weighing 130 pounds and lift it high in the air above his head. At the Steinway factory he impressed employees by lifting weights of up to a thousand pounds.[2]

William was a gifted tenor and noted with pride "I am in good voice," "I am in splendid voice," "I am in excellent voice," and even "I am in magnificent voice."[3] He participated in performances by New York's oldest and foremost German choral society, the Liederkranz, established in 1847.[4] He served nine terms as the group's president, longer than anyone else. Although the society passed a resolution in 1858 that no president could succeed himself, it found a way to circumvent its rule by reelecting William in alternate years.

He was also a talented pianist who enjoyed dealing with and entertaining the growing roster of performers who used a Steinway. But he was not overawed. He liked to joke, for instance, that six-times-married Eugène d'Albert could be billed as the "Bluebeard of the Piano" if he wed once more.[5]

Whereas William's father was one of thousands of Europeans who flocked to America to make a fortune, William was one of New

York's leading citizens. The newspapers regarded him as the spokesman for the city's large German-American community - not Carl Schurz, former Washington correspondent of the *New York Tribune* and Secretary of the Interior during the 1877-81 presidency of Rutherford Hayes, nor another friend, toy tycoon F.A.O. Schwartz. In 1871, William was appointed by a mass meeting of New Yorkers to the influential Committee of Seventy, organized to destroy the grip on the city's government of the Tweed Ring. The ring, under William "Boss" Tweed, had plundered millions of dollars from municipal coffers.

When William and his family first settled in New York, they lived in a crowded tenement. By 1871, William had a home in each of New York's two most fashionable areas. In Manhattan, he lived at 26 Gramercy Park, down the street from Samuel Tilden, a leading Democrat who ran for president in 1876 and lost. In 1870, William moved into a $127,500 twenty-seven-room mansion on fourteen acres along the waterfront of Long Island.

The estate had piqued his interest partly because it overlooked the property for the new factory he began the same year as part of Steinway Village. The house's bell-tower gave him a bird's eye view of activity at the plant. The location's further appeal was that it was near the estates of such fellow dignitaries as Gardner Howland, business manager of the *New York Herald*, Congressman Charles Tracey, and Alexander Stevens, president of the Sixth National Bank.

William was motivated to build the four-hundred-acre Steinway Village, one of the first company towns in the United States, by a mixture of self-interest and altruism. He was certain that the provision of good homes at low prices would so please his employees that they would not strike. Convinced that Manhattan was a hotbed of strike-inciting "Anarchists and Socialists," he believed that if his workmen were removed from contact with them and "the other temptations of city life in the tenement districts," they would be "more content and their lot a happier one."[6]

Moreover, business was so good that Steinway & Sons had outgrown its Fourth Avenue premises in Manhattan in less than a decade. William wanted more room and shipping facilities near the water, as well as a basin for the storage of logs in order to keep them moist and prevent them from cracking. He also was eager for space for a lumberyard, a steam sawmill, and a foundry.

He found an ideal spot in the northern section of Long Island. Besides the four hundred acres, then farm and woodland, there was a half mile of waterfront and a navigable canal. In the early 1870s, the sawmill, foundry, boiler and engine houses, and a factory for drilling, finishing, and japanning the frames and other metal parts for the pianos were completed. These were followed by a large dock and a 100-foot-wide by 300-foot-long basin, for the millions of square feet of logs. Subsequently, in 1877, facilities were added for keyboard making, woodcarving, and drying the lumber.

The rest of the village was created simultaneously. It was a massive project entailing the grading of main streets, laying of sidewalks, planting of trees, and the erection of a fire station. For the workers, most of whom at that time lived in two-room tenements, William built two-story brick or frame houses with a parlor, dining room, and up to four bedrooms on lots as big as twenty-five by a hundred feet. He charged between $300 and $800 for vacant lots and $1,700 to $4,000 for the homes.

Besides Steinway workers, William sought to attract other buyers through long, glowing newspaper advertisements. They boasted of "ground that is high and dry at all times, and from the nature of the soil, conducive to health, precluding the presence of all malarious diseases." They further referred to "beauty of scenery and all the desirable features of City life, such as the purest quality of water, perfect sewerage and drainage, and use of excellent gas at moderate price."[7] Hundreds of New Yorkers were persuaded, and Steinway Village grew quickly. By 1890, it had seven thousand inhabitants.

Although William made a healthy profit, having paid just $300 per vacant lot, he was not greedy, as was another company town builder, railroad baron George Pullman. In his company town of Pullman, Illinois, Pullman charged rents one-fourth higher than comparable houses fetched elsewhere.

William also took into consideration the residents' family lives, building a school for eight hundred children, several churches, a library, a post office, and a free public bath with fifty dressing rooms, bordered by a big park. He persuaded grocers, bakers, pharmacists, and other merchants to come to his town, as well as suppliers of piano parts.

He also started the Steinway and Hunters Point Railroad, a horse-drawn streetcar that linked the factory, by a fifteen-minute ride, with the ferry to Manhattan.

When the Association for Improving the Condition of the Poor asked if the parcels of farmland that remained undeveloped could be used to grow food by the "deserving poor," William readily agreed to provide the land gratis. The association provided the tools, seeds, and fertilizer and plowed the land for which it was repaid in potatoes, beans, oats, and other crops. It sold the food at neighboring markets and used the cash for the following year's expenses. When it honorably offered the surplus over and above its costs to William, he rejected the money. "I am not in the habit of doing charity by halves," he said. "It is my desire that the surplus instead be employed in furnishing seed, fertilizer, and agricultural implements for the next season."[8]

Unfortunately for William, his grand design of extricating his workers from the influence of the "Anarchists and Socialists" in Manhattan was only in its infancy when a citywide dispute arose in 1872 over labor's desire for an eight-hour day rather than the ten-hour one legislated in 1836. Two-thirds of Steinway's workers were still at the company's Fourth Avenue location, in the heart of Manhattan, when the controversy erupted. At first, William thought Steinway & Sons would not be affected because none of his employees attended an industry-wide union meeting on May 23 that called for a walkout.[9] But five days later, the Steinway workers decided to join the strike which by then included a demand for higher wages as well as shorter hours.

The following day, May 29, at an 8:00 a.m. meeting, an ailing William tried to conciliate the workers. "I cannot meet your demands without raising prices by one-third and such an increase will destroy our export trade and severely damage the domestic market," he pleaded. As a compromise he offered either a 10 percent wage hike for a ten-hour day or nine hours at the old salary. At the same time, he requested the workmen to vote on "whether to deal with me directly or whether you will be dictated to by others."[10] The employees voted overwhelmingly in his favor and adjourned until 2:00 p.m. to discuss the offer.

Feeling he had everything under control, William went for lunch with his brother Albert. As they ate, William received a startling report. Several thousand non-Steinway workers, in wild excitement over the news of the compromise he had arranged, were marching against the Fourth Avenue factory. Alarmed, William sent for the police to provide protection, and by the 2:00 p.m. deadline twenty officers had surrounded the building. At the second confrontation with his workforce, William faced a now-hostile group, many of them incited by rabble rousers from other firms and by the huge quantity of beer they had consumed during their noon break. The workers insisted on their demands. Quietly, a worn-out William replied: "I have nothing more to say. You must go with the other strikers."[11]

The next morning William obtained 150 copies each of the *Times*, *World*, and *Sun* newspapers, clipped out the stories about the march, and sent them to the company's dealers. In an accompanying letter, he fumed that "the unreasonable and unwarrantable demands of the workmen will force the prices of pianos to a point altogether beyond the reach of people of moderate means. All piano manufacturers and dealers will be seriously crippled for a long time to come. Unless the workmen are subjected to a long strike, they will in a few months again demand and strike for higher wages."[12] Having given this discouraging prognosis, William proceeded several lines further on to inquire whether the dealers would prefer his yielding and "your having to pay an additional sixty to a hundred and twenty dollars per piano"[13] depending on the size.

Unsurprisingly, the dealers balked at what would have been a one-third price increase. When William notified his employees of the dealers' refusal, they were persuaded he had tried his best and accepted his offer of a 10 percent salary raise for ten hours' work. But once again, he was checkmated by the opposition of strikers at other businesses. When William arrived at the factory a little after 6:00 a.m., on a rainy Wednesday, June 5, he found forty policemen already on guard and an immense crowd of those outsiders antagonistic to the settlement yelling at employees who entered the building. By 7:30 William requested the police to drive away the crowd. This was done by 10:00 a.m. without violence or force. The police also increased their contingent to three hundred; they stayed throughout the day and were given lunch by the company.

When a citywide labor demonstration on Monday, June 10, turned out to be a "grand fizzle"[14] of only two thousand marchers, not the forty thousand predicted, William believed the dispute would soon end. But the picketing continued. For the next two weeks the police stayed on guard by the factory, repelling a rush on it by one hundred outside strikers on June 15. But by June 23, one month after its outburst, the strike collapsed, and William did not have to budge from his original offer.

The early 1870s also demonstrated the astuteness of William's 1866 decision to open the 2000-seat Steinway Hall music and lecture auditorium on East Fourteenth Street. His canny placement of the auditorium on the second floor, reached by sweeping staircases near four display rooms of pianos, resulted in many impulse orders by concertgoers, and as the hall was connected by private telegraph to both factories, these could be filled quickly.

The hall happened to be across the street from one of William's favorite German restaurants and in 1882 he loaned money to August Lüchow, an employee there, toward its purchase. Under Lüchow it became New York's leading German restaurant and in gratitude, he set aside an upstairs banquet room as the "Steinway Room." There, William ate Lüchow's forty-five cent lunch special regularly with his senior executives. It normally began with a dozen oysters; when August Lüchow halved the number to cope with rising costs, an annoyed William went elsewhere for several days. But within a week he returned and made no further complaints. On another occasion, he was astounded to see a junior Steinway executive eating the forty-five cent lunch. "How can you afford to eat here on your salary?" he demanded. The employee flushed and did not return until his salary was higher.[15]

Many of the famous people of the day appeared at Steinway Hall, attracting huge crowds. Attendance was sold out for a reading by Charles Dickens in December 1867. William was not overwhelmed by the great novelist. He recorded the author's appearance in one terse sentence: "Met Charles Dickens at our Hall."[16] The hall was also where the National Woman Suffrage movement held its 1872 convention with the Reverend Henry Ward Beecher guaranteeing the hall's rent. The meeting was dominated by Victoria Woodhull, spiritualist, quack healer, stockbroker, and advocate of free love. She formed the National Radical Reform Party, also known as the "Equal Rights Party," on whose platform she ran for President later that year.

That same year marked William's initial foray as impresario when he persuaded the phenomenally talented Russian composer and pianist Anton Rubinstein to make his American debut at Steinway Hall. The Rubinstein visit occurred shortly after the labor dispute was settled at Steinway's Fourth Avenue factory. It launched what came to be regarded as one of the best-ever advertising campaigns: the unpaid-for endorsement by famous performers of Steinway pianos in return for free use of the pianos at concerts.

Had Vera, Rubinstein's extravagant wife, not spent money faster than the forty-three-year-old Russian genius earned it, he might have instantly rejected William's proposal for a grueling tour of two hundred concerts - seven per week - across the United States, as well as in

Toronto and Montreal, Canada.[17] Franz Liszt, no slouch himself in doing concert tours, warned that what William wanted was a "steeplechase de concerts."[18]

But because William offered a tantalizing $200 a performance, Rubinstein accepted gratefully. However, he was certain, as were many in Europe at that time, that America was an untamed land of tigers, crocodiles, Indians on the warpath, and uncouth Yahoos with little or no musical knowledge. Most worrisome, though, was the rumor that American paper currency was worthless. Consequently, he made three stipulations: semimonthly payments in gold coins, an insurance policy against "Red Indians," and no performances in beer gardens.[19] Rubinstein changed his mind about the gold coins when William impishly presented him with a sack containing the money. Staggering under the 140-pound weight, Rubinstein quickly asked if he could have a certified check instead.[20]

William took a huge gamble in hiring Rubinstein. American audiences were unaccustomed to the European concept of solo performances. Instead, they liked musical spectaculars with sixteen people playing eight pianos and huge choruses backed by two orchestras. William also feared a hostile reaction to Rubinstein's insistence on a program of the classical greats. Consequently, he urged Rubinstein to conclude his recitals with some showmanship - variations on *Yankee Doodle Dandy* - as a concession to popular taste. Sure enough, audiences were delighted.

The tour started unpromisingly, commencing with the arrival in the blazing heat on September 10 of a wan Rubinstein, tottering from ten days of seasickness en route from Liverpool to New York. The hot spell had not abated by the time of his opening concert on September 23, and the sweat poured down his face as he performed works by Handel, Beethoven, Mozart, Schumann, and several of his own compositions. The concert went well until the pianissimo middle of his D Minor Concerto. Then smack into the quiet moments came the sounds of kindling wood being split outside and of a dog being trained to jump rope. The crisis was overcome only by William's paying the perpetrators a bribe to stop.[21]

Despite the interruption, the concert was an enormous success with standing ovations and enthusiastic shouts of approval. The critics, too, were laudatory. But the highlight for William occurred some weeks later, just before Rubinstein embarked on his cross-country appearances. Calling at Steinway Hall in the hope of finding letters from his wife and children, Rubinstein was overjoyed to receive a bulky package of correspondence and photographs. To express his happiness, he sat down at a piano and played for William and his staff until midnight.[22] William was spellbound as Rubinstein rippled through *The Erlking*, the thrilling musical version written by Franz Schubert when he was just eighteen years old of German writer Johann Goethe's poem about an evil spirit that preys on children. The choice of composer was extra touching to William because Schubert and William's father were born in the same year. "It was as if we heard the voice of the little child, the clattering of the horses' hooves, the wild entreaties of the Erlking, as plainly as if we had witnessed it all ourselves," William excitedly said afterward. "I think truly it is a day that can never be repeated in all the course of my life."[23]

Subsequently, however, the relationship between the two soured. An overworked, exhausted Rubinstein with good reason complained to William about the punishing schedule, which frequently required him to board a train immediately after a concert. There were no recriminations about his exposure to a cholera epidemic. What upset him was that his weariness would detract from what he viewed as an obligation: a perfect performance at each place. "Each day I feel unhappier and think often of breaking my contract," he wrote William. "The tour becomes daily more difficult, more unbearable. We play so often in the same town that now I, with the longest repertoire in Europe, have reached the end of it and must study and memorize new pieces. I cannot give the public always the same. But we travel every day and I have no time to practice."[24]

Nevertheless, somehow the conscientious Rubinstein did find time to learn new pieces, and when he wound up the marathon in New York, he summoned up the energy to play seven farewell concerts at Steinway Hall. Finally, on May 24, 1873, Rubinstein sailed home. Unfortunately for him, his wife had spent in advance the money for which he had endangered his health. But in the United States, Rubinstein had wrought wonders for the cause of classical music. Moreover, as he had performed everywhere on a Steinway, with that acknowledgment printed at the bottom of every program, the name Steinway was irrevocably linked with the immortals of music.

For William, Rubinstein's triumph turned out to be a delightful contrast to the disastrous appearance in the fall of 1875 of the German pianist Hans von Bülow on behalf of Steinway's principal rival, Chickering & Sons. The tour began well with von Bülow introducing Tchaikovsky's new B Flat Minor Concerto in Boston, Chickering's home base, and next performing at the gala inauguration of Chickering's new concert hall on Fifth Avenue in New York, four short blocks north of Steinway Hall.

Unhappily for Chickering, von Bülow's good behavior quickly evaporated as he began to vent his fury on the piano over his wife, Cosima, Liszt's daughter, having just abandoned him for Richard Wagner.[25] It so happened that Wagner played a Steinway and would write the Steinways in 1879, when they were remodeling his piano: "I miss my Steinway Grand as one misses a beloved wife."[26] During one performance, von Bülow tore off the Chickering sign that hung on the side of the piano, pitched it on the floor yelling "I am not a traveling advertisement," and, as the finale, stuck it on the rear of the piano and kicked it.[27]

Tiffs among piano firms for the endorsements of illustrious performers were as common in William's day as they have been in the twentieth century. Indeed, the practice gave rise to a quip of the period: "Instead of saying 'Herr Wischer uses the Hammerschlag piano,' the announcement ought to read 'The Hammerschlag Piano Company uses Herr Wischer.'"[28]

The year after the von Bülow debacle, William was in the unaccustomed position of being embarrassed by the wavering affections of a performer. At first he reacted benignly when pianist Sebastian Bach Mills, normally a Steinway loyalist and one of the soloists at the 1866 gala inaugural of Steinway Hall, elected to play at a Pittsburgh concert the piano of Decker & Sons, a New York firm established three years after Steinway. But when Decker's Pittsburgh agent publicized this change of allegiance, neglecting to mention it was temporary, William's attitude changed. He framed a caustic letter in reply to the *Music Trade Review*, the industry's bible, which was covering the dispute. "Mr. Mills always uses our piano when he has his choice but, for money, he has to play others once in a while," he wrote.[29] Shortly afterward, William became involved in yet another testimonial scrimmage, this time against his friend and competitor Albert Weber. Each firm was eager for a touring English Opera Company headed by impresario James Henry Mapleson to endorse its piano. The first round went to Steinway, which supplied the singers with pianos both at the theater and at their hotel rooms in New York. The grateful troupe gushed about the Steinway's "richness and astonishing durability of tone."

Pleased, William repeated the strategy when the singers moved on to Philadelphia. That started the fray with Weber. While the group was at dinner, Weber had the Steinways carried out of the hotel rooms and replaced with his own pianos. William retaliated by sending up his movers to put back the Steinways that Weber's men had left in the corridor. There was a fight, which the Weber side won. Subsequently, Weber hosted the opera company at a post performance champagne supper, and as the evening progressed, the intoxicated singers signed a paper that said Weber pianos were the best they had encountered.

In 1876 William incorporated Steinway & Sons, and two years later, he designed Steinway's lyre logo: a stylized S on either side of an ampersand astride the strings.

All was well with the business, but William's personal life was in turmoil due his wife's unfaithfulness. William and Regina Roos, a native of Buffalo, whose family also was involved in music, were married in 1861; she was eighteen and William twenty-five. William gave her $100 in cash and a $142 clock as a wedding present, and they honeymooned at Niagara Falls.[30]

William started writing a meticulous, well-organized diary about his joys and sorrows in personal and business matters three days before his wedding and continued for thirty-five years until November 8, 1896, three weeks before his death from typhoid fever.

Regina was tall, with an hourglass figure, but when she wore her brunette hair pulled back severely in a bun, she looked plain and older. William's and Regina's marriage seemingly was happy. There were four servants to run the household, expensive velvet, lace, and satin dresses for Regina, as well as hundred-dollar cash gifts on her birthdays, carriage drives in Central Park, dinners at Delmonico's, evenings playing whist at a penny a game, hosting musical soirées, and dancing or attending the theater and operas.[31]

Devoted to Regina, in 1862 William sat for hours at her bedside as she recovered from losing a baby just before it was due and again, the following year when a baby was stillborn.[32] Then in 1865, George Augustus was born, followed the next year by Paula Theoda, the Theoda being in honor of William's oldest brother, Theodor.

Save for Regina falling ill with diphtheria in 1870, all was well with their marriage insofar as William was concerned. In February 1875, he was saddened by the death of his sister Wilhelmina and then stunned later in the year when he learned of his wife's unfaithfulness. On 18 September, he confronted Regina about her affair with a New Yorker named Louis Stern during the years 1868 and 1869. One of the addresses where William charged the acts of adultery had occurred was 107 East Fourteenth Street, their home adjacent to Steinway Hall and later one of its warerooms.[33] The other address was their home near the Steinway factory.

William also cited Stern, rather than himself, as the actual father of Alfred, the "splendid, long healthy boy"[34] whose birth William had welcomed ecstatically in 1869, the day after Regina's twenty-sixth birthday. William had been so joyful that George and Paula had a baby brother, he had given the servants champagne. After the confrontation with Regina, William heartbrokenly poured out his misery in his diary. "I suffer the tortures of hell and pass a perfectly sleepless night, the most terrible I have ever lived through by the discovery I make."

Incredibly, after this showdown, Regina continued to live on at 26 Gramercy Park, and on New Year's Eve she even joined William for a midnight supper and they congratulated each other on the New Year.[35]

Brooding about the evening as well as all of 1875, William stayed up until 3:00 a.m. Anguished, he confided in his diary: "By a superhuman effort I continue not to show my mental sufferings too apparently, while my wife seems to enjoy herself very much and thus pass from the year 1875, the most horrible I have ever lived through, into the year 1876 with the settled conviction in my mind that for me all enjoyment of life is forever gone and only praying to the Almighty God to extend my life long enough that I can put all our firm's affairs as well as my private matters into such shape as not to distress my brothers, yet to take care of my children properly, and shield them from disgrace."

It was not until May 1876 that this miserable period in William's life reached a climax. On the evening of 15 May, his divorce complaint was served on Regina. After taking it upstairs to read, she dashed back to the parlor and began an argument with him that was so loud the children awoke, screaming. Two days later, she obtained a passport made out to Regina Roos and child. Before she left on 20 May, William gave her 2,000 francs as part of the divorce settlement. He had agreed to pay her $2,500, an amount less than his lawyer's fee.[36]

Regina's parting from William and their children was like a scene from a pulp novel. After she kissed George and Paula farewell, a weeping William drove her and Alfred to the docks to board the steamer *Labrador*. Ending their marriage in civilized fashion, they drank champagne. Then, a still-crying William kissed Regina and Alfred good-bye as Regina pressed a small package into his hands for him to open at home. As the *Labrador* pulled out of the harbor, both Regina and William sobbed uncontrollably. William was so distraught that a friend had to support him. At home, he again broke down when he opened the little box and found Regina had returned her wedding ring accompanied by an affectionate note.[37]

In June, just one month after Regina sailed for France and two months after the divorce decree became final, she was joined in Paris by Louis Dachauer, a nationally acclaimed organist, with whom she had also committed adultery. French by birth, Louis, who was the same age as William, had won first prize at the Paris Conservatory of Music for original compositions before emigrating to the United States where one of his pieces, *Dachauer's Mass*, was regularly performed at churches.[38] Regina and Louis moved into a home he owned in Lorraine, posing as husband and wife.

As time passed, William grew less sentimental about Regina. By September, one month after the divorce was finalized, he was referring to her as Madame Reg. Roos.[39] He was relieved there was no unpleasant publicity due to having settled out of court. When on 10 March 1877, he received his lawyer's bill for handling the divorce, he thought the matter was confined to the past. He haggled over the bill, negotiating the price down from $3,500 to $2,000.[40]

It was with utter consternation[41] then, that he read the 24 March 1877 edition of *The New York Times*. In its page-six divorce column, a relatively new feature, the paper disclosed Regina's infidelity in connection with the Dachauer divorce suit filed by Louis's wife, Maria.

The *Times* reported: "A number of divorce cases were brought before the courts yesterday in one form or another. Perhaps the most singular of them was brought by Maria Dachauer against Louis Dachauer on the grounds of her husband's alleged adultery. Mrs. Dachauer charges her husband with having had improper intercourse with one Regina Roos Steinway, the wife of William Steinway. The latter, Mrs. Dachauer says, has since obtained a divorce from his wife on account of such improprieties. Mrs. Dachauer says her husband committed adultery with Mrs. Steinway at the latter's home in Gramercy Park, and also at his own residence."

Three weeks later, on 15 April, William gained vengeful satisfaction when he learned that Louis Stern, to whom he had referred in his diary as "Judas Stern," had lost his job a little more than a month after he had been discharged by his previous employer on 4 March.[42]

Despite his bitterness at Regina's duplicity, William sent her and Dachauer money from time to time along with photographs of George and Paula. In August, 1878, Louis died from injuries he had suffered in an accident the previous month. By 1879, William had largely succeeded in blotting out his unhappiness, but it was revived on the rainy night of 29 March 1879 when he spotted Louis Stern in the audience at a New York Philharmonic concert at Steinway Hall of Beethoven's Ninth Symphony.

"My enjoyment was marred by the sight of Judas among the audience," he wrote in his diary.[43] Six months later, on 20 September, William took fourteen-year-old George out for dinner and then later at home "revealed in brief lines I am divorced from his mother and what she did. He expressed no surprise. It is quite a load off my mind."[44]

On 12 January 1881, Regina died of typhoid fever. On receiving word by cable of her death, William telegraphed her brother, George, as to whether she was to be buried in Buffalo or France. George's decision was France, and William paid for Regina's burial expenses and offered to take care of any debts incurred by her.[45]

Subsequently, William managed to expunge the notoriety of Regina's unfaithfulness. For example, the 1895 edition of *Contemporary America Biography*, published by the Atlantic Publishing and Engraving Company, incorrectly said he "lost his first wife by death in 1876." In actuality, it was the year of their divorce.

William did keep in touch with Alfred, who received his medical degree in Heidelberg and set up practice in Munich. When Alfred broke his leg in 1891, he wrote William requesting 500 marks for sunbathing to heal the fracture. William cabled the money immediately and in his will he bequeathed $25,000 "to Dr. Alfred Roos, a nephew."[46]

As William recovered from the pain of his divorce, he suffered additional family sorrow. His brother Albert died of typhoid fever on 14 May 1877 at the age of thirty-seven. It was to Albert that he had primarily confided his grief about Regina. Also, it was Albert who had supervised the construction of Steinway Village and been in charge of the purchase of the most modern machinery, heating, and lighting for the new Long Island City factory. He had likewise taken charge of the company's display at the 1876 Philadelphia Exhibition.

As was his father's, Albert's funeral was held at Steinway Hall. On this occasion, the New York Philharmonic provided the accompanying dirges. While flags in the district were lowered to half mast in his honor, eight factory workers who had known him from his youth served as pallbearers. Then, three months later, William's mother died at the age of seventy-four. After twenty-seven years in New York, all that remained of the original Steinways were William, Theodor, and Doretta, who had married Jacob Ziegler, a furniture maker.

With time William's gloom lifted and he applied himself to his vast array of interests with his usual zeal. His whirlwind of family, business, and public activities over the next two decades left a lasting imprint on both Steinway & Sons and the United States.

## Chapter III
# *William: The Last Twenty Years*

In August 1880, William, then forty-four years old, remarried. The matchmaking was handled by his brother, Theodor, while he was in Hamburg that year to launch Steinway & Sons' first - and still only - overseas manufacturing branch. Theodor's choice was twenty-six-year-old Elizabeth Ranft, the eldest daughter of a former Brooklyn resident, Richard Ranft, who had moved to Dresden, Germany. After a brief introductory conversation with Elizabeth, William proposed on the eleventh of August.[1] They were married five days later and honeymooned in Vienna, sightseeing at such landmarks as the Schönbrunn, the Hapsburgs' palace.

The heavyset Elizabeth, whom William called Ellie, was not as physically attractive as Regina but she had personality traits Regina lacked. William found her to be a good, honest, and loving wife, as well as kind to George and Paula. It gave him great pleasure that each New Year's Eve she expressed her thanks to him for all he did for her.[2]

William and Ellie had three children: William Richard, born in 1881, Theodore Edwin, born two years later, and Maud Emily Louise, born in 1889. The family spoke German as well as English, and divided its time between the Long Island mansion in the summer and Gramercy Park the rest of the year. William was a devoted and doting father, although he was extremely displeased the time ebullient young William, called Willie as a child and Billie later in life, requested a Steinway factory superintendent to build an enormous doghouse with lumber from the factory yard and to charge it to his father. The bill was so steep that William threatened to cut off Willie's allowance for a year.

While William's family life was serene, the labor situation at Steinway & Sons was not. The workers had grown to resent the harsh discipline that Theodor Steinway had imposed. Stern and inflexible, Theodor's genius in piano design did not extend to labor relations. He had never shed what William labeled his "German ideas about workingmen."[3] Theodor's concepts were far more rigid than those prevalent in America. For instance, while the ten-hour day prevailed in both the United States and Germany, Theodor subscribed to the German dictum that employees could not refuse extra work.

Additionally, he believed that workers, like soldiers, should follow orders. Theodor did not view himself as a martinet; indeed, his ultimate objective was laudable. He was determined that every piano should be flawless and was equally certain this could be achieved solely through "every workman making only one and the same product so as to achieve an absolute perfection in his work." Thus, he ruled that an employee must forever remain in his own particular department and never assist a fellow worker.

The stipulation did have the virtue of preventing the theft of piano construction secrets. Even today, when all but a few of Steinway's patents have expired, there are no blueprints for its pianos. Instead, patterns are made in-house by one person who parcels them out to the thirty departments. These departments, of which the largest - the soundboard division - has just twenty-three people, range from case parts to case assembly, action production, action assembly, tuning, and polishing. So successful is this protective policy, nobody has ever left Steinway to start a piano manufacturing company on his own.

Moreover, the practice instilled pride in the workers about the expertise of their respective departments. It was customary for some to sign their work. The regulators signed the eighty-eighth key with their initials or name as symbolic of their infusion of the piano's personality - its tone. Regulation is done by hardening and softening the felt of the hammers so the sound will not be too brilliant or too mellow and by checking that the keys depress and rebound evenly. The inspectors who did the final checking inscribed their initials on the side of the third key from the top. But because each item was scrutinized before the next operation, the workers began to fear dire repercussions if something bearing their name was deemed imperfect.

Consequently, officially they stopped autographing. However, it was the practice of tone regulator Ramon Parada, a thirty year employee who retired in 1988, to write his name on the side or bottom of the top key. Parada took tremendous pride in his work, which involved forty tests performed six times each on every note. Like most workers at the factory, he made some of his tools. They were simple but effective, such as a tab from the lid of a milk carton he used when he plucked the strings to prevent his fingers from being hurt.[4] Parada reserved his signing for pianos he regulated on significant days - unhappy ones, such as the day President John F. Kennedy was assassinated and the day the attempt was made on President Ronald Reagan's life, and happy ones, such as when the Yankees or the Mets won the World Series.[5]

While Theodor's assignment rules had logic, his decrees on workplace conduct were extremely strict. "All workers are to maintain a clean, orderly and moral existence, keep the benefit of the factory uppermost in their mind and protect it against harm," he declared. They had to hand in an identification card on arrival at work and reclaim it before going home. Those who lost their tag were fined fifty cents and required to pay for a new one. If they arrived late for the day shift, they were fined twenty-five cents; if at night, they lost 10 percent of their wages that week.[6]

Mistakes either had to be corrected on their own time or paid for if someone else did the repair. Moreover, they were subject to summary dismissal for the pettiest of reasons. For example, one employee was fired for "looking too much around," another for "standing away from his work without making an excuse," and a third "because he whistled although forbidden to do so." Several more were fired for their refusal "to pay for imperfect work," "not following their foreman's instructions" or for "participating in strikes."[7] Understandably, the workers chafed under this yoke. Although William conceded that Theodor's rules created "much consternation and dissatisfaction" and claimed that he himself disliked the "rigid control," he did little to ease it.[8]

The workers' resentment finally boiled over in September 1882 due to the harsh treatment by the general superintendent Adolph Sommer, who zealously applied Theodor's dogma. The breaking point erupted after nine piano lids, approved at the Steinway Village factory, were rejected as unfit because of cracks by the Fourth Avenue plant where the parts were assembled. Sommer fired the two lid makers without pay, in line with Theodor's summary-dismissal injunction. The two men requested that he reconsider, maintaining they were blameless and that either the wood was of poor quality or the varnishers had applied too thin a veneer.

When Sommer denied their claim, all eight hundred Long Island City workers went on strike. The five hundred Fourth Avenue workers took similar action. The walkout occurred while William and Theodor were in Germany, leaving their young nephew, twenty-five-year-old Charles Herman, the second of their brother Charles's three sons, in charge. He proved to be as tough as his uncles, unwilling to even consider firing the unpopular Sommer, although his dismissal would have defused the strike.

"Discharges or transfers of employees are not permissible without the positive order of Steinway & Sons to do so," Charles Herman stated. "Therefore, I positively refuse to discharge him."[9] Then he proceeded to reject the demand that the lid makers should not bear all the blame. Said Charles: "To be able to produce absolutely faultless instruments, we must hold every workman responsible for the accuracy of his work according to our system of thirty years' standing under which the Steinway piano has attained its worldwide reputation as the most durable instrument. We must positively decline to change these fundamental principles of our business."[10]

The strikers held their ground, thinking they had William at a disadvantage since it was September, the peak season for piano orders. They reckoned he would cave in out of anxiety for production to resume. In an effort to thwart the entry into the plant by non union strikebreakers William hired on his return, some strikers resorted to firing shotguns into the air to frighten them away.

But they misjudged William. As in 1872, he stood fast against the pressure. His lone concession was to dispatch Sommer to the Hamburg plant - but just for six months. Otherwise, he was unyielding. He requested the Long Island City Police Department to throw a protective cordon around the site to prevent outright violence. Then, knowing that the strike fund was small and that the strikers lacked support from employees at other piano factories, William issued eviction notices to all those workers who rented company-owned houses and had not paid their installments for two months. By mid-November, sixty days after the wildcat strike exploded, it was over.

All remained calm until 1886, when the issue of the eight-hour day cropped up again, although it did not lead to a strike. Once more, William was opposed to a shorter work day, despite the fact that many pianomakers were reconciled to the idea. This time, too, William was victorious, and his triumph aroused wide support from other captains of industry. "Thank you for your firmness in holding to the ten hours' rule," the Furniture Manufacturing Association wired him.[11] The *New York Sun* editorialized that the "eight-hour movement was defeated because it was impossible for it to be successful without ruin to both employer and employed."[12]

The eight-hour issue was not resolved in William's lifetime. When another strike flared up over this contentious matter in 1890, William again refused to budge. On business in Europe at the time, he wired

Charles Herman, who, as his personal assistant, was in charge, to remain firm. "Never yield regular work day less than ten hours," his instructions read.[13]

Concurrent with bringing Steinway's workers to heel, William was involved in two projects typical of his penchant for thinking on a big scale: the development of a summer resort at North Beach on Long Island Sound between Flushing and Bowery bays, east of Steinway Village, and tunnels under the East River linking Long Island with Manhattan.

Just as with Steinway Village, in the development of the North Beach project William was motivated by a combination of goodwill and the profit motive. The complex, which opened in 1886, had hotels, boating, picnic grounds, a menagerie of rare animals plus an aviary, carousels, and a Ferris wheel. It featured an exciting novelty - electrically lit night bathing. There also were nightly dances, except Sundays when concerts were held instead.

From a public spirit viewpoint, William had visualized North Beach as a way to get rid of what *The New York Times* described as a "great number of impudent roughs who indulge in nude bathing in the waters of Bowery Bay, to the disgust and annoyance of the respectable residents."[14] As an astute businessman, he had figured North Beach would be a moneymaker and, consequently, traffic would increase on the streetcar line he owned, the Steinway and Hunters Point Railroad.

The ambitious scope of the project - the steamboat pier alone cost $50,000 - dictated that William bring in a partner. He settled on beer baron George Ehret. The two had much in common. Like William, Ehret was a German-American who had built a multimillion-dollar business from scratch. A year younger than William, he had emigrated to New York from Germany in 1857, seven years after the arrival of Henry Engelhard Steinway and his family.

Ehret worked for other brewers for a decade and then established his own firm, Hell Gate Brewery. At that time, American brewers made malt beer well, but their methods of brewing lager were primitive. Ehret was a leader in installing new methods of making lager and his business boomed. He also was one of the first brewers to use artificial ice-making machines and refrigeration.[15]

Like William, Ehret invested much of his money in real estate. He became the second largest landlord in New York after the John Jacob Astor estate. It was said of him that he never raised the rent or evicted a tenant for inability to pay it.[16]

Besides being self-made millionaires, William and Ehret shared an interest in music and supported needy performers. Both were prominent in New York's German-American community. They were alike, too, in that they thrived on complex, massive business challenges. Thus, when William approached Ehret with his scheme, he received an enthusiastic reaction. The faith of both men was justified. North Beach was a huge success. The chance of any hooligans causing trouble was prevented by a police patrol of thirty officers. As a further precaution, a jail was built close by.

Today, there are no remnants of the project. Instead, the Grand Central Parkway runs along the shoreline and La Guardia Airport juts out from what was the site.

Engrossed in the North Beach project, William paid little attention to the birth in the 1880s of three pianomakers -Schimmel of Europe, Baldwin of the United States, and Yamaha of Japan - that ultimately would overshadow Steinway & Sons in terms of volume of sales. Schimmel, which became Steinway's chief European competitor, was the first of the trio to make its appearance. In 1885, just five years after Steinway & Sons established its Hamburg branch, then thirty-one-year-old Wilhelm Schimmel opened a factory in Leipzig, in central Germany. The son of a schoolmaster who also was a tailor, Schimmel first apprenticed as a cabinetmaker specializing in accordions and violins. Today, the company is Western Europe's leading pianomaker. Its annual production exceeds the combined output of Germany's thirteen other pianomakers, including Steinway.

The advent of Schimmel was followed in 1887 by the establishment of Baldwin and Yamaha. In their heart of hearts, the Steinways would come to speculate that Baldwin might not exist if William had not made a snap decision in January of 1887. Without advance notice, he withdrew the Cincinnati dealership from Dwight Hamilton Baldwin and awarded it to M. Steinert Company of Boston. His reason was that Steinert, a Steinway representative for longer than Baldwin, had decided to open a branch in Cincinnati.[17] Actually, that city was one of Steinert's two original locations when Morris Steinert launched his business in 1860. When the Civil War began, Steinert, a Northern supporter, sold his Athens, Georgia store and moved to Boston. At the same time his son, Fred, who ran the Cincinnati store, sold that outlet to Dwight Baldwin.

Baldwin did not seem the type destined to become a dynamic presence in the business world. Born in 1821 in Pennsylvania, he intially intended to be a minister but found the circuit-riding expected of a preacher in the mid-nineteenth century too demanding. His other interest was music, and he began teaching throughout Kentucky and Ohio, finally settling in Cincinnati in 1856. As his students frequently consulted him as to the brand of piano to buy, Baldwin decided in 1862 to become a dealer. By 1887, he had stores throughout Ohio, as well as in Louisville and Indianapolis. He was a curious hybrid of devoutness and commercialism. He refused to send out mail on Saturdays because he did not want letters travelling on the Sabbath, yet he kept his stores open on Sundays.[18]

When Baldwin lost the Steinway franchise, his young partner, Lucien Wulsin, urged him to become a piano and organ manufacturer. Wulsin had as unlikely a background as Baldwin. A Southerner by birth, he served in the Ohio Cavalry on the side of the North during the Civil War. Badly wounded, he was discharged at the age of twenty. He enrolled in penmanship and bookkeeping at a Cincinnati commercial college and, on graduating, became a bookkeeper for Baldwin. By 1872, he was a partner. Baldwin's manufacturing started with organs in 1889 in Chicago, then the hub of the organ industry. In 1890, he branched into pianomaking, initially concentrating on uprights, because Steinway & Sons specialized in grands. The following year he moved Baldwin's headquarters to Cincinnati.

Once again, Baldwin's days as a preacher shaped the business. He forbade a line of pianos to be named Dwight as he was a teetotaler, and he was afraid the name would conjure up connotations of Dwight, Illinois, where there was a sanitarium for alcoholics.[19] Baldwin died in 1899, three years after William. Childless, he bequeathed his entire estate, save for a bequest to his widow, to the Board of Home and Foreign Missions of the Presbyterian Church. Wulsin and three partners subsequently purchased the company from the Baldwin estate.

Since the 1890s, Cincinnati has been Baldwin territory, and Steinway has had to switch dealers several times. Ironically, Steinert chose to withdraw to concentrate on New England instead; it remains one of Steinway's biggest dealers. The rivalry between Steinway and Baldwin in Cincinnati often verged on the farcical. "We had to compete on every grand piano sale against Baldwin; everyone first examined the Baldwin and then came to us," recalls Frank Mazurco, a former Steinway salesman in Cincinnati who became the company's vice president of sales and marketing in 1985.[20] That is, of course, the Steinway version of the direction shoppers took to make comparisons.

The vying of the two firms for performers also had amusing moments. "Whenever performers who used the Steinway came to

Cincinnati to play with the Cincinnati Orchestra, which used a Baldwin as its house piano, Baldwin would romance them," Mazurco says. "The president of Baldwin and members of Ohio's Lazarus department store family, who were well connected with the Cincinnati Orchestra, would meet the performers at the train station or airport and host them at dinners. Often, both Steinway and Baldwin would have welcoming committees cheek-to-jowl."[21]

At the same time as Dwight Baldwin launched his business, across the world in Japan what is now the world's largest pianomaker, Yamaha, began under far less auspicious circumstances. Torakusu Yamaha was the son of a Samurai who worked as a surveyor and taught Torakusu and his brothers mathematics, engineering, and science. Torakusu Yamaha, like Dwight Baldwin, was not initially interested in pianos. Instead, he first made watches. When his business fared poorly, he switched to making medical equipment. He got into pianomaking by chance. According to company lore, when he was in the remote rural village of Hamamatsu, fifty miles from Osaka, local officials asked him to fix their Mason & Hamlin organ. There were few organ repair technicians then in Japan, and those that did exist rarely traveled to Hamamatsu. Thus, Yamaha was asked to help because of his mechanical aptitude.[22]

Sensing the potential of the organ business, Yamaha decided to switch careers. To get launched, he is said to have made drawings of the Mason & Hamlin's reed organ mechanism, which was then unfamiliar to the Japanese whose chief musical instruments at the time were forms of the harp, flute, and guitar. As the first manufacturer of such organs, Yamaha loosened Japan's dependence on imports of the instruments from the United States. He also prospered because he organized his production in the style of the American assembly line. By 1890, three years after setting up his business, he had fared so well that his staff had grown to one hundred.

In the 1890s, Japanese musical tastes shifted to upright pianos, also imported from the United States, in preference to organs. Spotting the trend, Yamaha branched into piano production in 1900 under the name Nippon Gakki Company (Japan Musical Instrument Company). By 1910, he also was making some grand pianos. Yamaha was retained as the brand name and, in 1987, as recognition that Yamaha was better known than Nippon Gakki, the company became Yamaha Corporation. In its first year of piano production, the firm built only two. Today, its annual production ranges between 200,000 and 250,000. By contrast, Steinway currently makes about 4,500 a year.

Back in the late 1880s and 1890s, William paid little heed to the birth of these piano companies. After all, Steinway & Sons reigned supreme. A tight-fisted Thomas Edison wrote in June 1890 from his Orange, New Jersey, laboratory: "Gents - I have decided to keep your grand piano. For some reason unknown to me it gives better results than any so far tried. Please send bill with lowest price."[23] Others were willing to spend much more than Edison. Also under William, Steinway's business in hand-painted and decorated *art case* pianos reached its peak. The company had started taking orders for such custom-designed pianos in 1855, just two years after its establishment. Actually, while Steinway did the elaborate carving on the case and legs, paintings and other decoration were applied by artists - many of them located in Europe - commissioned either by Steinway or directly by the purchaser. Between 1855 and 1930, when demand dried up due to the depression, Steinway received several hundred orders from the United States and Europe for *art case* pianos.

New York's exclusive set, the so-called *Four Hundred*, felt their Fifth Avenue and Newport, Rhode Island mansions were bare unless they contained an art case Steinway. The fifty thousandth Steinway, a magnificently decorated instrument, was sold to Lord Nathaniel Rothschild, head of the British branch of the fabulously wealthy banking family. Frederick Vanderbilt purchased a concert grand and had it decorated in Paris with small portraits of opera composers on the side of the piano and a floral and white gold-leaf pattern for his wife to place in the drawing room of their Hyde Park, New York mansion. He had hired the famous architect Stanford White to sketch the design. Mrs. Vanderbilt was a music lover who hosted concerts and other musical events at their estate.[24]

How much Vanderbilt paid for his wife's piano is unknown but in 1920 it was listed by Steinway-London at 600 pounds sterling (approximately $180,000 at today's prices). Another idea of the cost of such artwork is provided by an order from Henry G. Marquand, a man of many careers including railway tycoon, major shareholder in the Newport Casino in Newport, Rhode Island, and first president of the New York Metropolitan Museum of Art. He paid $1,200 for his grand, then shipped it to London where painter Sir Lawrence Alma-Tadema applied $40,000 worth of magnificent artwork. A small version of Sir Edward Poynter's well-known painting *The Wandering Minstrels* was reproduced above the keyboard, the music stand was cut in a honeysuckle design, the case encrusted with ivory, coral, and mother-of-pearl inlays, and the legs carved in the shape of lions. The names of Apollo, the Greek and Roman god of music, and the Greek muses of the arts were inscribed within ribbon-tied laurel wreaths on the lid. On Marquand's death in 1903, the piano was sold at auction for a mere $8,000. In 1980, it was auctioned again, this time at Sotheby's, where it fetched a price commensurate with its appearance - $390,000, the most paid to that date for a musical instrument.

A less aesthetic display of conspicuous consumption was manifested by the rags-to-riches Edward Doheny. He began as an impoverished prospector who tramped across the western United States for twenty years hoping to make a big strike in gold. Instead he struck oil in 1892. One of his first purchases was a sentimental gesture - a Steinway piano with a sculpted bust of a little boy, probably his son, at each end of the keyboard. John Howland Steinway, however, classified it as the "worst ever art case piano, the ultimate in bad taste."[25] Other wealthy purchasers included financier Jay Gould and industrialist-art collector Henry Frick.

Royalty showered awards and Royal Warrants on the firm in appreciation of pianos made for them. Awards included the Order of the Red Eagle of Germany(third class), the French Legion of Honor, a gold medal from the King of Sweden, and the Order of the Lion and Son of Persia. By Royal Warrants Steinway was appointed pianomaker to the rulers of England, Italy, Norway, Persia, Portugal, Romania, Russia, Spain, Sweden and Turkey.

The issue of warrants by both Queen Victoria and the Prince and Princess of Wales prompted William to discard his usual mixture of restraint and pomposity in advertising. He was the first piano manufacturer to advertise regularly, but his advertisements normally were small and hard to distinguish from surrounding ones for such products as Dr. Warner's Health corset ("secures health and comfort of body with grace and beauty of form") and Dick's Tasteless Medicines ("for sale by all druggists").

Moreover, the fine print of Steinway ads practically necessitated a magnifying glass, destroying the impact since the ads were wordy. A typical one ran:

> In perusing the pamphlets of the limited number of piano firms who deserve to be classified as real "manufacturers" among the large number of "compilers" who buy nearly every portion of their pianos *ready-made* the amused reader very soon finds that each manufacturer not only claims to make the best piano,

> but in several instances it is asserted that all other pianomakers have fraudulently appropriated their own inventions and ideas without, however, adducing the slightest proof for their absurd statement, or even naming or attempting to describe any of their alleged inventions.
>
> One of the older houses (notoriously the very last to adopt the Overstrung System), unblushingly concludes a ridiculous tirade against its competitors by the preposterous sentence that "Every vital point in the construction of the perfect piano of today has been the original and exclusive work of -, viz. themselves.
>
> Messrs. Steinway & Sons do not claim to any such thing, being conscious of the fact that good pianos were made in Europe and America before their house even existed. What we do claim is: The Steinway piano is a distinctly original creation, whose highest standard of excellence is the result of the progressive improvements made in building up a new and perfect system of piano construction by Steinway & Sons.
> Respectfully,
> Steinway & Sons

After receiving the two British Royal Warrants, William exploited them by abandoning such low-key promotion and splurging on something that would appeal to the desire of ordinary mortals to hobnob with the rich and titled. A double-page advertisement, in purple and gold inks, that ran in the *Musical Courier* announced the royal honors and then listed 174 top-drawer Steinway purchasers in order of titled precedence, commencing with five dukes and duchesses followed by twenty-seven earls and countesses, nine marquesses and marchionesses, and down the ladder to lords, barons, viscounts, sirs, honorables, generals, admirals, and colonels. It went on to suggest: "You too can be a duke - well, not quite, really. But you can acquire a tinge of the celestial dukeishness by buying the same brand of piano as did his Grace."

It was partly due to William's many contacts with performers that Austrian violinist Fritz Kreisler made his U.S. debut at the age of thirteen in 1888. The opportunity arose for Kreisler from the desire of Edmund Stanton, the manager of the New York Metropolitan Opera House, also home of the New York Philharmonic until 1892, to book Moritz Rosenthal, a talented twenty-six-year-old pianist, during his

U.S. tour. As Rosenthal was a Steinway artist, Stanton asked William to put in a good word for him. The Polish-born Rosenthal had moved to Austria where he was impressed by Kreisler's playing, and he, in turn, suggested that Kreisler be included in the program.

William and Stanton basked in the reflected glory of the Rosenthal-Kreisler concerts. "Master Kreisler," as he was billed, made his debut in short breeches, though he had wanted trousers.[26] Rosenthal and Kreisler began in Boston and then traveled to New York, where Kreisler received warm reviews. "He has a most agile and accurate left hand and if his manipulation of the bow were as excellent as his tone formation, he would be a violinist, young as he is, who could measure himself with some of those who stand highest in the world's admiration," the *New York Tribune* commented.[27]

Throughout this period, William was expanding his outside interests. He became active in the Democratic Party and a friend of President Grover Cleveland. In 1886, during Cleveland's first term, William presented him with a grand piano for his wedding that year at the White House. In 1888, William was chosen to represent New York on the Democratic National Committee and was a delegate to the convention that nominated Cleveland for a second term. Cleveland lost the election. William was a delegate again in 1892 when Cleveland once more became the Democratic candidate, and that time he won.

Around the time of Cleveland's election campaigns, William twice rejected the nomination for Mayor of New York, even though being nominated guaranteed election. By the early 1890s, he was listed in the Social Register, the tabulation of High Society that first appeared in 1887.

Another new interest was Gottlieb Daimler's revolutionary high-speed internal combustion engine. It is likely that William and Daimler became acquainted through a Steinway executive who was a brother of Daimler's associate, Wilhelm Maybach, designer of the first Mercedes car.[28] During a visit to Germany in 1888, William asked Daimler to give him a demonstration of the new combustion engine. An obliging Daimler picked William up at his Stuttgart hotel and drove him ten miles, up and down hill, to his factory at Bad Canstatt in forty-eight minutes. Impressed, William installed the Daimler motor on his Long Island City streetcar line.

With the ten-horsepower engine, the trolley could carry thirty-five passengers at a speed of twelve miles an hour. William subsequently obtained the rights to manufacture the motor in North America, and he built a plant near Steinway & Sons' Long Island factory.

Starting with ten-horsepower engines, the factory rapidly added sixteen-, then twenty-, and twenty-five-power ones. Soon the engine was in every sort of machine from knife grinders to electric power stations. An elated William had to expand the premises sixfold.

It was about this time that William started to deliberate about who in the family would succeed him. His children from his first marriage, George and Paula, both married in 1888. Paula's husband, Louis von Bernuth, who came from Germany in the 1860s, was one of many young Germans whom William helped get settled in America. Handsome and bright, Louis was of tremendous assistance to William at the factory, as well as in his real estate and transportation ventures.

But helpful as Louis was, he could not succeed William because the presidency was restricted to those bearing the Steinway name.

George, who suffered from delicate health, withdrew from the business around the time of his wedding, at the age of twenty-three, to Ottilie Roessler of New York. Although they had three daughters born in quick succession in 1889, 1890, and 1892, the marriage was not a success. George spent considerable time traveling and in 1895, while he was in India during a trip around the world, Ottilie obtained a divorce. In 1897, George, who had remained a shareholder after his departure from the business, was named to the board of directors to fill the vacancy created by William's death the previous year. George's directorship was brief; he died in 1898 while sailing for Rotterdam on a trip he hoped would improve his health.

William's sons by his second marriage, Willie and Theodore, were still youngsters. Thus, when his sixty-year-old brother, Theodor, informed William in 1885 that he wished to return to Germany, William asked him to go over his construction methods with three of their nephews - the younger two sons of their brother Charles, Charles Herman, the one who had been inflexible during the 1882 strike, and Frederick Theodore, as well as Henry Ziegler, the second oldest son of their sister Doretta. Both Henry and Charles Herman were then twenty-eight; Frederick was three years younger.

William's precaution proved wise: Daily cables throughout late 1888 and early 1889 from Germany reported on Theodor's deteriorating condition from asthma and heart trouble, largely caused by constant smoking, according to his doctors.[29] Despite his failing health, Theodor befriended Ferrucio Busoni, a promising Italian pianist living in Germany, by mapping out a U.S. debut for him.[30] That tour never materialized because on March 12, 1889, Theodor, who was childless and whose wife had predeceased him, died on the eve of a recuperative trip to Italy. Shortly after Theodor's death, an English syndicate sought to buy Steinway & Sons for $4 million, but William rejected the bid.

William's relationship with his nephews Charles Herman and Frederick Theodore was cordial; that with their elder brother, Henry William Theodore, was not and culminated in a lawsuit. Henry, who had previously worked at the Hamburg branch, became a member around 1890 of Steinway & Sons' board of directors, which was made up entirely of family. Convinced that Steinway Village and the Hamburg operations were a financial drain on the company, Henry was at odds with the rest of the board. After a year of bickering, William demanded at the end of 1891 that he resign or face prosecution. For twelve days, Henry refused to hand in his resignation; when he did, William incorrectly believed he was rid of this "brute."[31]

Instead, Henry filed a lawsuit against Steinway. The case, which came to trial in December 1894 in the New York Supreme Court, revolved around Henry's allegations of the harmful effects on the company of Steinway Village and the Hamburg plant. "The vast sums of money expended on developing Steinway Village have no immediate relation to the objects for which the firm was incorporated," Henry claimed. Hamburg, he added, was a burden because it acted as a competitor rather than as an overseas arm. He further maintained that the price of pianos was artificially inflated due to the New York and Hamburg operations overcharging each other for goods.

In its February 1895 decision, the New York Supreme Court dismissed all of Henry's charges, pointing out that "as industrial conditions change, business methods must change with them and acts become permissible which at an earlier period would not have been considered to be within corporate power." The Court also implied that Henry's purchase of more stock in Steinway & Sons around the time he filed his suit indicated approval of how the company was run. The main point at issue - the extent of a corporation's power - was deemed so important by Harvard University's Law School that it included the case in its curriculum.

Henry, who was just thirty-nine when the court case ended, never worked again. A bachelor, he lived off the inheritance from his father and his shares in the business. His chief occupation was fishing, and he died in 1939 at the age of eighty-three from pneumonia contracted during a fishing trip.[32] He bequeathed the bulk of his estate to New York's Lenox Hill Hospital. The only bequest to his family was $10,000 to Billie, William's eldest son by his second marriage.[33]

While the court battle rocked the family, William's preeminence in the musical world also was under attack. In 1889, plans were announced for a music hall at Fifty-seventh Street and Seventh Avenue with Andrew Carnegie as the principal sponsor. In a display of hubris that paralleled his cancellation of Dwight Baldwin's franchise as a Steinway dealer without notice, William airily dismissed the prospects of the new hall. "Mr. Carnegie's hall will never pay," he predicted. "The public can only stand a certain amount of this sort of music. As to educating the masses to an appreciation of high-class music, that cannot be done to such an extent as to encourage unendowed enterprise to go into business."[34]

For once, William was in agreement with his chief rival, Frank Chickering, who echoed William's sentiments that not enough people were interested in music to warrant another hall. "First-class concerts have always gone a-begging in Chickering Hall, with a seating capacity of fifteen hundred," Chickering stated.[35] But the New York Philharmonic's outgoing conductor, Theodore Thomas, who was about to move to Chicago to head its new orchestra, punctured William's and Chickering's arguments as self-serving.

He said: "At present New York has no place in which orchestral concerts can be effectively given. Steinway Hall is well enough as far as it goes, but it is not large enough and is ill-appointed besides. With a perfect music hall we shall be able to reach that part of the public which does not at present go to hear music from a sense of duty. Something more - comfort, even luxury - is required."[36] The Philharmonic's new conductor, Walter Damrosch, raised a further argument in the proposed hall's favor: Performers would not have to declare allegiance to a piano company to play in it, as those who appeared at Steinway and Chickering Halls had to do.[37]

Nevertheless, the hall's developers remained concerned, especially as Metropolitan Opera house manager Edmund Stanton agreed with William and Chickering. Stanton maintained that three halls would be too many because "New York has more music today than she can stand, and as for the stimulation of a great popular interest in classical concerts, I don't believe it can be done."[38]

Another cause for concern was the hall's location in what was then the "Uptown" of Manhattan, a considerable distance from the theater district, which at the time was much farther south near Steinway and Chickering halls. However, these doubts were offset by the fact that the district had become an area of fashionable residences whose millionaire owners were the audience at which the hall was targeted.

Even before the hall's five-day gala opening beginning May 5, 1891, with Piotr Ilyich Tchaikovsky as the guest conductor, it became evident it had won the public's affection. All tickets were sold weeks in advance. Newspaper reviews were ecstatic about the lavish decor and excellent acoustics. It quickly replaced the Steinway and Chickering auditoriums in popularity. Within months, William closed the auditorium at his hall, although he retained the showrooms. Chickering Hall remained open until 1895. However, there was a major consolation for both companies: As Carnegie Hall was not an extension of another pianomaker, the performers had to obtain instruments from existing suppliers, such as Steinway and Chickering. The hall also bought house pianos; from the outset, at least one has been a Steinway.

During his appearance at Carnegie Hall's dedicatory concerts, Tchaikovsky dealt a blow to Steinway's prestige by publicly praising the Knabe piano, made by Baltimore-based William Knabe & Company, which had been established fourteen years before Steinway & Sons. "The Knabe has a rare sympathetic and noble tone color, and perfect action," he wrote.[39] Cynics said his endorsement likely was prompted by Knabe largely paying his expenses.[40]

William had to find a way to erase the damage to Steinway's image from the closure of its auditorium and Tchaikovsky's testimonial to the Knabe. The solution was provided by his nephew, Charles Herman. Then head of Steinway's European operations, Charles heard an exciting young Polish pianist named Ignacy Paderewski play Beethoven's *Emperor Concerto* in London early in 1891. Impressed, Charles cabled William, suggesting that he book Paderewski for a U.S. tour later that year, beginning at Carnegie Hall. Although Paderewski was not regarded highly by many of his musical contemporaries and critics often were lukewarm, he had both a romantic and a melancholy history coupled with sex appeal, a potent combination in box-office promotion.

At the time of his trip to the United States, Paderewski had two mistresses; nonetheless, his image was that of a widower with an invalid child, and the public sympathized with his plight. Nearing his thirty-first birthday, he had thick reddish-gold hair, so appealing to his female fans that they tried to cut off his locks. His past was intriguing, too. His mother had died when he was three years old and his father had lost his money during the 1863 rebellion in Poland against Russia. Fortunately, some wealthy Poles learned of Paderewski's musical ability and paid for his education in Warsaw.

Paderewski earned $10 million overall in his piano-playing career and even served as Premier of Poland in 1919. But in his youth, he saved for months in order to buy new shoes and travel to Paris to hear the lionized Anton Rubinstein. On his arrival, he learned the five performances were sold out. Rubinstein's manager refused to find some way for the up-and-coming pianist to hear one of the recitals. Later, at the height of his fame, Paderewski always stipulated that some seats for his concerts be held for young students.

Paderewski made his professional debut in 1887, and one of his first performances was in Berlin. As he played an encore, the bored conductor, Hans von Bülow, yawned in full view of the audience. Time had not improved his temperament since he kicked the Chickering piano twelve years earlier. Thereafter, Paderewski refused to perform in Germany.

It had been twenty years since William had persuaded Anton Rubinstein to do seven concerts a week. With Paderewski, he made a marginal concession - an average of six concerts a week. While Paderewski occasionally had a day off, he sometimes had to play twice a day. All told, the contract called for eighty concerts at a lump sum of $30,000. That fee seemed generous, but on a per-concert basis it came to just $375, not much of a gain over Rubinstein's $200, considering it was two decades later. However, Charles Herman offered an attractive sweetener: an account at a London bank for Paderewski to draw against so he could devote all his time to preparation for the tour.

Later in his career, when he was the toast of the music world, Paderewski's fee escalated to as much as $25,000 a performance. His hands were insured for $100,000. In London, the Steinway branch would send a piano van to Victoria Station to pick up his luggage and take it to the luxury Carlton Hotel where he stayed. For his United States tours, William and his successors hired a private Pullman car with a bedroom, dining room, and sitting room for him. Paderewski was also given a special upright that could be taken apart to get it into the small compartment he used for practicing. There it was reassembled, and on arriving at his destination, Paderewski would order his car to be unhitched from the train and pulled onto a siding where he could play undisturbed by curiosity seekers.

By then, Paderewski also had a substantial entourage: two chefs, a masseur, valet, secretary, tour manager, tuner, personal treasurer, and, sometimes, a physician. He arose late, had brunch at 1:00 p.m. and dinner after his performance. Every night he and the master chef would engage in the same repartee. "Mr. Charles, your Boeuf Wellington is magnificent and your soufflé was very good" was the sort of compliment Paderewski would pay. Mr. Charles invariably replied, "Yes, and the soup was very good, too."[41]

But in 1891, Paderewski had none of these comforts. Like Rubinstein, he was seasick during the Atlantic crossing and exhausted when he reached New York on November 11. There, he had a reception that made him more miserable. Charles Tretbar, William's liaison with performers, greeted him brusquely and deprecatorily: "We hear you have had brilliant successes in London and Paris but let me tell you, Mr. Paderewski, you need not expect anything like that in America. We have heard them all, all the pianists, all the great ones, and our demands are very exacting. We are not easily pleased here. You should not expect extraordinary houses."[42]

The insults continued. Tretbar took Paderewski to a hotel so dirty that bugs crawled in the bed and mice scampered behind the walls.[43] The next day, Paderewski vehemently protested to William, and he was moved to better quarters at the Windsor Hotel at Fifth Avenue and Forty-sixth Street. Paderewski liked it so much that he continued to stay there even when he could afford more luxurious accommodation. Coincidentally, Louis Dachauer had stayed at the Windsor back in 1876 when his wife had the divorce writ served on him, naming William's first wife, Regina, as his partner in adultery.

Worried that the advance sale of only $500 worth of tickets for Paderewski's three performances, starting November 17, presaged a nearly empty Carnegie Hall, Tretbar sought to fill it by handing out free tickets. But Paderewski's tremendous success opening night resulted in lines at the box office for tickets to his other two performances. Tretbar promptly telegraphed the holders of the complimentary tickets to return them if they did not intend to use them. None did.

Paderewski's debut performance consisted of Saint-Saëns' *Concerto No. 4* in C minor, six Chopin works, and his own composition, *Concerto No. 1,* opus 17. The reviews were laudatory with some passing criticism. *The New York Times* started off with derogatory personal remarks but proceeded to praise him: "Paderewski is his name. It is not a pretty name, and it is not a pretty man; but he can play the piano. Yet he is not the ideal pianist. His program was arranged with cunning. He began by disappointing some of his auditors. Next he interested them and finally he conquered them. He played Saint-Saëns well but not incomparably. In the Chopin numbers he deepened the conviction that he had a wide range of sentiment, a gentle, melancholy poesy, the gift of pathos in music.

"It is a great gift and who can make it reach and touch his hearers through the medium of the piano is a musician of personal influence. His own concerto was a fitting climax. The work itself demands respect; its themes are musical and admirably divided between piano and orchestra. His performance of the solo part was a wonderfully brilliant piece of piano playing."[44]

Paderewski, however, felt he could have done better. Immediately after the concert, he started to practice in his hotel room for his appearance the next day with an entirely different program of Beethoven, Schumann, and Liszt. When the hotel manager said the late-night session disturbed other guests, Paderewski hurried down to Steinway Hall. After the night watchman admitted him, Paderewski placed two candles on top of a storeroom piano and practiced for the next ten hours even though the heat had been turned off for the night. He only stopped when it was time for a 10:00 a.m. rehearsal with the New York Philharmonic.[45]

His marathon rehearsal resulted in great acclaim. After his second peformance which was on his thirty-first birthday, the audience rushed onto the stage in approval, and the following morning the *Times* waxed enthusiastic: "The success of Ignacy Paderewski is assured. No pianist has made such a sentimental impression here since Anton Rubinstein. Paderewski is a great artist."[46] Even with such notices, Paderewski practiced for seventeen hours before his third concert.

The rave reviews combined with Paderewski's romantic aura touched off what the *Musical Courier* dubbed *Paddymania,* a precursor of the 1920s fervor for Rudolph Valentino, the 1940s craze for Frank Sinatra, the 1950s passion for Elvis Presley, and the 1960s swooning over the Beatles. Women mobbed Paderewski on the stage, pulled scissors out of their purses to snip off a piece of golden-red hair, and kissed his hands and clothing.

The rest of Paderewski's tour also was a resounding triumph. He was guest of honor at eighty-six parties[47] and invited to give private performances at soirées of the Vanderbilt-Astor set. The wining and dining combined with the energy he poured into his concerts often made him too tired to fall asleep. He would unwind with several hours of cribbage and bridge. But the ordeal was worth it. Paderewski sailed home with $95,000. The extra $65,000 came from twenty-six additional concerts arranged by William, who gave Paderewski the entire proceeds.

When Paderewski offered some of the money back, William grandiloquently refused, saying "To have discovered you is enough."[48] This was an overstatement as Paderewski already had had many triumphs in Europe. In any event, an overjoyed William presented Paderewski with a set of $400 diamond shirt studs to express his gratitude.[49]

When Paderewski returned to the United States in 1893, there again was a frenzy over him, but this time it revolved around which make of piano he would play at the World's Columbian Exposition, being held in Chicago in honor of the four hundredth anniversary of Columbus's discovery of America. The burning question was: Would Paderewski perform on a piano manufactured in the host city or on one produced by that New York outsider, Steinway & Sons?

What came to be known as "The Great Chicago Piano War" capped a year of intense emotional ups and downs for William. The year began gloomily as his pet project, underwater tunnels linking Manhattan and Long Island, was put on hold due to a tragic construction accident that killed five people and injured twenty others.

William's involvement dated back to 1890, when he obtained control of the financially strapped New York and Long Island Railroad Company, which had been formed to build the tunnels. William realized that the underwater passageway would make transportation across the East River far quicker than the ferry trip. That same year New York Mayor Abram Hewitt appointed him to the City's Rapid Transit Commission. Construction on the tunnels commenced in May 1892. It took months of digging and blasting before the actual tunneling could begin and so by December 28 the work had progressed a mere thirty-two feet. Then suddenly that day there was an enormous explosion caused by a worker's attempt to thaw one hundred pounds of frozen dynamite cartridges by placing them in a steam box, a common procedure.[50]

Due to this explosion plus a series of other setbacks, work on the tunnels was halted. William feared the enterprise was stillborn. Although bedridden with a high fever and a swollen left hand and elbow, he anxiously tried to save it, even chairing meetings from his sickbed.

His efforts were unavailing. Not until 1902, six years after William's death, was the project revived by his friend, banking tycoon August Belmont, Junior. He wanted to name it "Steinway Tunnels" as a tribute to William, but the final choice was "Belmont Tunnels" in recognition of the swift completion of the project under his direction. Belmont sold the tunnels to the City of New York in 1913, and they are now used by the Number Seven IRT subway line.[51]

Concern over the failure of the tunnel project was eclipsed by William's preoccupation with his family's health. While he himself was ailing, first twelve-year-old Willie and four-year-old Maud developed chicken pox.[52] Shortly after they recovered, Ellie, who had nursed the children and was caring for a still-weak William, caught a chill after going out one day on social calls and getting her feet wet.[53]

By the next day, March 2, the chill became pneumonia, and William called in three doctors. He was grief-stricken when they said there was no hope. Ellie died the afternoon of March 4. The day after was William's fifty-seventh birthday. It was a poignant day that oscillated between birthday greetings and funeral preparations.

William had to stifle his sorrow so as not to spoil the pleasure of Willie, Maud, and ten-year-old Theodore, when they brought bouquets of flowers at dawn to his bedside. Throughout the day, the doorbell kept ringing as congratulatory birthday cables were delivered. In the midst of this clamor, the doctors returned to perform the autopsy on Ellie on which William had insisted. His distress was somewhat assuaged when they told him her death, which was peaceful, was also merciful. They had discovered she had a terminal kidney illness, which would have caused considerable pain and killed her within two months.[54]

Following a quiet, family-only funeral for Ellie, William sent money to Seesen for an *Elizabeth Pavilion* to be erected in her honor in the ten-acre-park he had donated the previous year. He wanted people to be able to sit in the pavilion and gaze at nature - at the manmade ponds he had suggested, as well as the many foreign trees he had recommended be imported, ranging from American Douglas Fir to Persian Black Walnut and Japanese tulip trees.[55]

The nagging problem of what to do about the Columbian fair urgently required his attention. Originally New York was to be the host city. William was one of the hundred leading citizens appointed to the planning committee. At a public meeting at City Hall, he opened the subscription list with a cheque for $50,000. When the fair was relocated to Chicago, William halved his contribution.

At that time, the rivalry between New York and Chicago in matters of civic pride was at its zenith. Ludicrously, which piano would be on the stage in the fair's music hall at the opening concert became the symbol of the struggle. The contretemps was touched off when the judicial panel for selecting the pianos was announced. Customarily, such contests featured a neutral lineup of distinguished experts from around the world. This time the Chicagoans selected a panel of one - Chicago Musical College director Dr. Florence Ziegfield, the father of Florenz Ziegfield, the soon-to-become legendary Broadway producer. Ziegfield had an obvious conflict of interest: W.W. Kimball, Chicago's leading pianomaker, was on the college's board of directors.

Enraged at this favoritism, the New York piano manufacturers led by William, along with most other eastern firms, withdrew from the fair. A fair official tried to entice them back with the suggestion that they display their wares without entering them in competition. But the Chicagoans ingenuously protested, albeit to the disbelief of many, they bore "fraternal and cordial intentions to treat all alike, whether from East or West."

These were the preliminary skirmishes of the Great Chicago Piano War. The main bout erupted when the Chicago pianomakers instructed Theodore Thomas, newly settled into his position as the first conductor of the Chicago Symphony Orchestra, that a Chicago piano was to be used at all concerts at the fair. An irate Thomas viewed this as a shameful intrusion of commerce into art. He was a foe of considerable stature. A native of Germany, he had been a child prodigy on the violin who made his debut at the age of six. Later, he accompanied Jenny Lind and other famous singers and was influential in the development of chamber music performances in the United States.

Subsequently, he became a conductor, first of the Brooklyn Philharmonic and next of the New York Philharmonic. The founders of the Chicago Symphony lured him away with the offer of a permanent orchestra and pledges of financial support to build up a first-rate ensemble. Thomas believed the interference of Chicago's pianomakers clashed with his mandate. He told them to keep out of his domain and emphasized that he would stand by his commitment to performers that they could play the piano of their choice.[56]

His statement, of course, was a reference to Paderewski, who was coming from New York after a visit to the ailing William. Thomas had invited Paderewski to appear at the two opening concerts and the pianist not only had agreed but had graciously waived his fee in honor of the occasion. As always, Paderewski planned to play a Steinway.

But the fair's director refused to permit a Steinway piano on the grounds. The impasse that sparked gained international attention.

The newspapers grabbed hold of the story as a lion does raw meat. The Chicago publications attacked the New Yorkers; the New York papers threw brickbats at the Chicagoans. They both jibed at Paderewski. He suffered in silence until a particularly nasty editorial in the *New York World*, which, despite its base in New York, decided to take an Olympian view. It said: "The determination of the World's Fair directors not to allow Paderewski to play a Steinway may be rather small business for World's Fair directors, but it is certainly not very generous on Mr. Paderewski's part to sell himself to a piano firm. It sounds as if Mr. Paderewski is less of a world than a Steinway artist."[57]

Paderewski rushed to set the record straight, backed by William. In an indignant letter to the editor of the *World*, Paderewski wrote: "Throughout the wide world any artist is permitted to use the instrument of his choice, and I do not understand why I should be forced to play an instrument of a manufacturer strange to me and untried by me, which might jeopardize my artistic success." William's attached note reiterated Paderewski's declaration. It read: "Permit me to state that we have no contract of any kind whatsoever with Mr. Paderewski, who is at liberty to follow his own artistic inclinations and preferences as to the use of an instrument best adapted to his requirement."[58]

What both omitted to mention was that the previous year Paderewski had indeed signed an exclusivity document that declared: "Mr. Paderewski promises during his stay on the North American continent that he will play only pianos of the House of Steinway & Sons, New York, and that he will not use any pianos of any other American piano manufacturer, nor give any testimonials on their behalf."

Written in German, the document was not technically a contract because it was headed "U bereinkommen" (a gentleman's agreement).[59]

Ultimately, a face-saving solution to the stalemate was reached: The fair's officials redefined the music hall as a separate institution unconnected with the fair. Consequently, Paderewski could play a Steinway, "the instrument of his choice," and the day after his historic May 1 concert, William laconically summed up the affair: "Paderewski played on a Steinway grand in spite of all the opposition."[60]

As the Great Piano War receded into memory, William, a man of firm convictions vigorously and widely expressed, crystallized his views on two of the pressing issues of the day - the Sunday *blue laws* and *free silver*, rather than the prevailing gold standard. Thus, he was ready when *The New York Times* dispatched a reporter to interview him first on the blue laws. The *Times* regarded William with marked respect. It stated: "William Steinway is never so busy with the multitudinous affairs of his firm that he cannot find time to give expressions to views on topics of interest to Germans and the community in general. That his German fellow-citizens consider him the representative of their best interest was positively demonstrated when a *Times* reporter approached a number of leading local Germans for the purpose of gathering their opinions. All said that no one in the community could better give the sentiment of the German-Americans than Mr. Steinway."[61]

When asked by the *Times* man to give his views on a more liberal Sunday, William made it plain he favored relaxation of the laws. He answered:

> The enforcement of the law has fallen with the greatest severity upon the working classes, who are compelled to live in small, ill-ventilated rooms of crowded tenement houses - where they have to sleep in the very rooms in which cooking, washing and ironing are done - generally with a numerous family.
>
> Take the many thousands of New York's skilled workingmen. In order to be at his work promptly at 7:00 a.m. the workingman must arise at 5:30. He eats his breakfast while the smaller children are still asleep, hangs onto a strap of either a surface or elevated car for perhaps half or three-quarters of an hour or even longer; then performs his day's work, again hangs onto a strap and arrives at his home, tired and jaded, after 7:00 p.m. when his youngest children are again asleep. So he does not get a glimpse of them until the Sunday following his hard week's work.
>
> Take our last tropical summer. The average workingman has neither the room nor the means to keep an icebox. Thus, last summer he was compelled to buy everything - meat, vegetables, delicatessen - on Saturday night and keep it in the sultry atmosphere of the living and sleeping room of himself and his family. Instead of being able to go to some garden on Sunday where he and his family could listen to good music and he and the other grown-ups could take a light cool beer or light wine mixed with cool seltzer water, the family is

compelled to remain in the dingy tenement house rooms in rainy weather or walk the streets in good weather.

Thus, certainly, instead of being a day of rest and recreation and harmless amusement, the Sunday is a veritable day of hardship and castigation. This state of affairs is entirely unworthy of the City of New York, the greatest cosmopolitan city on earth.[62]

Having delivered these comments, William waited for a question. No doubt it did not take him by surprise. "What modifications of the law would you favor?" the reporter queried. William had a well-balanced response calculated to quell the concerns of readers who might fear a cessation of the blue laws would lead to wanton disorder on the Sabbath.

"My idea would be to issue licenses only to persons of good character," he recommended. "I believe the sale of perishables, meats, vegetables, delicatessen, ice and flowers should be allowed up to 10:00 a.m. Further, all saloons should remain closed until noon or 1:00 p.m. so as to protect the portion of our population which attends divine service. Then open the saloons until 11:00 p.m. or midnight. In addition, there should be more severe punishment of drunkenness than heretofore for it is good for mankind to foster self-control and moderation in everything."[63]

He concluded amiably with a joke that the *Times* passed on to its readers: "I believe in Frederick the Great's expression, 'In my domain everyone may go to eternity in his own style.' "[64]

William was as adamant an opponent of *free silver* as he was a proponent of open Sundays.

The silver issue was an outgrowth of the 1896 panic, a much more devastating and widespread collapse of the economy than what had occurred in 1873. For the first time since that depression, William had to close some departments. That Steinway & Sons weathered the crisis was primarily due to William's sale of many of his stocks and bonds and his using the proceeds to bolster the firm. Other companies were not so fortunate. Many became bankrupt as orders languished and creditors foreclosed mortgages. Tramps roamed the countryside in search of shelter and food; in the cities, long lines of unemployed waited outside soup kitchens.

People were desperate for a miracle, and the Silverites led by William Jennings Bryan thought they could provide it. All that was needed, they argued, to restore prosperity was to increase the money supply through unrestrictred coinage of silver. The issue symbolized the chasm between farmers and big business. The farmers believed currency reform would put an end to all their other miseries - steep tariffs, shipping, and warehouse fees. Conversely, big business was convinced free silver would bankrupt the government, whereas the gold standard, which they labeled *sound money*, promised stability.

William belonged to this latter school of thought. As the leader of New York's German-American community, he was the natural choice of its business leaders to be chairman of the *German-American Sound Money League*. At a mass meeting in October 1896, William made what would be his last major address before his death the following month. To a cheering audience he gave a rousing speech. "We are confronted with a crisis which threatens our very existence as a recognized great and honored Nation. The problem stares us in the face whether the people of this country by means of inflammatory appeals to class prejudice and by bold assertions without a show of argument, could be so easily deceived as to declare for commercial ruin and repudiation. In the words of our beloved Schiller: '"Contemptible is the nation that would not sacrifice its all for its honor.' "[65]

A measure of William's importance was the celebration of his sixtieth birthday earlier that year on March 5. Congratulatory messages flowed in from around the world, Steinway Hall was filled with floral arrangements and gifts, and delegations from the company, German-American societies, and City Hall called upon him to extend their best wishes. At the regular meeting of the Liederkranz, yet another affectionate tribute was paid. William was overwhelmed when a chorus of one hundred sang birthday greetings - "Steinway, William Steinway, Sei Gegrüsst" - composed for the occasion by the choral society's musical director. Afterward, the society threw a party for him at which the members gathered round him to shake his hand and applauded and cheered his thank-you speech. They serenaded him with his favorite songs and presented him with a mammoth floral wreath in the shape of Steinway's lyre trademark.[66]

In an interview with *The New York Times*, a member of the Liederkranz summed up why William was so beloved: "It may be possible to find his equal as a prominent American, likewise as a German, but Mr. Steinway has no equal as a cosmopolitan in the civilized world. In Italy, Spain, France, Germany, England, Russia, America, and in all other countries he has contributed largely to the advancement of art, as he makes no distinction in this branch, claiming rightly that art has no country, but belongs to the world. In charity, although he seldom lets it be known, he has also contributed much in all sections of the globe."[67]

By that time, Steinway did have a large international business, and William's known charitable activities included the establishment of six scholarships in Seesen, three for boys and three for girls, and division of his $5,000 Rapid Transit Commissioner salary among fifteen municipal charitable societies. He contributed more than $100,000 to the city's then-leading opera company, Abbey, Schoeffel and Grau. "Mr. Steinway did more financially toward giving grand opera to New York than any other man," a director of the company commented at the time of William's death.[68]

Eight months after William's birthday, his friends were stunned when he fell ill with typhoid fever, the disease that had killed his brothers Charles and Albert. Despite his weakness, William rose from his sickbed to vote for Republican William McKinley for President because McKinley supported the "sound money" in which William so fervently believed. That belief had led him to switch from his previous unswerving allegiance to the Democratic Party.

William's friends were heartened on November 22 when his physician, Barnum Scharlau, reported an improvement in his condition. Said Scharlau: "He has a good physique and this is depended upon to pull him through to a complete restoration of his health."[69] His prognosis was too optimistic. A week later, William suffered a relapse and he died the next day, November 30, at 2:30 a.m. His was the second death to shock the music world that month: William's chief competitor, George Chickering,who had taken over management of his family's business after the death of his brother, Frank, had died on the seventeenth.

The youth who had bemoaned the loss of $240 in back wages forty-three years earlier had become a multimillionaire whose estate was valued at $2,500,000.[70] Mayor William Strong ordered the flags on all city buildings to be lowered to half mast, befitting a man who had played such a prominent role in New York. "Mr. Steinway was one of our most public-spirited and liberal-minded citizens and it will be long before his place is filled," the mayor said.[71]

After a family service at 26 Gramercy Park, William was accorded a public funeral on the scale of that for a statesman.[72] The invitation-only ceremony at 1:00 p.m. on December 2 at the Liederkranz Hall on East Fifty-eighth Sreet was attended by two thousand. They included all the members of the Rapid Transit Commission and delegations from German societies in New York, Boston, and Philadelphia, as well as from the American College of Musicians. Also in the congregation were the Mayor of Long Island City and Abram Hewitt, the former mayor of New York who had appointed William to the transit commission. Mayor Strong was a pallbearer.

The hall was draped in black. At the entrance was a life-size portrait of William, with a spray of hyacinth above it and the words "Our President" inscribed in violets below. At the front of the hall were banks of flowers. One tribute of German ivy and white roses was in the shape of a grand piano, with a keyboard of violets including a wreath in the shape of the Steinway lyre. The Kriegerbund, a society of decorated veterans of the 1870-71 Franco-Prussian War, formed a guard of honor around the coffin. The pallbearers wore white silk sashes from shoulder to waist and black rosettes.

Following the playing of the funeral march from Beethoven's *Eroica Symphony*, William's close friend, Carl Schurz, stepped forward to deliver the eulogy in German. Normally a skilled orator, Schurz faltered after a few sentences. "Forgive me," he said. "I loved him." His place was taken by Julius Hoffman, acting president of the Liederkranz since William's death. He, too, was unable to hold back his tears. "We thank you for the love you have shown us," he said, sobbing. "At all times but once you have given us happiness. The once you brought us sorrow was when you left us."

As the mourners strove to control their weeping, *Ave Maria* and *Into Thy Hands I Commend My Spirit* were sung by members of the Abbey, Schoeffel and Grau Opera Company. Chopin's *Funeral March* concluded the service. Steinway & Sons employees had waited outside in columns. After the casket was lifted into the hearse, they marched alongside as an escort to the Twenty-third Street ferry. There, the coffin was loaded onto a boat and taken across the East River to Green-Wood Cemetery in Brooklyn. As it was placed in the Steinway mausoleum, the male chorus of the Liederkranz sang hymns. Henry Engelhard Steinway and his sons now were all dead, and the continuation of the dynasty was in jeopardy.

# Chapter IV
## *The Nephews*

Thirty-one years were to elapse before the direct line of descent from William again ran Steinway & Sons. When William died, his eldest son, George, already had dropped out of the business and Willie, at age fifteen, and Theodore Edwin, at thirteen, were too young.

Two of his nephews, Charles Herman and Frederick Theodore, who had learned construction methods from William's brother Theodor, filled the interregnum. The elder of the two, Charles Herman, was president for twenty-two years. He was not formally appointed president until April 1897, six months after William's death, although he assumed William's responsibilities immediately. When he died in 1919, his three-year younger brother, Frederick Theodore, succeeded him and served as president until his death in 1927.

Charles's business habits were regimented and methodical. He spent one-third of the year in London and another third in Paris, where Steinway had company-owned dealerships. Insofar as ocean liner schedules permitted, he arrived on the same date each year. At most, his visits varied by a matter of days.[1]

He also gained a reputation as a generous patron of orchestras, choral societies, and almost every young pianist who came to the United States. His enthusiasm stemmed from the company's association with the music world and his own pleasure in music. An accomplished pianist who had studied in both the United States and Europe, he also wrote several compositions in the style of his friend Victor Herbert.[2]

Competitors as well as employees referred to Charles as "The Boss." Unlike his uncle William, Charles did not like to give interviews or have his name in the newspapers. However, he was readily accessible to his workers. It was he who began the custom of the Steinway president placing his desk among those of the office staff at Steinway Hall. Anyone could ask "The Boss" a question merely by walking up to that desk.[3]

Whereas William had enjoyed games that displayed his physical prowess, Charles took pride in his ability at billiards, becoming one of New York's best amateur players. "It is perhaps an outgrowth of the family constructive genius and skill of hand that his chief sport is a game requiring a true eye and a steady hand," *The New York Times* wrote. He also gambled at the racetrack.[4]

The immediate challenge Charles faced on becoming president was to fend off a takeover bid from the same English syndicate William had rejected in 1889. By remaining independent, Steinway stayed aloof from the turn-of the-century impersonal associations being stitched together in the United States of formerly family-owned pianomakers. In 1903, six years after Charles rejected the English offer, the Weber Piano Company was swallowed by the then fifteen year-old Aeolian Company of New York as part of Aeolian's strategy to make pianos of varying quality and sell them by affixing a recognized name. Often, the connotation of craftsmanship remained but not the essence. Aeolian received a marvelous boost when shortly after it acquired Weber, it snared Paderewski to play a Weber piano after the pianist, miffed over a difference of opinion, parted with Steinway & Sons. The rupture, however, was shortlived. Paderewski quickly returned to the fold and the reputation of Weber hurtled downward. Later, Aeolian purchased a dozen more pianomakers including Mason & Hamlin.

Five years after Aeolian bought Weber, a rival consortium, the American Piano Company, was established. Based in Rochester, New York, it gobbled up both Chickering & Sons and William Knabe & Company. In 1932, as the depression squeezed the lifeblood out of the piano industry, Aeolian and American merged to become the Aeolian American Corporation.

Charles Herman was far from a caretaker president. He enlarged the Hamburg factory and rectified a glaring omission - the absence of a store in that city - by opening one in 1904, a quarter century after the factory's establishment. Dissatisfied with the financial report sent from Hamburg, Charles brought Theodore Ehrlich, a promising Hamburg employee, to the United States, trained him as a bookkeeper, and then sent him back. He also added a company-owned dealership in Berlin in 1909 and expanded the U.S. network.

For the important position of concert and artist manager - the person who deals with the performers - he hired the charming Henry Junge, a native of Germany who had taught violin in England and later represented Thomas Edison's business interests at an exposition in Paris. At the request of President Theodore Roosevelt, Charles placed Junge in charge of the White House musicales that the President had introduced. Junge encouraged Charles to present Steinway's one hundred thousandth piano to the White House as a gift, in a well-publicized ceremony in 1903. The concert grand was patriotically decorated. The shields of the original thirteen states were painted around the rim and the underside of the lid depicted the greeting of the nine muses by the young American Republic. The tops of the legs were carved in the shape of eagles with spread wings.

Junge was equally skilled at accommodating the desires of lesser officials. When Carl Engel, the head of the music department at the Library of Congress asked if Junge could find him an inexpensive piano, he graciously sent him one on loan until he could afford to buy it. The accompanying note was typical of his way with words: "I sincerely trust that the realization of having a little 'Steinway baby' in your home infuses you with proper parental affection, although it is at present only a stepchild. But after you have realized that its tongue is not a blatant one and that it 'coos' very ingratiatingly when your caressing digits coax dulcet melodies from its pretty mouth, you might, one day, be tempted to adopt it legally to shower your fatherly blessings upon it."[5]

On April 18, 1906, Charles was stunned to learn that the store and entire stock of Sherman Clay & Company, Steinway's San Francisco dealer since 1892, had been destroyed in a devastating earthquake. He was impressed, though, by Sherman Clay's determination to keep functioning by filling orders from its Oakland store. To show his gratitude, he shipped Sherman Clay twelve grand pianos free of charge in December "as a Christmas gift and token of our appreciation."

More sales to the rich and famous were made. Five-and-dime store magnate F.W. Woolworth ordered a luxury grand with painted panels. Another lavishly decorated grand was purchased by Evalyn Walsh McLean, the owner of the allegedly jinxed forty-four-and-a-half carat Hope diamond. The Chinese Embassy in Paris had its piano decorated with a lacquer and bronze design depicting Chinese mythology. The company, however, drew no attention to the purchase of two Steinway concert grands by well-known Los Angeles madam Pearl Morton for her brothel. She kept the pianos in the big room that took up the whole front of the house. It was furnished in stereotypical whorehouse decor: cut-glass and gold chandeliers, tables with gilt legs and glass or marble tops, red plush curtains, red carpets, and full-length mirrors on the walls. One of Mrs. Morton's girls would play John Philip

Sousa marches for frequent client Earl Rogers, one of the greatest criminal lawyers of his day.[6]

In handling temperamental performers, Charles proved to be as adept as William. He instructed the workmen to humor the many changes requested by hard-to-please Gustav Mahler. Mahler wanted a bigger tone. To get what he desired, he first suggested that some hammer felt be removed. "No good," he said about the result, and ordered more to be filed off. "No good," was still his opinion after the second try. Finally he asked that holes be drilled in the hammer. That he liked. "Das ist, Das ist," he rejoiced.[7]

Josef Hofmann, a Steinway artist ever since William Steinway had wooed him away from Weber following his 1887 debut at the age of eleven, was encouraged to suggest modifications that would make him happier at the keyboard. Hofmann, who had short fingers and a smaller-than-average hand span, asked for the keyboard to be made four inches narrower so that his fingers could more readily stretch the eight-note distance of octaves. He further requested that the sides of the keys, normally made of wood, be of ivory just like the top part, so he would not get splinters in his fingers, and that the *fallboard*, the part of the piano directly above the keys be highly polished. He believed glossiness provided a helpful reflection.[8]

Charles also decided Steinway needed a fresh advertising approach. During William's presidency, when Steinway & Sons reigned supreme, there had seemed to be no need for "hard sell" advertisements. A proud statement of accomplishments was deemed sufficient. But Charles Herman was president in an era when Steinway & Sons no longer was the biggest. Recognizing that it could not continue to claim paramountcy in size, Charles laid the foundation for what has been Steinway's promotional approach ever since - an emphasis on reputation.

In 1900, four years after becoming president, he approached the country's largest advertising agency, the thirty-one-year-old Philadelphia firm of NW Ayer Inc. Thus began one of the most durable relationships between a client and an advertising agency. It lasted until 1969, when Ayer reluctantly severed the tie because Yamaha was a client of a Los Angeles agency that Ayer acquired that year. As Yamaha's billings for its piano, motorcycle, and sports equipment businesses were $1.9 million at the time and Steinway's only $200,000, Ayer chose to retain the new rather than the longtime client, a position that Steinway accepted without hard feelings.[9]

At the outset, Ayer found it difficult to persuade Charles of the wisdom of a radical step to admit that Steinway actually engaged in the sale of pianos. The initial advertisement diffidently stated that Steinway received other pianomakers' instruments as trade-ins. The second murmured that Steinway rented its pianos, and the third edged nearer with the disclosure that the company was willing to sell used pianos. But not until the fourth Ayer advertisement, framed in 1901, did Charles permit mention of the fact that the firm sold new Steinways.

Having cast aside decorum, Charles gave the green light for even bolder advertising, and Ayer branched into testimonial advertisements. The first, run in 1902, said that the German Kaiser had so liked his Steinway piano that he had conferred the Order of the Red Eagle on William. "We leave it to the American public to form its own conclusion," the ad read. Testimonials by musicians began in 1904 with one from Richard Strauss. It was followed the next year by a glowing endorsement by Paderewski that said:

> My joy in the grandeur, the power and the ideal beauty of the tone and the perfect mechanism of the Steinway is unbounded. All who play your Pianos can but thank you. I do and at the same time congratulate you most heartily.
>
> Your very devoted,
> I.J. Paderewski

But the reference to Steinway that received the most attention during Charles's presidency was not the creation of an advertising caption writer. Instead it was "I know a fine way to treat a Steinway" in Irving Berlin's snappy 1915 tune, *I Love a Piano*. Steinway had played no role in Berlin's choice of lyric.

Charles's personal life lacked the stability that characterized the clockwork way he ran Steinway & Sons. Both he and his wife, Marie Mertens, a French brunette with an eighteenth-inch wasp waist,[10] were unfaithful. He had a mistress and she a lover. Charles and Marie lived lavishly. Marie was so pampered that she never even put on her stockings herself; a maid performed this chore for her.[11]

Of their two children, Charles far preferred his daughter Marie Louise, nicknamed "Kitten," to his son, Charles Frederick. Marie Louise, born in 1893, was one year younger than her brother. It was to her that Charles dedicated one of his compositions, *The Toronto Rose*.

He believed she had more business acumen than her brother, but the unwritten rule of the Steinway business was that it was a male preserve. Marie Louise led the sheltered life of the rich young woman of the turn of the century. She had a governess until she turned twenty-one. Six months a year were spent in Germany and Switzerland to soak up foreign languages, and she mastered five. She also learned the many accomplishments then expected of women - how to sing, play the piano, and do petit point.

She was a talented singer who performed with aplomb works by Grieg, Debussy, and Mozart at a concert staged by her teacher. But behind her sedate exterior lurked a live-wire personality similar to that of her mother. Like many of her generation, Marie Louise felt her upbringing to be unbearably straight-laced and boring. In defiance, she cut off her braids and bobbed her hair long before that style was in vogue, flaunted scarlet nail polish, was daring enough to smoke, and married young to Bronson Batchelor, a prominent pioneer in the U.S. public relations industry. He had her model as a nurse for one of the posters he concocted for the American Red Cross fund-raising campaign during World War I.

In his will, Charles Herman, who died October 30, 1919, at the age of sixty-two, made evident his love for Marie Louise and his contempt for Charles Frederick, but did not reflect adversely on his wife's infidelity. At the time he died, they were separated and she was living in Pasadena, California. The will reversed the usual procedure whereby the heir apparent receives the bulk of the estate and the women only jewelry and other personal effects. Marie Louise and her mother each were left one-third of the $5 million estate. Charles bequeathed Marie Louise his scarfpin but left his gold watch and chain as well as other jewelry to Charles Frederick.

Charles also placed Charles Frederick on a strict allowance by locking his third of the estate in a trust fund from which he was to receive just $100 a week. As Charles Herman explained: "I make this provision for my son because I am of the opinion that he is lacking in business ability, and is not competent to take charge of and prudently use, manage, and dispose of money and property." A supplementary clause underlined Charles's lack of confidence in his son's management of money. Half the hundred-dollar allowance was to be paid directly to Charles Frederick's wife, Florence.[12]

After Charles Herman's death, Marie and Marie Louise continued their fun-loving ways. Marie, then in her fifties, married a twenty-one-year-old French captain, Edward Lefebvre, whom she had met dancing, a favorite pastime. When Marie told her doctor of her wedding plans, he warned her: "If you marry this boy, it will kill you." She laughingly replied: "I can't think of a better way to die."[13] A year later, just as her doctor had predicted, she did die. She willed her money to Lefebvre but included a proviso that effectively eliminated his allure as a prospective bridegroom, although perhaps not as a boyfriend. The inheritance would revert to Marie's estate should Lefebvre remarry. He wound up on skid row.[14]

Tennis was a major passion of Marie Louise's, and she ranked among the top twenty female players of her generation. But it was not her skill on the tennis court that amazed New Yorkers so much as her attire. In 1926, seven years after Charles's death, she gained front-page newspaper attention for daring to play without stockings. On June 17, the *Daily Mirror*, the gossip sheet of the day, made her the lead story under the heading "Society Matron's Bare Legs Shock Forest Hills Club." An accompanying full-length picture showed a grinning, obviously unabashed Marie.

With tongue firmly in cheek, the *Mirror* described the earth-shaking incident:

> The fashionable and aristocratic West Side Club is today a house divided. The apple of dissension, the slim provocative foundation of the tiff which has split the once tranquil club into two bitterly protesting factions, the very modest and the very modern, is nothing less perturbing than a pair of shapely unclad legs.
>
> And the owner of the disconcerting - ah, limbs - is no one less lovely or less patrician than Mrs. Bronson Batchelor, the former Marie Steinway, noted society beauty and heiress to Steinway piano millions. This Summer - Oh, shocking indiscretion! - she has been wont to slip off her silk stockings in the clubhouse before going out to play. Her distracting ankles, more conventional members of the club observed in horror, were adorned only with a gold slave bracelet.

Marie Louise divorced Batchelor at a time when it was rare for a woman to end a marriage. She married again, to George Bartow Pfingst, a Philadelphian in the silk business who was younger than she and a keen tennis player. Barbara, her six-year-old daughter by her first marriage, and her governess accompanied them on their honeymoon to Hawaii. When a busybody inquired about her ménage, an irritated Marie blasted him with a sharp rejoinder: "This man is my brother and this is our child."[15] Besides tennis, Marie occupied herself with occasional interior decorating and bit parts in silent movies. Actress Kay Francis was a close friend.

Marie Louise died in 1959. Long before her death, the fortune that her father had so confidently thought she would handle wisely petered out. She spent her later years making electronic switching boards in a Connecticut factory.[16]

Charles Frederick, who had been brought up as a *bon vivant*, dancer, and tennis player and not trained in the business, developed a drinking problem,[17] something that plagued several members of the different branches of the Steinways. Although he became company secretary, it was a titular position. Primarily, he spent his time cataloguing the mineral properties of a stone collection he assembled and raising flowers and vegetables.[18] In 1969, he died at the age of seventy-seven.

Unlike his brother Charles Herman, who was relatively young when he became president, Frederick Steinway was fifty-nine when his turn came. As a youth, Frederick had displayed independence in his choice of a major at Columbia University. Mining engineering was a peculiar selection for a young man destined for his family's business. But Frederick believed it was the best way to obtain the mechanical training necesssary to understand piano construction. After graduation, Frederick, like his forebears and successors, started at the bottom of Steinway & Sons sorting lumber. In 1891, at the age of thirty-one, he became factory manager and held that position until he became president.

Frederick had a lovable personality interlaced with a strong sense of family pride. When a dealer once had the temerity to suggest that Steinway, always the most expensive piano house, lower its price by $85, Fredrick quickly squelched him. "Delivery will be delayed because it will take some time to remove the name Steinway from the keyboard," he said. That ended the discussion.[19]

Frederick's hobby was the breeding and racing of trotters, and his horses won many trophies. He named one of his most promising colts in honor of his close friend Josef Hofmann. When the automobile took over the highways, Frederick disposed of his stables and switched to golf.

It was in 1920, shortly after Frederick became president, that Steinway's most famous advertisement was created. The inspiration came from NW Ayer, the company's advertising agency, which had decided Steinway needed a memorable slogan. The assignment was given to a recently hired whiz kid, twenty-eight-year-old Raymond Rubicam. Rubicam believed that "the way to sell is to get read first and the way to get read is to say more about the reader and less about yourself and your project. Mirror the reader to himself and then show him how your product fits his needs."[20]

As Rubicam flicked through the old Steinway ads, he noticed the references to how the piano was the favorite of many great composers and musicians. The phrase "The Instrument of the Immortals" flashed through his mind. But how to illustrate the ad? Rubicam recalled that Steinway & Sons had recently commissioned paintings from prominent American artists such as N.C. Wyeth, Charles Chambers, and Harvey Dunn that would evoke musical visions. On display in Steinway Hall, their subjects included Schubert composing the *Erlking*, the piece William so loved, Anton Rubinstein playing for the Czar of Russia, Beethoven communing with nature, the death of Mozart, the musical version of Shakespeare's *Midsummer's Night Dream* as if seen in the mind of its composer, Mendelssohn, and portraits of Chopin, Wagner, and Liszt.

But when he asked for permission to reproduce the paintings, Frederick refused, explaining that he was opposed to the commercialization of these musical greats. Undaunted, Rubicam got the same effect by dressing a model as an Old Master and having Ayer's art department photograph the model at the piano, bathed in a shaft of light to indicate inspiration from on High. Underneath Rubicam wrote: "There has been but one supreme piano in the history of music. In the days of Liszt and Wagner, of Rubinstein and Berlioz, the pre-eminence of the Steinway was as unquestioned as it is today. It stood then, as it stands now, the chosen instrument of the masters - the inevitable preference wherever great music is understood and esteemed." An Ayer vice-president, Gerald Lauck, then suggested that Rubicam's "The Instrument of the Immortals" be used as the headline.[21]

Because Steinway & Sons still regarded slogans as undignified, Frederick consented to the ad's being run only once. When, for the first time in twenty years, a Steinway ad triggered a surge in sales, Frederick rescinded his edict. However, he would not yield on his opposition to the use of the paintings in the Steinway art gallery. Notwithstanding, Rubicam remained unwilling to abandon the Old Masters theme. He hired some of the artists plus new ones to sketch renowned musicians, opera scenes, and interpretations of famous musical compositions. The drawings were reproduced in color on double-page spreads in the *Saturday Evening Post*, the first time the magazine had run four-color ads.

The advertising campaign drew enormous attention to Steinway. It boosted Rubicam's career, too. Within three years of his "Instrument of the Immortals" brainwave, he cofounded Young and Rubicam with John Orr Young. When he died in 1978, Y&R was the largest advertising agency in the United States.

However, one drawback to Rubicam's brilliant slogan never occurred to him: A printer's error can ruin it, as happened with a ghastly misprint in the October 23, 1969 issue of the *Globe and Mail* of Toronto. A dropped letter turned the expression into "The instrument of the immorals."

In his eight years as president, Frederick made several important decisions besides that of agreeing - albeit reluctantly - to more dynamic advertising. Realizing that the German operations had outgrown their facility, he ordered the construction of a new plant in Hamburg in 1923. At home, he realized the potential of a new mechanical gadget - the player piano, for which even such distinguished performers as Hofmann were making player roll recordings. Frederick searched for a way for Steinway to cash in on this craze without losing its prestigious image. He concluded the answer was to arrange a deal with Aeolian whereby Steinway would build the instruments with a space for the player piano machinery and Aeolian would make and install the equipment.

In 1925, one year after the new Hamburg factory was completed, Frederick moved Steinway & Sons into its present hall at 109 West Fifty-seventh Street. William's masterpiece on East Fourteenth Street which had cost $250,000 in 1866, was sold in 1923 for $600,000. Fifty-seventh Street, the new location, was an ideal choice because it was New York's premier music address. Carnegie Hall was down the block, and major performers' agents as well as other music stores were nearby.

Steinway Hall, notwithstanding its imposing name, is basically a music store, the only place in metropolitan New York where a new Steinway piano can be bought. But to refer to Steinway Hall as a store is akin to describing the Sistine Chapel as merely a place of worship. Its grandeur is due to Frederick's belief that customers should feel as if they had been transported into the presence of the musical immortals. Steinway Hall has twelve showrooms reached by walking through a spectacular rotunda that serves as a reception area. Forty-five feet in diameter, it is two stories high with pillars of Italian marble trimmed with green marble from Tinos in the Greek archipelago. The domed ceiling is handpainted with music themes, and a dazzling nineteenth-century Viennese chandelier is suspended from the center. Between the columns there are busts of several musical titans.

The large front window has nonreflective contoured glass on its lower half so passersby can get a clear, unobstructed view. The lights are kept on at night so people can peer in then, too. The overall impression can be daunting for timid shoppers. "When I walked in the first time, I thought Paderewski would step out from behind a plaster bust," jests John Brimingham, co-owner of the company from 1985 to 1995.[22]

The new hall was opened on June 15, 1925, the date William's granddaughter, Betty Steinway Chapin, the daughter of his youngest son, Theodore Edwin, was born. The year was a golden one on Broadway, featuring Al Jolson, *Hamlet* with Ethel Barrymore and Walter Hampden, Arthur Hammerstein's *Rose Marie*, and Noel Coward's *Hay Fever*, but these hits were eclipsed by the splendor of the hall's official inaugural in October. As *The New York Times* reported: "More persons of note in society and music thronged the building than New York's greatest concert halls shelter in a day."[23] The crème de la crème included Sergei and Mrs. Rachmaninoff, Mrs. John D. Rockefeller, Mrs. E.H. Harriman, Mrs. Andrew Carnegie, Mrs. Marshall Field, Frederic Juilliard, S.R. Guggenheim, and George Eastman, founder of the Eastman Kodak Company. Josef Hofmann was the principal guest performer, playing Beethoven, Chopin, and his own *Sanctuary*, which he had written under the pseudonym Michael Dvorsky.

In all that he accomplished, Frederick was supported by his wife, Julia Dorothea Cassebeer, his first cousin once removed and a granddaughter of Doretta Steinway. The two were leading patrons of music. They assisted struggling young artists and made their Park Avenue apartment a glittering salon where the musical stars of the day gathered.

In his will, Frederick, who died July 17, 1927, left his entire $1.9 million estate to Julia.[24] She proved to be an astute investor who, unlike many in the family, pulled out of the stock market before the 1929 crash. Frederick had foreseen trouble in the market before his death and had made a similar suggestion to others, who believed he was sadly mistaken.

One such incredulous person, a prominent piano dealer, confided in an acquaintance at Steinway that he believed Frederick's line of thought indicated "he is getting a little old. When I explained to him that I am now worth two million dollars, Mr. Steinway recommended that I think about putting twenty-five percent in bonds." The dealer did not and after the crash was forced to live in a corner of the repair shop at his store. His bank would not even allow him to withdraw $10 a week.[25]

After Frederick's death, Julia always wore black dresses with a lace bodice and a lace or floral decorated hat. Until she died in 1957 at the age of eighty-six, she was the matriarch of the Steinway family. Gracious and forthright, she was the "dowager empress" to her family and "Queen Victoria" to Steinway employees.[26]

When she swept into the concert and artist (C and A) department, employees were overwhelmed. Winston Fitzgerald, who has impeccable manners, recollects their first somewhat acerbic encounter shortly after he joined the firm as assistant C and A manager in the mid-1950s. "One day I was alone in the office and standing at my desk with my hands in my pockets, when in walked this regal woman," he recounts. "She looked at me and said, 'Young man, never let me see you with your hands in your pockets again.' Then she smiled and we became fast friends."[27]

The Steinway children and in-laws adored "Aunt" Julia, knowing that her grand dame manner was only a pose and that basically she was extremely kind-hearted. The youngsters found the gorgeous decor of her apartment and the butler and the cook intimidating but were quickly set at ease when chocolate mousse, a favorite of theirs, was served or Aunt Julia pretended not to notice when they avoided eating a delicacy like crabmeat by hiding it under a lettuce leaf.

She also had a knack for the thoughtful gesture such as giving Charles (Charlie) Garland Steinway's bride, Sarah (Sally) Shields, a prized ring as a wedding gift rather than to a Steinway girl. (Charles Garland was Charles Herman's grandson.) Aunt Julia had a talent for repartee, too. Once when Charlie complained to her that her cook and butler made more than he did as a troubleshooter for the sales department, she joked that he and Sally could have their jobs.[28]

Eleanor Ziegler Lodge, a niece, thought of Aunt Julia as a grandmother because her own had died when Eleanor was an infant. Julia's mother had started taking Julia to New York Philharmonic concerts at the age of six, and Julia started Eleanor young, too. She taught Eleanor not to applaud during the pauses between symphony movements and introduced her to the stars of the musical world. "She had a box in the middle of the hall and one night somebody leaned over from the next box and said 'hello"; it was Jascha Heifetz," Eleanor recalls, still with some awe.[29]

Frederick had briefed Julia about the business, and she continued to follow its progress after his death as well as to carry on their shared love of music. Her business acumen caused her nephew, Henry Ziegler Steinway, the last of Willliam Steinway's descendants to serve as president, to turn to her frequently for advice. "She was a wonderful, marvelous woman and I talked to her all the time when I became president both to keep her informed and get her thoughts," he says.[30]

Julia had become a member of the New York Philharmonic's auxiliary board, a woman's organization, in 1923 four years before Frederick's death, and she continued the association afterward, serving on the Philharmonic's board of directors from 1934 until her death. It was her practice to do trenchant postmortems of Philharmonic guest performers with the staff of Steinway's *C* and *A* department, ticking off the reasons why Pianist A should not have played an all-Chopin program and Pianist B was not suited for a particular Prokofiev sonata.[31]

Nevertheless, her nephew Henry Steinway Ziegler, who is Eleanor Lodge's brother, describes Julia as the "nonmusician that musicians would have voted as their most important friend." She was one of the few persons Vladimir Horowitz and Artur Rubinstein allowed backstage during performances.[32]

The Horowitzes consulted her in 1952 as to the proper price range for tickets for a performance with the New York Philharmonic for the musicians' pension fund. Their provisional approval was subject to her saying she favored a range from $3 for a seat in the rear balcony to $125 for one in a box near the stage. Julia was the only outsider Horowitz saw when he began a twelve-year retirement in 1953.[33] She also was a close friend of Toscanini, Rachmaninoff, Hofmann, Richard Strauss, and Edward MacDowell.

The Steinway art collection included an interpretation of MacDowell's *Indian Suite No. 2*, a favorite of Julia's, and the dirge from this piece was played in memoriam to her by the Philharmonic the night of her death. Her fellow Philharmonic directors included philanthropist William Rosenwald, whose ownership of a crucial block of Steinway shares helped tip the vote in favor of the sale of the company in 1972 to CBS, and William Paley, the head of CBS.

Perhaps Julia was best summed up by her friend and admirer, Dame Myra Hess, in a letter to the editor of *The New York Times* after Julia's death. "With the passing of Julia Steinway we have lost one of the most beloved personalities in the musical life of New York," Dame Myra wrote. "Always modest about her musical knowledge, she had an unerring instinct and her presence at a concert, whether it was given by a world famous artist or a young beginner, became a ritual and a benediction to the occasion.

"In all she did Julia Steinway was the true expression of herself, for with her dynamic vitality there was a rare combination of dignity and warm humanity, illuminated by the brilliance of her wit."[34]

Steinway Hall continued to be Frederick's legacy. Throughout the years, a roll call of celebrity customers has shopped there - Ethel Barrymore, Paul Newman, Dustin Hoffman, Diane Keaton, Mitch Miller, Isaac Stern, and Muhammad Ali.

The most famous room at Steinway Hall is one the public does not see, although it is but a few seconds' ride down the wood-paneled elevator located off the rotunda. This shrine is known as The Basement and is always referred to in capital letters as opposed to the basement, in small letters, where it reposes. The Basement is spoken of reverentially because that is where the concert pianists come to select instruments from the company's "piano bank." All told, Steinway has a bank of 330 pianos worldwide (260 in the United States), for use free of charge by Steinway artists.

Sixty Steinway pianos are reserved for The Basement, although it can only accommodate thirty-five. The rest are out on assignment or are being lovingly tinkered over by Steinway Hall's concert and artist technicians. Although there is an impression that pianos located there are special, blessed by divine inspiration from their exposure to the history within The Basement's walls, they are not made especially for that destination. Instead, they are selected at random from the Long Island factory. Bank pianos generally are retired after five years. They are still as strong as ever but performers, like car buyers, want the newest model. Retired pianos are put up for sale at Steinway Hall or at a franchised dealer, where their pedigree often helps clinch the transaction.

Among the owners of such blueblood pianos was Academy Award-winning actress Greer Garson, who used to play two-piano duets of favorite concertos at her house in the evening with Metro-Goldwyn-Mayer's head hair stylist Sydney Guilaroff before he set her hair for the next day's shooting. One of her Steinways had been used by Artur Rubinstein for three days at rehearsal before a Los Angeles recital. As the actress later informed an amused Rubinstein and Oscar Levant, when they were guests at her home and performed an impromptu duo classical and popular program, she had had her doubts as to whether his rehearsal piano was "the good, *slightly* used Steinway" she was seeking. She had finally told the salesman, "I'll take it, but if Mr. Rubinstein played De Falla's *Ritual Fire Dance* on it even once, I expect a two thousand dollar discount."[35]

Unlike its competitors, Steinway does not lend pianos to professionals for concerts unless they already own a Steinway. Its position is that such ownership is a fair exchange for performers wanting Steinway to supply them with pianos for careers that can last as long as sixty years.

What about the struggling young performers who cannot afford to purchase a Steinway? New, the lowest-priced Steinway, a forty-inch-high upright retails for around $10,000. A well-maintained Steinway, Baldwin, or other well-known name that is twenty-five years old fetches about 40 to 50 percent of the price of a comparable new model; at fifty years, 30 to 40 percent; and at seventy-five years, 25 to 35 percent.

Richard Probst, Steinway's concert and artist manager from 1986 until 1991, had a ready reply for those saying they were too impoverished to buy even an old, forty-inch Steinway at approximately $1,500. "I agree with Dizzy Gillespie who said that the chances of true talent not coming to the fore are, One, slim, and Two, none. If a person has truly great talent, it will come to the fore and he or she will cease to be poor. After all, they can always give concerts without being a Steinway artist."[36] However, the concert and artist department willingly counsels pianists who want to turn professional even if they do not own a Steinway.

Steinway can afford to take this attitude as its roster of well-known artists numbers 400 while Baldwin, which does provide pianos to promising music graduates, has only 250. Under Jack Romann, C and A manager at Baldwin for twenty years until his death in 1987, much of the emphasis was on young people. His view was that "the first thing an artist needs is the tool of their trade, so we lend them a piano for their home and help them get auditions with top New York managers."[37] This policy continues.

Glamorous memories must accompany visitors to The Basement because its dowdiness is not the least evocative.[38] Pianos that will stand alone on huge concert stages are jammed together. There are jarring noises which cannot be muffled, from the heat and plumbing. There is no attempt to coddle the pianos with a humidity and temperature-controlled environment since no such protection exists in the concert world. It is only when the blue fire door is slid shut that visitors can picture Rachmaninoff doing his first run-through of his third Piano Concerto on this very spot.

It is here that Horowitz would tease Steinway employees by trying out new pianos and then puckishly declare he would stick with the one he had since 1935. Steinway staff refer to the piano as "Mr. Horowitz's Old Cannonball" because of its sonorous tune and flattered the pianist by calling him "Maestro," a term usually reserved for eminent conductors. Here, also, Richard Rodgers played the score of *Oklahoma!* for potential backers and Albert Einstein played his violin between train connections. Here, too, Josef Hofmann, Josef Lhévinne, Artur Rubinstein, Van Cliburn, Myra Hess, Percy Grainger, Rudolf Serkin, Vladimir Ashkenazy, Carmen Cavallaro, Gary Graffman, Glenn Gould, Cllifford Curzon, Rosalyn Tureck, André Watts, Roger Williams, Elton John, Byron Janis, John Browning, Daniel Barenboim, and on and on have selected pianos for concerts.

Oscar Levant and Maryla Jonas, a protegée of Artur Rubinstein, joked and hammed it up here in a discussion on the difficulty posed in some Chopin pieces by thirds, the simultaneous playing of two notes separated by another. And Brazilian pianist Guiomar Novaës, who was married to a wealthy architect but did not like to flaunt her wealth, would appear in the drabbest of clothes. Described by Winston Fitzgerald as a person "who was flighty about everything except the piano," she once addressed a letter to him as "Churchill Fitzgerald."[39]

When Placido Domingo wanted a locale for a television program that resembled a cozy salon, he chose a Steinway Hall showroom, scheduling the recording for after the hall's business hours. The session lasted until 3:00 a.m., primarily because the Italian vocalist accompanying him suggested an Italian song that Domingo did not know and so had to learn that evening. There was a time when performers often conducted their search for the piano of their preference after the hall closed, entering the premises through a back entrance. However, today the hall closes at 6:00 p.m. and anyone wishing to enter later must have a pass.

With the death of Frederick, the presidency of Steinway & Sons reverted to William's direct descendants. Two more generations held the position during the next forty-five years until the firm passed entirely out of the family's hands.

**Above :** Henry Engelhard Steinway (courtesy of Seesen City Hall)

**Above :** William Steinway (courtesy of Seesen City Hall)

**Left :** Early piano built in 1836 by Henry Engelhard Steinway in kitchen of his Seesen home. (courtesy of Seesen City Hall.)

**Above :** Henry Engelhard Steinway's factory in Seesen. (courtesy of Seesen City Hall)

**Below :** Map of Long Island Plant in the early days.

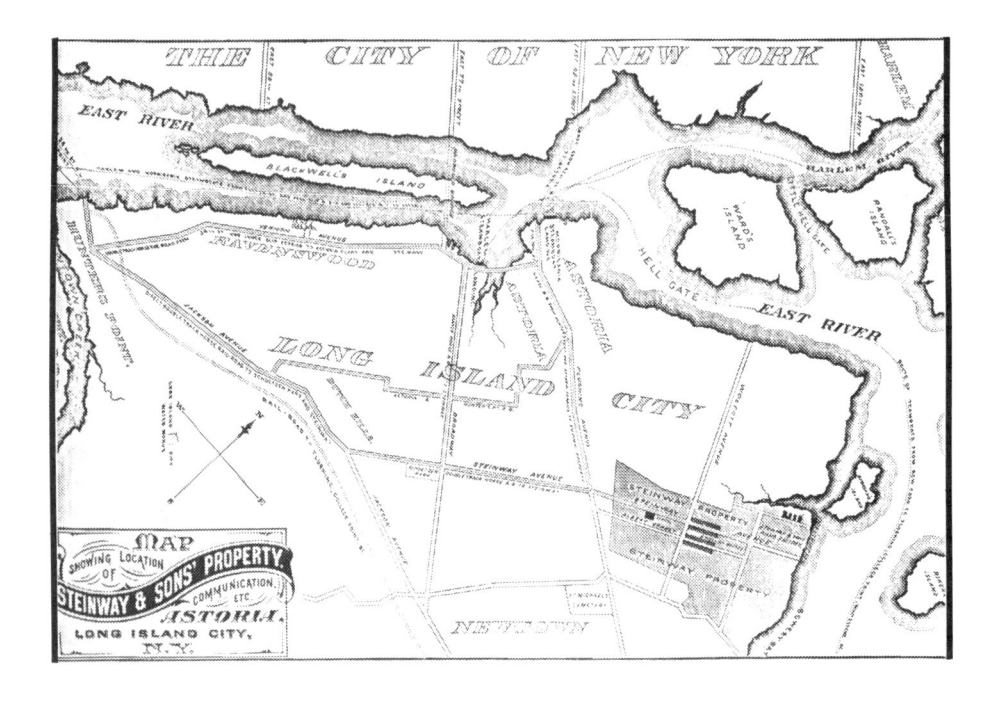

**Above :** Foundry, Metal Works and Lumber Yards at Long Island Plant.

**Right :** Long Island factory today.

**Left :** Hamburg factory (photo by author)

**Above :** Steinway Hall Rotunda 109 W. 57th Street, New York.

**Left :** Boston area headquarters of the Birminghams (photo by author)

**Right :** Park donated to Seesen by William Steinway in memory of his second wife. (photo by author)

# Chapter V
# *Theodore Edwin: The Early Years*

Some members of the Steinway family say that the next president of Steinway & Sons, Theodore Edwin, William's youngest son, did not want the position. Instead, they say he suffered from a drinking problem and an inferiority complex that caused him to want to be surrounded by yes-men. They further describe him as a dreamer and as being primarily interested in stamp and book collecting, as well as in participating in amateur theater.

On the other hand, whether out of a sense of duty or because he really desired the position, Theodore remained president well past the normal retirement age. Forty-four when he succeeded Frederick in 1927, he held the position up to the age of seventy-two in 1955. Then he served as chairman until his death two years later. The result was that of all Steinway's presidents, he served the longest except for his father, whose regime was thirty-one years, three longer than Theodore's. Because of the longevity of Theodore's presidency, the media referred to him as "Mister Music." Although his critics claim that in large measure he left the running of the business to others, Theodore made excellent executive appointments and pulled Steinway & Sons through the Great Depression. Moreover, important features were added to the Steinway piano during his tenure.

At the time of Frederick's death, Theodore was one of William's three direct male descendants. The other two were his two years older brother, Billie, and William's grandson, William Steinway von Bernuth, the son of Paula von Bernuth, William's daughter by his first marriage. He was nine years younger than Theodore. Whether he would have been appointed president had he wished the position is debatable, since it was considered essential to bear the Steinway surname to be eligible. As it so happened, he did not want to go into the family business. Instead, he pursued careers in education and public service. Before World War II, he was assistant to the dean of engineering at Purdue University in Indiana and coach of the university's wrestling team. After serving in the war as a colonel, William returned to New York where he helped find employment for the disabled. Later, he worked in Washington at the Veterans Administration.

Billie, on the other hand, was deeply committed to Steinway & Sons. He joined the firm in 1899 at the age of eighteen and served a ten-year apprenticeship, typical of the on-the-spot training required of all family members. Although he did not become president, Billie made an impact on the company as European manager for thirty years and then as the company's "goodwill ambassador." He outlived Theodore by three years, serving as chairman after Theodore's death in 1957.

Why Theodore became president rather than Billie is a subject on which the Steinways are close-mouthed. There appear to be three reasons. First, although Steinway & Sons was intended to be a dynasty, it was never a requirement that the presidency be held by the eldest son, and as it so happened, it never was. Second, Billie's role as general manager of Steinway's European operations was regarded as vital. Fluent in German, he had held the position since 1909. Third, the family regarded his wife, Marie, a former showgirl whom he met in Germany and who spoke English poorly, as unsuitable for the head of their august company. "Everyone in the family was very polite to her but did not really see her," says one relative. By contrast, Theodore's wife, Ruth Gardner Davis, traced her lineage back to the *Mayflower* Pilgrims. As it turned out, Ruth and Theodore continued the Steinway dynasty, having six children, four of them boys, whereas Billie and Marie were childless.

If Billie harbored a grudge toward Theodore regarding the presidency, it was never apparent. The lack of ill feelings stemmed from their close relationship as they grew up. Following the death of their mother in 1893, when they were twelve and ten years old respectively, their father, William, had asked Paula and her husband, Louis, to move in with him and take care of them and their four-year-old sister, Maud. Paula, only fifteen years older than Billie, and Louis continued to do so after William died three years later.

Maud, nicknamed "Cookie," grew up to be a five-foot seven-inch beauty, with a tiny waist, who rarely laughed and who preferred books to sports. She attended every performance of the popular Shakespearean husband-and-wife team of Edward Hugh Sothern and Julia Marlowe and was a follower of theosophy, a form of religious contemplation somewhat akin to Buddhism. A smart dresser, she ignored what was in vogue, preferring flowing Grecian-style clothes and long strands of pearls.[1]

Maud and Meta, Paula's daughter who was six months younger, struck up a lifelong friendship. It was through William, Paula's other child, that Maud met her unconventional husband, Raymond Paige. When Louis von Bernuth died in 1906, William was just fourteen years old but already weighed two hundred pounds. He tended to be a bully. Convinced that a man was needed to rein him in, Paula wrote Yale University asking for a suggestion as to "the strongest, most athletic person" she could hire for the summer.[2]

Yale's recommendation was Paige, the captain of the football team. He had a riches-to-rags background. He was the son of an Ohio banker who lost his savings of $1 million in the 1890s panic and had to sell his mansion, which was so large it had a ballroom, as well as his fine horse and carriage. Suddenly Raymond was in the position of having to work his way through school.

But he still craved the good life. Tall, handsome, and charming, he was the quintessential wheeler-dealer. He went to New Haven's leading tailor and offered: "If you will make me daytime, sports, and evening clothes without charge, I will bring you enough new customers to pay for them." Then he went to the city's best restaurant and made a similar arrangement: "If you give me my meals free, I will make certain your tables are filled."[3] Raymond fulfilled his end of the bargains and so did the others. On Raymond's first day on the job at the Steinway mansion, a petulant William wanted to drown him, but Raymond soon had his young charge behaving properly.[4]

Throughout his long life, Raymond kept jumping into one venture or another. He invested in cotton mills, imported pearls from the Orient and rubber tires from Russia. In addition, he had a straw hat factory. Maud's marriage to him did not last. She never remarried but he did twice.

Paula died in 1931, four years after Theodore became president. Ever since her husband's death in 1906, she had worn mourning black. During the last years of her life she lived with Meta, who never married, in the Wyoming, a huge apartment house on Manhattan's West Side close to Carnegie Hall where they loved to attend concerts, plays, and lectures. Part of each year they spent in Europe, setting aside one trunk for pillows to provide the osteoporosis-stricken Paula with cushioned comfort.[5]

She also suffered from diabetes but refused insulin, preferring to stave off the illness by altering her diet. She had requested that her funeral service be conducted in the living room of her apartment and that Maud, who had a melodious speaking voice, deliver some readings. Maud bought bunches of tulips, draped them inverted over the coffin, and recited from Goethe as well as from ancient Greek writers.[6]

Theodore yearned to attend Yale but instead, like Billie, he joined the family business at the age of eighteen. He learned to take apart and reassemble the twelve thousand parts of the piano almost blindfolded. Theodore was less extroverted than Billie and not as dapper a dresser. He looked forward to vacations when he could wear his favorite jacket, an ancient garment with holes in it. He liked to tease his brother that "My fifteen-dollar raincoat does the same job as the hundred-dollar one you bought at Brooks Brothers."[7]

As president, Theodore began his work day at 8:00 a.m. It was his custom to have the same taxi driver pick him up each day at his home on East Sixty-fifth Street and take him to Steinway Hall. Late in his life, he moved three blocks north to Sixty-eighth and Lexington. His office looked like a museum due to his collection of model pianos, old German books, photographs of his forebears, and a mask of Paderewski. He perpetuated the custom started by his uncle, Charles Herman, of working at a desk outside his office so as to be accessible to employees.

Normally moderate in temperament, Theodore turned gruff when Steinway traditions were questioned. He inevitably became huffy when a performer or orchestra leader wanted to intensify the pitch of the piano. Pitch refers to the exact vibration of a tone expressed in cycles per second. The A above middle C is the standard for establishing the pitch, and since 1939 the internationally accepted pitch has been A440. Some performers and orchestras, however, prefer as high as A444, maintaining that it produces a more brilliant sound. But opponents of the higher pitch say that it upsets the balance of the tension within the piano, thereby seriously damaging it. Concert tuners further say that while only a few hours are necessary to tighten the strings to heighten the pitch, it takes a half year to wholly restore the normal level.

Thus, tuners and piano manufacturers are very reluctant to increase the pitch. This was the stand taken when Eugene Ormandy, the esteemed conductor of the Philadelphia Orchestra, requested a Steinway tuner to soup up the pitch to 442 1/2 for a Carnegie Hall concert. "I'm terribly sorry, we don't tune our pianos above 440," the tuner said. Fuming at this lack of deference, Ormandy snapped, "I'm the music director and I want 442 1/2." Just as adamantly, the tuner replied, "I'm the tuning director and I shall tune at 440." Ormandy stamped over to the telephone and called Theodore. "I insist upon 442 1/2," he angrily told Theodore. The fact that it was the great Ormandy making the demand made no impression on Theodore. "Don't be a damn fool, Gene," he said. That ended the dispute. Ormandy settled for 440.[8]

Another time, Theodore snuffed out the request of William Francis Gibbs, America's foremost naval architect, who, as part of his emphasis on fire precautions on his oceanliner, the *United States*, requested Steinway to encase the ship's piano in aluminum. Actually, Gibbs's demand bordered on the hypocritical in that parts of the ship the passengers did not see, such as the bilge keels, were made of wood. Also, whenever he went on board, he carried a small piece of wood on which to superstitiously knock for good luck. An exasperated Theodore silenced Gibbs with his offer to douse a piano with gasoline to prove it was fireproof. Gibbs immediately backtracked, assuring Theodore such a demonstration was unnecessary.[9]

Despite the disdain with which he treated Gibbs's idea, Theodore himself had tested material other than wood for pianos. In 1935, Steinway collaborated with American Steel & Wire and Smith-Corona Typewriters in the experimental design of an all-steel, rustproof piano. However, the plan got no further than the drawing board.[10]

Theodore was as renowned as one of the world's foremost philatelists as for being Steinway's president. Liechtenstein, which annually issues a stamp bearing the picture of a prominent philatelist, chose him in 1972 as the first American for this honor, over such collectors as President Franklin Delano Roosevelt and Cardinal Spellman.

The study in his house was set aside as a stamp room. Theodore's favorites were those with a musical motif, even if as infinitesimal as a bugle carried by a cavalryman. His wife, Ruth, did not share this passion even though he tried to pique her interest by buying stamps that were predominantly green, her favorite color. After Theodore's death, she momentarily bewildered a stamp auctioneer when she called to say she had green stamps she wished to sell. His immediate thought was she had supermarket trading stamps.[11]

In 1920, before he became president of Steinway, Theodore proposed a wager to a fellow member of the New York Stamp Collectors' Club. It was based on an adaptation of Jules Verne's *Around the World in Eighty Days*. The challenge was for each of them to send a postcard around the world, one to the west, the other to the east, and see which route turned out to be the quickest. They arranged a relay system through the International Stamp Exhibition then being held in

New York. Theodore's card bearing the likeness of New York Governor Al Smith was mailed westward and the other man's, with a picture of Vice President Calvin Coolidge, eastward. Theodore's card arrived back in New York after a fifty-five day journey, the winner by six hours.

After he became president, Theodore hosted receptions at Steinway Hall at which Steinway artists played for up to four hundred international stamp collectors. In 1933, when Germany issued a set of nine stamps in honor of Richard Wagner, each with a scene from one of his operas, Theodore bought 250 kits. He had "with the compliments of Steinway & Sons" inscribed on the covers and distributed them to acquaintances.

Theodore was also a book collector - especially opera libretti by Wagner and works of H.G. Wells, which he eventually donated to Bard College in New York, the university his third oldest son, John Howland, attended. He wrote sonnets for Ruth and for his daughter Betty - once when she was frightened as a child of a thunderstorm and later, on the occasion of her marriage. Theodore's other enjoyments were woodworking and tinkering with cars, usually with Josef Hofmann, his closest friend in the musical realm. Hofmann had more than sixty automobile-related patents to his credit, particularly in shock absorbers. Theodore's drinking problem might have had some connection with Hofmann's - he became an alcoholic in his later years. Hofmann died in 1957, the same year as Theodore.

Among Theodore's most important contributions was whom he selected to fill two positions vital to Steinway's success. In 1928, a year after becoming president, he promoted Roman de Majewski, a count from Poland, to lead the wholesale division, which handles sales to dealers. Majewski managed the department up to 1965. The other astute appointment was making Alexander Greiner manager of the C and A department in 1934. Greiner, who had served as a captain in the Czar's army in World War I, held the position until 1957. Between them, Majewski and Greiner created a golden era of good relations for Steinway.

Majewski initially was brought to Steinway by Frederick Steinway, Theodore's predecessor, as the result of a chance encounter at the home of their mutual friend, Ignacy Paderewski. One day in 1910, the celebrated pianist invited Frederick and Julia, during their regular sojourn in Europe, and Majewski, whose father and Paderewski were friends, for lunch at his Lake Geneva, Switzerland, estate. His drawing room contained two Steinway grands. As Majewski departed, Frederick casually remarked, "When you visit the United States, please call on us and we will have lunch together at Lüchow's."[12]

Eleven years elapsed until Majewski took him up on the invitation. In between the dashing, enterprising Pole obtained the Warsaw agency rights from a wide range of foreign companies. Then, in 1917, he joined the Polish Cavalry and served for three years as a lancer during the conflict between Poland and Russia after the Bolshevik Revolution. On his return to civilian life, he went into the business of exporting chairs to the United States. As he exuberantly reacted to his initial success by sending shipments that far exceeded actual orders, he soon went broke.

In the fall of 1921, he sailed to New York to try to retrieve some of his investment by disposing of the chairs at a fraction of their cost to Macy's Department Store. While walking to Macy's, he passed the Fourteenth Street Steinway Hall. It was approaching noon and, impulsively, he decided to drop in on Frederick to ask him to honor the 1910 luncheon invitation. Frederick remembered and took Majewski across the street to Lüchow's. He listened sympathetically as Majewski explained his plight.

When Frederick offered him a job as an assistant to the concert and artist department, Majewski confided, "But I know nothing about pianos. I studied violin for eleven years with very poor results and the piano for four, with even worse results." Frederick waved away the seemingly insurmountable obstacle by saying that Majewski's knowledge of English, French, German, and Russian would be an enormous asset in handling the great pianists who had come to the United States after the war.

Tall and debonair, Majewski's trademarks were ascots and elegantly folded handkerchiefs. He was a stickler for punctuality, expecting his assistant, Richard Gigax, to pick him up at his Park Avenue apartment at precisely 8:12 a.m. "I would park a block away at 8:05 and both turn on the car radio and consult my wristwatch so as to make certain I would pull up in front of the building at 8:11," Gigax recalls. "At exactly 8:12, a smiling Roman would walk out the apartment door."[13]

Majewski was expert at keeping dealers happy. He threw annual black-tie parties for them in the ballroom of the Hotel Pierre in New York or the Conrad Hilton or Palmer House in Chicago, at which a Steinway artist would perform. He was the first in the piano industry to institute week-long sales training sessions for dealers and their sales staff. The concept was adopted by competitors, some of whom even nervily requested that Majewski supply his agenda. Another Majewski innovation was a course for tuners, held at the Long Island City factory.

Realizing the wonderful advertising value of having Steinways shown in close-ups on a movie screen, Majewski regularly visited Hollywood to promote their use in motion pictures. His favorite tactic was to have a Steinway artist play for the studio bosses and film stars. He chose Eugene List as his demonstrator after List gained international attention for playing several private concerts for Churchill, Truman, and Stalin during breaks in their conference at Potsdam, Germany, in 1945.

The major change that has occurred in the three decades since Majewski was wholesale manager has been the increase in the number of brands carried by piano dealers. Some dealers franchised by Steinway carry Yamaha or Kawai, the leading Japanese imports to the U.S.; a few also handle the Austrian-built Bösendorfer, but there is no crossover with Baldwin, Steinway's chief American rival.

Steinway's policy always has been to franchise only one agent per territory so that dealers will not cannibalize one another's business. By contrast, its competitors, which produce thousands more pianos, often have several representatives in a district. Occasionally, Steinway's rule leads to tugs of war over customers who live in one city but decide to make their purchases in another. Steinway's philosophy is to get the money and then iron out the complications, quite often through a split of the commission.

As representative stock, Steinway requires a dealer in a small community to carry a couple of uprights and a couple of grands. A dealer in a big city must feature several hundred thousand dollars' worth of Steinways: at least one each of its five grand and three upright sizes. On average, Steinway charges 20 percent or more than Baldwin, almost twice as much as Yamaha, and more than double the price of Samick, a Korean import. Hence, some dealers are reluctant to carry Steinway because of the heavier outlay for stock.

In the days when piano stores consisted of several floors, Steinway would request that one room be set aside for its pianos. At one time Steinway sold through department stores, but it ceased the practice because it disliked being subject to the frequent changes in market leadership among chains. Also, according to John Steinway, it became discontent with "the pianos being jumbled in with refrigerators and rugs. Moreover, often the dust was so thick, you could write your name on it. We were displeased, too, with the modern store philosophy of 'sell the merchandise and kiss the customer good-bye.' It clashed with our philosophy of ongoing service."[14]

The pullout is not one-sided, though. Many department stores have elected to narrow their focus to clothes in the belief that they are more profitable than furniture and appliances, which take up far more space than racks of clothing.

Whereas the wholesale department's ultimate target is the general public, the concert and artist department deals with the much smaller circle of professional performers. The job of concert and artist manager ideally should be held by someone with a knowledge of music and the combined skills of a lion tamer and psychiatrist. Alexander Greiner was an expert in both pampering and pacifying artists. Like all good C and A managers, he sympathized with the unique dilemma of concert pianists.

Most arrive in a city hours before the concert, uncertain as to whether the piano they will encounter that night will be friend or foe. No other musical performer faces this predicament, as their instrument travels with them. A host of potential horrors lies in wait for pianists, such as a pedal or key suddenly dropping off, a string snapping, or a leg collapsing. The stage may slope so that unless the piano is wedged underneath, it may roll away during the performance. Vladimir Horowitz insisted that a level filled with water be used to detect any slants.

The audience makes no allowance for a pianist and piano being strangers to each other, the performer's plane being delayed, or his or her suffering from a cold. They have paid $25 or so for a ticket and expect their money's worth. Only an Alexander Greiner understands that the performer often is a nervous wreck and exhausted from a grueling tour seemingly fiendishly arranged so that the schedule hopscotches from day to day across the country and time zones.

The best way for people to comprehend what concert pianists undergo is to imagine how they would feel if they knew their financial wherewithal for the next decade depends on what they do in two hours alone on the stage before two thousand or more people. A professional pianist can't say, "Gosh, this isn't a good night but you can hear me next Thursday in Cleveland." Pianists live on the strength of their performances, and no one knows better than the artist what piano is the easiest to play and provides the widest palate of colors and nuances.

Greiner's background was perfect for someone who had to tread the minefields of C and A life. The son of a prosperous glassmaker, he attended the Moscow Imperial Conservatory of Music and, on graduating, sold pianos. After the revolution, as a supporter of the overthrown czar, Greiner was in danger and fled the country. What happened next is shrouded in mystery. Greiner told Winston Fitzgerald, his assistant at Steinway, that he escaped, mostly by foot, into Western Europe, and got a job with the Red Cross.[15] But *The New York Times* obituary on Greiner says he went to the Orient and worked as an interpreter for the U.S. Consulate.[16] On emigrating to America, he headed for Steinway & Sons, which hired him immediately because of his musical background and fluency in seven languages.

Years later, in 1955, Greiner, the foe of communism who had almost lost his life in 1917, gladly served as interpreter for Emil Gilels, the first Russian pianist since the revolution to tour the United States. Gilels wanted a Steinway, and Greiner offered to contact Steinway's Hamburg factory and arrange for shipment of the piano from there to Gilels's home in Russia. Gilels accepted the offer and peeled off one hundred twenty-dollar bills from a thick wad of money for the instrument.

Of medium height, soft-spoken, and elegantly dressed, Greiner and his beautiful brunette wife, Alexandra, nicknamed "Mimosa" by Josef Hofmann because of her fondness for the flower, held many parties for performers at their East Fifty-seventh Street apartment. Childless, they treated Winston Fitzgerald like an adopted son. Greiner made everyone feel important. When New York Metropolitan Opera conductor Fritz Reiner called on Greiner and referred to Fitzgerald as working for Greiner, Greiner quickly corrected him, saying "This young man does not work for me but with me."[17] Greiner also loaned pianos free of charge to promising students at the Juilliard School of Music.

Greiner never lost his thick accent. Once, when he ordered two fifteen-dollar bouquets of roses to be sent to Myra Hess, one from him and Alexandra, the other from Theodore, the florist thought he had said fifty dollars.[18] As a result, Dame Myra was astonished to find her room filled with roses.

No matter how difficult or bizarre the requests of Steinway artists were, Greiner unflappably filled them. Once he received an urgent telegram from Florida by Paderewski. "Left trousers of my dress suit in New York suite. My daughter also forgot twelve turtles. Believe they are in the kitchen sink." Greiner located the trousers and the turtles and expressed them to Paderewski. Just as imperturbably, he had a piano delivered by elephant in India and retrieved six uncrated pianos after the overthrow of the sultan who had ordered them.[19]

In 1947, when the Buenos Aires Port Authority told Artur Rubinstein it would take three weeks, due to congestion, to unload the piano from the boat on which he had had it shipped, Rubinstein frantically telephoned Greiner. Greiner said if Rubinstein was willing to bear the heavy expense, he would immediately send another piano by cargo plane. Thrilled at the prospect of getting the piano in under twenty-four hours, Rubinstein replied that he would be delighted to pay.[20]

Greiner's quick response further mollified Rubinstein who had been offended that Steinway's "Instrument of the Immortals" advertisements referred to Paderewski, Hofmann, Rachmaninoff, and "others." He had resented being lumped alphabetically with the list of "others" in fine print well below the headline. As "R" is near the end of the alphabet, Rubinstein was almost in last place.

He had exploded at what he regarded as second-class treatment, telling Greiner, "I want you to know whenever I talk about Baldwin, Bechstein, Bösendorfer, Erard, Knabe, Mason & Hamlin, and Pleyel, I never omit to mention the Steinway piano."[21] Greiner did not misunderstand this alphabetical rearguard ranking of Steinway, and from then on Rubinstein and others of his generation who deserved star billing got it.

Not long after this incident, Steinway-London developed a ruse to avoid collision of egos between Steinway artists. It posted a pageboy in front of the store to warn if a star was headed toward the premises in case another one already there would feel upstaged. The manager would quckly invite one or the other out for coffee.[22] Nowadays such tactics are unnecessary because there is more collegiality among performers.

Steinway employees looked forward happily to Rubinstein's visits. He always courteously telephoned in advance to inquire when it would be most convenient for him to come in. On arrival, Rubinstein, a skilled raconteur, entertained the staff with anecdotes about his tour and then ran his fingers two or three times up and down the keys of three pianos. "Never offer me more than three," he told Robert Glazebrook, then chief technician at Steinway's London branch and later its manager. "If I can't find one from a selection of three, I'm not doing my job properly." Thus, his visits, anecdotes included, never lasted longer than thirty minutes.[23]

Performers anthropomorphize pianos. To female pianists, pianos are masculine; to men they are feminine. For Rubinstein, pianos had the charms, wiles, and furies of women. Some pianos he described as big and husky; others as placid, sensitive, and poetic; and still others as green-eyed, red-haired passionate seductresses. If he planned a program of Spanish music, he wanted "a wild-eyed babe"; for Brahms, "a strong, Germanic poem."[24]

Rubinstein was easy to please, whereas the late British pianist Clifford Curzon was not. Some performers prefer the keys to react to a surface touch, but Curzon felt the sound should come from a deeper one. He also found a mellow tone more desirable and made his feelings very clear one afternoon when he tried out a piano at London's Royal Festival Hall on which Rudolf Serkin was scheduled to play that evening. The piano had been tuned for the brilliance Serkin liked. Normally quiet and gentlemanly, Curzon could be acerbic when aroused. He jumped back in horror from the piano, crying out "How could anybody play this? This isn't a piano - it's tin cans!"[25]

During Greiner's C and A days, freight rates were still reasonable, which enabled pianists to ship their favorite piano from The Basement around the country for their tour. All that was necessary was to lower a wooden flag at the back of the hall on Fifty-eighth Street and the truck driver from the railway would know he was to stop.

Sometimes terrible mishaps occurred. One of the worst involved a piano from The Basement, a favorite of Myra Hess. She asked that it be shipped to Chicago for a concert. The day of the concert arrived and there was no piano. Dame Myra had to use a Steinway from the local dealer, Lyon & Healy. It was not until weeks later that the piano was discovered in a boxcar on a railsiding in Chicago. It had been dropped, and when the Lyon & Healy people removed it from the packing crate, they found the keyboard competely jammed.[26] On other occasions, Dame Myra would wire Steinway that "I am going to divorce husband one and use husband two" to indicate her selection of piano.[27]

Far more serious than the inconvenience Dame Myra underwent in Chicago was what happened to Jerome Kern in 1936 when Steinway movers damaged a piano of his.

When Kern moved from New York to Los Angeles, Steinway had graciously agreed to ship his beloved German-made Blüthner piano. The Blüthner firm shares the same founding date - 1853 - as Steinway, but unlike Steinway, remains family-owned today. Largely handmade, as is the Steinway, the Blüthner piano has won many awards and is known for its particularly full treble and its romantic tone. Kern felt Steinway was the most skilled in the United States in piano cartage. Unfortunately, the movers were overly zealous in securing the Blüthner in the crate so that it would not slide; the nails they used went through the crate into the soundboard.

Kern believed only that piano provided him with inspiration. Thus, when the damaged Blüthner was uncrated, his shock was so great that he had a massive heart attack followed by a stroke. Steinway repaired the piano and Kern recovered, going on to write more hit songs. His playing, however, was never thought to be quite the same again.[28]

Pianists often agonize for hours in The Basement over which piano to select. Once when a performer finally had narrowed the choice to two, one that he liked for its touch, the other for its sound, Greiner decided enough was enough. "Let's go for lunch," he said, giving a secret signal to the workmen. While Greiner and the pianist were gone, the workmen switched the position of the two pianos. On their return, the performer, carefree after several martinis, tried the pianos again and reached an instant decision that he preferred the one on the right.[29]

A teenage Byron Janis could not be fooled by such tricks. In the mid-1940s Janis won a wager against Joseph Messerschmitt, whom Greiner had appointed head tuner at Steinway Hall, over whether there are clear distinctions between pianos. "All pianists are crazy; there isn't much difference; it's all in your head," Messerschmitt maintained. "I bet if I cover the serial numbers of five pianos, the most you could identify would be three." Gleefully, Janis distinguished all five, effectively ending the argument.[30]

It was during Theodor's presidency that yet another Japanese pianomaker was established - Kawai Musical Instruments Manufacturing Company. Founded in 1927, the year Theodore became head of Steinway, Kawai since has become second worldwide in terms of piano sales, behind Yamaha. Kawai produces about 70,000 pianos annually - about one-third of Yamaha's volume and fifteen times more than Steinway's. In 1988, Kawai purchased the electronic keyboard manufacturing and distribution assets of Lowrey Pianos and Organs, a leading U.S. producer of home organs.

Indirectly, Kawai is an offspring of Yamaha. In 1890, three years after establishing Yamaha, founder Torukusu Yamaha spotted twelve-year-old Koichi Kawai riding a wooden bicycle, the first Yamaha had seen. When Kawai said he had designed and built the bicycle, Yamaha quickly hired the youngster. Kawai worked with Yamaha for the next thirty-seven years. At Yamaha's death in 1927, he left to start his own business. During its founding year, Kawai became the first Japanese pianomaker to devise its own action for upright pianos.[31] Hitherto, Japanese firms had had to import actions at considerable expense from the United States or Germany.

Besides strengthening the wholesale and concert and artist departments by hiring Majewski and Greiner, Theodore was in charge in the 1930s when significant innovations were made to the Steinway piano, and it was also during his regime that Steinway introduced the baby grand to the world. While these developments were not as spectacular as the contributions conceived by his uncle Theodor, they were still notable.

They were devised by two of Theodore's relatives. Frederick Vietor, a grandson of Albert Steinway who had died in 1877, was responsible for refinements to the action and soundboard. Henry Ziegler, the youngest son of Doretta Steinway Ziegler, designed the baby grand.

Frederick, eight years younger than Theodore, was senior vice president in charge of the factory. He worked with Paul Bilhuber, a vice president who was Steinway's acoustics expert, to develop an extra-fast repetition action so that trills could be played even more rapidly. Their research was prompted by a complaint Josef Hofmann sent Vietor in 1932 that he did not find Steinway's action "quick enough." "Could it be made more sensitive and responsive?" he requested.[32] Four years later, Vietor completed work on an accelerated action that enabled notes to be repeated 14 percent faster.

A delighted Hofmann had Steinway make his four pianos with the high-speed action. But because most compositions do not require such speed of response, Frederick's invention did not become standard equipment. The Long Island City factory incorporated it but the Hamburg one did not. Other manufacturers also decided against the technique.

Frederick's other innovation was the diaphragmatic soundboard, in which the thickness is tapered from nine millimeters at the center to six at the edge. Its purpose is to produce a freer, more unified vibration across the board. It is credited for producing the Steinway "sound" in which the bass is much deeper and bigger than in most makes of pianos. Some critics of the sound maintain it can overwhelm the upper treble notes.

How people react to sound is highly subjective. Rarely is there agreement, because tastes differ widely. A comparison of fine pianos is as unfair as contrasting the relative merits of a beautiful yellow rose and an equally beautiful red one. It boils down to personal preferences.

The piano is one of the most difficult instruments to capture on records because the sound begins to decay the moment a note is struck. The general impression is that the sound curves from a Steinway last longer than from a Baldwin. Says longtime record producer Jack Pfeiffer: "I am very impressed by the Baldwin but it is less warm and sustained, especially in the bass. There is a center to each tone: if it is very defined, the pitch of that note will come through more prominently and the center is more defined with a Steinway."[33]

Noted jazz and classical pianist Peter Nero says he finds "the rate of decay in the sound from notes very quick in other pianos, especially the Baldwin. When you strike a note, the initial impact is there but the tone drops off very swiftly. Baldwin is very percussive and therefore is good for pop jazz. But for lyrical playing it sounds thumpy. A Steinway has resonance and a singing tone."[34]

Baldwin has many devotees, though, such as Jorge Bolet, Dave Brubeck, Peter Duchin, Ferrante and Teicher, Luciano Pavarotti, André Previn, George Shearing, and Stephen Sondheim. On its honor roll are the late Bela Bartok, Leonard Bernstein, Benjamin Britten, Eddie Duchin, Walter Gieseking, José Iturbi, Igor Stravinsky, and singers Kirsten Flagstad, Jeanette Macdonald, Ezio Pinza, Lily Pons, Rosa Ponselle, Helen Traubel, and Richard Tucker.

Perhaps the best-known Baldwin endorser was Liberace, who never forgot how Baldwin assisted him in his early career. Some years ago when Baldwin hosted a party for him, Jack Romann, who was master of ceremonies, asked Liberace if he would like to say a few words. Liberace's touching reply was: "In the days when I was a nobody and playing at the Waldorf-Astoria's Starlight Roof, the piano was awful. The tuner suggested Baldwin might help me out. Baldwin got a piano to me later that day and never asked me to pay cartage. I'll always remember that."[35]

So grateful was Liberace that whenever he was in New York, he spent part of a day at Baldwin's Manhattan store, autographing pianos for purchasers. He would draw a candelabra and sign "With love, Lee." Each appearance resulted in more than $100,000 in sales.[36]

Nonetheless, Baldwin's hardest task is to battle the carefully cultivated Steinway image that dates back to Henry Engelhard's and Theodor's passion about quality and William's advertising campaigns that emphasized this commitment. Although the quality of Steinway pianos flagged sadly in the 1960s and 1970s, public good will toward the company has remained relatively steadfast because Steinway has implanted the impression that its pianos epitomize fineness and prestige.

"The Steinway myth is so ingrained that it is fatiguing to overcome," Romann would say half-jokingly. "Steinway has honed its image zealously and guards it stringently."[37] As proof, both he and Baldwin's chairman, Richard Harrison, cited a left-handed compliment paid the Baldwin piano by *New York Post* critic Harriett Johnson in her 2 December 1986 review of a Jorge Bolet performance. She wrote: "Bolet's Baldwin Piano sounded throughout like the best Steinway and no higher praise can be bestowed."

Bösendorfer and Yamaha have their fervent advocates, too. Bösendorfer performers include André Previn, Victor Borge, and Oscar Peterson. Previn uses Baldwin in the United States and Bösendorfer in Europe where Baldwin does not have representatives. "To my mind the Bösendorfer is the perfect piano for chamber music and Mozart," he comments.[38] Borge, in one of his routines, would walk on stage, bow, sit down on the bench, poise his hands above the keys, and then jump up and address the audience: "The Steinway people have asked me to announce that I play the Baldwin."

Such Steinway stalwarts of the past as Glenn Gould and Artur Rubinstein played the Yamaha on occasion. Current Steinway regular Vladimir Ashkenazy owns two Yamahas in addition to six Steinways. One of the Yamahas is at his holiday retreat in Switzerland and the other at his home in Finland, where he spends justs a few days of the year. "It's cheaper to buy a piano than have one sent and a Yamaha is less expensive than a Steinway as well as being a sturdy piano," he explains.[39] Millionaire Gordon Getty, one of the world's richest men, who took up composing after the sale of Getty Oil to Texaco, does his work at a Yamaha grand. His late father, J. Paul, had owned a Steinway.

Actually, there is no standard Steinway, Baldwin, Bösendorfer, or Yamaha sound because no two performers share the same taste in how they want the piano voiced. Generally, if playing Mozart or Schubert, they wish a mellower tone to best express the subtlety and sensitivity of these composers. But if they are playing a percussive Prokofiev piece, they want a big, brilliant sound so that the piano will sing out over the hundred, and sometimes more, instruments in an orchestra.

In any given year, Mozart, Prokofiev, Beethoven, Brahms, Chopin, Rachmaninoff, and Gershwin may all be played on the same piano. As Roger Clemens, a longtime tuning expert, explained: "Whatever way the piano is voiced, it is ideal for only half the literature played. Some pianists can adjust but others are distressed that the voicing is not the optimum for what they plan to play. The St. Louis Orchestra has the perfect solution: it has three Steinway concert grands. Two are set aside for concerts, one voiced in a mellow tone, the second in a brilliant. The third piano is reserved for practicing and is maintained as meticulouly as the performance pianos."[40]

In recent years the preference of performers has swung from a rich, round, singing tone to a more brilliant one. Brilliance is in favor because it "cuts through the orchestra." There are some performers, however, who maintain all the fuss and bother is nonsense as it is the pianist who bears the ultimate responsibility for bringing forth spine-tingling sounds, not the piano. This school of thought is well articulated by Bach specialist Rosalyn Tureck, who states: "I don't agree that a piano has to cut through an orchestra. It is up to the pianist to produce a big sound that can be heard to the back of Carnegie Hall or the Royal Festival Hall in London."

Frederick Vietor did not confine his recommendations to piano construction. In the late 1920s, he suggested that Steinway Hall become a music department store and sell radios, organs, and records, beside pianos. The diversification, however, was shortlived, because Steinway could not compete against specialty stores that discounted extensively.

So impressed was Theodore with Fredrick's ability that he planned to take early retirement and have Frederick assume the presidency, even though that would break the tradition of only someone with the Steinway surname heading the business. But, in 1941, at the age of fifty, Frederick fell terminally ill with Hodgkin's disease.

In his final days, he was paid a touching tribute by his World War I army squadron, which had become part of New York's National Guard. Frederick was its commander when it was called into action, armed with sabers, in the early 1930s to quell riots in Harlem. Fortunately, the men did not have to use their weapons.

Just before the squadron, reactivated for duty in World War II, left for overseas, it staged a review solely for Frederick, knowing how much he had wanted to reenlist.[41] Shortly afterward, he died. It is through his daughter, Margery Vietor Kittredge, that the Steinways are linked to another well-known name: her son Charles is married to

Susan Cooke, the daughter of longtime PBS Masterpiece Theater host Alistair Cooke.

Simultaneous with Frederick Vietor's work on the accelerated action and diaphragmatic soundboard, the design plans were nearing completion for the baby grand which Henry Ziegler had proposed back in 1910 when his cousin, Charles Herman Steinway, was president. At five feet one inch, the baby grand - Steinway's Model $S$ piano - is a half foot shorter than the previous smallest one, the $M$. The baby grand capped Henry's distinguished career of refinements to the piano's construction. With a total of eleven patents, he is second only to the first Theodor in the number of patents granted to a member of the Steinway family.

It was not solely his inventions that made Henry Ziegler of pivotal importance to the future of Steinway & Sons. Due to the terms of his being hired by William Steinway in 1871 when Henry was fourteen, the Ziegler branch of the Steinway family came to play a decisive role in the sale of the company to CBS a century later in 1972.

Henry's mechanical bent as a boy was outstanding, but his father, Jacob, wanted him to join his successful furniture business. Wiliam was equally eager for Henry to join Steinway. To convince Jacob that Henry would have a better future at Steinway, William devised a solution that became a paramount factor at the time of the CBS bid. "I will give Henry $50,000 worth of Steinway bonds," William promised Jacob, "if you allow him to join our business instead of going into yours."[42]

Henry's grandson, Henry Steinway Ziegler, calculates that taking inflation into consideration, the bonds would be worth at least $1 million today. Also, according to him, his grandfather could have become president of Steinway had he agreed to legally adopt "Steinway" as his surname, but Henry refused.[43] The position went to Henry's cousin, Charles Herman Steinway, who was the same age, and Henry became vice president in charge of inventions and construction.

In 1941, eleven years after Henry's death, Steinway found it could not pay dividends on all the bonds outstanding due to the harmful impact on business of the depression followed by World War II. As did all the other bondholders, Henry's heir, his son Frederick Jacob, agreed to the firm's proposition that he accept shares in proportion to the value of the bonds. He died in 1968 and his shares passed to his two sons, Henry Steinway Ziegler, a lawyer, and John, an architect, and to his daughter, Eleanor. She is the wife of Henry Sears Lodge, the son of the late Henry Cabot Lodge who was Ambassador to the United Nations and a Massachusetts senator.

The exchange of the bonds for shares made the three Zieglers the largest shareholders in 1972. Since they were not in the business, they favored the sale to CBS. To be fair, it should be pointed out that the sale also was supported by the then-president, Henry Ziegler Steinway, Theodore's son, as well as by most of the other members on his side of the family.

The first Henry Ziegler, who long after his death so influenced Steinway's destiny, was called "The Governor" by Steinway employees because of his gruff demeanor. His mode of commuting to work provoked much comment. It was his practice, even as the car became the customary way to commute, to go from his Fifty-fourth Street townhouse down to Steinway Hall, still on Fourteenth Street, in his carriage pulled by his prized trotters. He would then spank the horses on their hindquarters, signaling them to return home by themselves. This routine ceased when the police told him passersby were unnerved by the sight of a riderless carriage. Subsequently, Henry's groom met him at the hall and took the horses and carriage back home.[44]

A compulsive inventor who drew or experimented on anything that was handy, Henry was particularly fond of writing his formulas on the inside of the closet door in his office. As was the case with Frederick, he split his time between Steinway's New York and European operations. Once, when he was overseas, the Long Island staff decided to use the opportunity to fix up his office. As part of the facelift, the inside of the closet door was painted. On his return, a desperate Henry scraped off the paint to reveal the formulas. The traumatic experience failed to cure him. The door continued as his favorite repository for ideas.[45]

At home, he used the furniture to test the new piano finishes he was constantly developing. The dining-room table underwent most of the applications as it was impervious to any substance Henry concocted. Indeed, his finishes were so indestructible that nothing could scratch or burn the table and it lasted, unscarred, through three generations.[46]

Henry was married to his cousin, Albertina Vogel, the exceptionally beautiful daughter of Wilhelmina Steinway Vogel. An extremely talented pianist, Albertina yearned to be a concert performer, but concert touring by women was deemed unacceptable behavior in the Victorian era in which she grew up. Her stage appearances were confined to accompanying a relative when he sang publicly. Later, she became an avid automobile driver in the early days of the car industry, driving a De Dion-Bouton, a popular car that was midway in price between the Pierce-Arrow and the Model T Ford.

Of Henry and Albertina's three children, Albert, their first, died in infancy. Their daughter, Eleanor Theodora, died in 1902 at the age of nineteen, just six weeks after her wedding. She had caught typhoid fever from one of her bridesmaids who unknowingly had the illness. Her death was a tremendous shock to her parents; they went into mourning for the rest of their lives.[47] The surviving child, Frederick Jacob, was fourteen when she died. He served for many years as a director of Steinway & Sons, but his chosen career was sculpting in a neoclassical style.

He shared a studio in New York and Paris with his teacher and friend, the noted sculptor Mahonri Young, the most famous descendant of the Mormon leader Brigham Young. Frederick exhibited successfully in Paris and went on to do a memorial at New York's Fordham University to World War I hero Major General Clarence Edwards, who had taught military science at the school from 1890 to 1893.[48] The bas-relief was commissioned by New York soldiers who had served under Edwards.

Frederick played the piano by ear and composed for fun. For his home, he had a copy made of Henry Engelhard's first piano, the one made in his kitchen in Seesen, Germany. He hired Betty Humby, the wife of Sir Thomas Beecham and a former concert pianist, to teach his daughter, Eleanor. When he was bedridden with heart trouble from which he died in 1968, Frederick whiled away the time by transposing Ravel's *La Valse* into another key in his mind because he was too ill to do it on paper.[49]

Henry's Ziegler's death in 1934 came one year before the baby grand finally appeared before the public during the depths of the Great Depression. As Theodore later gratefully acknowledged, it was the baby grand to which Steinway largely owed its survival. Previously, the company was in precarious straits. In 1929, immediately after the onset of the depression, Theodore launched a $2 million advertising campaign that ran until 1932. It largely was a continuation of the great musical moments illustrations in the *Saturday Evening Post* begun during his predecessor's presidency. At first, the ads worked wonders. The first year, they were primarily responsible for a 69 percent increase in Steinway sales when the piano industry as a whole plummeted below the average for 1921.

But as the depression worsened, the ads no longer helped. Instead, Steinway dealers lamented that business was dryer than the

Sahara. Their frustrations were summed up in the rueful comment of one to Theodore: "I can't put money in their pockets." In desperation, the salesmen called on universities, but they were just as short of funds. Invariably, their answer was, "We certainly need lots of pianos, but we have no money. Why not put them in free for advertising value?"[50]

Orders for art case pianos also dried up. One of the last, made for R.S. McLaughlin, Canada's foremost automotive tycoon, had an elaborate design of cherubs, monkey orchestra figures, floral garlands, scrolls, and exotic birds. It cost $10,500; its current value is $200,000.[51]

So bad was the situation that Theodore slashed salaries, laid off hundreds of workers, cut back production at the Long Island City plant to one day a week, and sometimes entirely, and asked Steinway's banks to waive its debt of $3 million. Throughout the entire decade from 1929 until 1939 the company paid out only one dollar in dividends to each of its shareholders. Notwithstanding, when the company was offered $1 million for the use of its name on a radio and a refrigerator, Theodore rejected the proposition as debasing.

Steinway's difficulties were compounded by the fact that its Hamburg operations were also being buffeted by hard times. In the wake of the collapse of Germany's economy after World War I, the Hamburg factory's production shriveled to just twenty pianos for an entire year. Fortunately for Steinway, the manager, Theodore Ehrlich, was extremely capable. It was he whom Charles Herman had handpicked in 1906 to be trained in New York for the position of Hamburg's chief accountant. Three years later Charles made him assistant to Hamburg's manager, Arthur von Holwede, a piano technician by training, whose association with the factory dated back to its 1880 establishment.

The tall, bald Ehrlich was a man of many talents. Besides excelling in finance, he was a skilled violinist who played chamber music with three members of the Hamburg Philharmonic Orchestra on Saturdays at his home. Ehrlich kept the Hamburg operations alive by squeezing a loan out of the New York office and paring the number of employees to a minimum. He also instituted an important change in policy regarding the lending of pianos to performers. Concerned that their free loan drained the financial resources of the already hobbled company, he decided it must stop. Aware, however, that such action would lose Steinway its roster of artists if the other German manufacturers were not to follow suit, Ehrlich invited his competitors to a meeting. The result was an agreement that all would charge rent.[52]

This pact could be construed as a cartel arrangement, but during those days when the firms were scratching out an existence, their survival was deemed more important. Today, nominal rental fees are the accepted practice in Europe. By contrast, in the United States, Steinway performers are responsible only for cartage and tuning fees, both of which are tax-deductible expenses.

Steinway's financial problems were not entirely due to the depression. It also was faced with a fundamental change in lifestyles. No longer was the piano the major mode of American entertainment. Increasingly, there were other amusements, such as the radio, movies, and the automobile. Moreover, many Americans had moved to small apartments from spacious homes. It followed that their taste in pianos shifted from big to small ones, and Theodore realized that Steinway's baby grand was ideally suited for the times.

In June 1935, he instructed Roman de Majewski to write an enigmatic letter to Steinway's seventy-five dealers. All it said was: "An important meeting will be held next Wednesday in the Steinway factory. You are invited to attend." The absence of any details triggered wild speculation throughout the industry. "Steinway & Sons is going to liquidate" was one rumor. "Steinway intends to borrow $2 million from its dealers" was another. Alarmed, dealers telephoned Majewski. Each was told, "I cannot tell you, believe me."[53]

Their emotions ranging from anger to fear, 125 people from the dealerships poured into New York City. When they arrived at Steinway Hall, they were loaded onto four chartered buses and driven to the Long Island City factory. The funereal expression on their faces deepened as they filed into a display room and beheld on a raised platform a solitary grand piano shrouded with a black velvet drape and surrounded by flowers.

Theodore thanked everyone for coming, dryly adding "It is remarkable you responded without asking why." Then, with a flourish, he flung off the velvet cover and declared, "Gentlemen, you are participating in the birth of a new Steinway."[54] There on the platform was the baby grand based on Henry Ziegler's 1910 concept. At $885, it was $75 cheaper than the fifty-two-inch-high Steinway upright and $140 less than the six-inch-larger "*M*," the next size grand. Simultaneously, Theodore announced substantial price reductions for all other models. Five years later, he introduced two small uprights - one forty inches high, the other, forty-five inches - priced at several hundred dollars below the taller fifty-two inch model.

While the baby grand's popularity carried Steinway through the depression, the 1930s remained one of the toughest periods the company has had to endure. Perhaps it was the strain that caused

Theodore to react unsympathetically in 1936 when Serge Koussevitzky, the great conductor of the Boston Symphony, sought his help in connection with the newly established Tanglewood Summer Music Festival in Massachusetts. The Boston Symphony has always been the festival's resident orchestra. As Tanglewood was to be a first in America, Koussevitzky believed Theodore, in his role as "Mister Music," should do his part to make it a success. He told Theodore the large number of pianos Tanglewood would require, hoping for special terms. Instead, Theodore quoted full price in line with Steinway's policy not to give discounts.

Steinway's stand had long-term repercussions. The infuriated Koussevitzky stomped over to Baldwin's New York office one block north of Steinway's. Baldwin gave him the red-carpet treatment, favorable prices, and a promise to foot the bills for cartage to and from the grounds and for maintenance. Ecstatic, Koussevitzky ordered more than one hundred uprights for the teaching studios at Tanglewood as well as thirty grands. When he informed his colleagues at other orchestras as to why he had switched to Baldwin and encouraged them to follow suit, Baldwin received an avalanche of new business.[55]

Baldwin soon became the official piano of most American orchestras and summer music festivals. Steinway officials profess indifference about this, pointing out that 90 percent of pianists still use a Steinway and that many orchestras, including Boston's, where the Baldwin is the official piano, also own Steinways.

The Koussevitzky incident also is primarily responsible for one of Steinway's most famous, durable and effective advertisements: the "box score" promotion. To counteract the impact of the Boston Symphony's affiliation with Baldwin, Paul Murphy, Sr., then president of M. Steinert, Steinway's Boston representative, advertised that "Eight out of ten soloists with the Symphony use the Steinway piano."[56]

Steinway expanded that theme into a regular campaign called "How the concert season stacks up." A drawing of a grand piano is shown for each time the Steinway is used by an orchestra. At the bottom, there is a tabulation for Steinway and for "all others."

Two years after the unpleasant confrontation with Koussevitzky, Theodore had a more cheerful experience when Steinway donated a piano - its three hundred thousandth - to the White House to replace the 1903 one, which had been retired to the Smithsonian Institute. President Roosevelt, with whom Theodore was acquainted through their mutual passion for stamp collecting, invited Theodore to show him the proposed designs at his Hyde Park, New York, estate one Sunday morning.

FDR suggested that the rim design contain five panels representative of American folk music - the Virginia Reel, a square dance, Indian war chant, Negro spiritual, and a Western cowboy song. The legs of the piano were carved in the shape of massive eagles and gilded. According to recently retired White House curator Rex Scouten, this caused countless headaches since the legs made the piano too broad to get through the front entrance of the White House. Whenever the piano has to be sent for an overhauling, the legs must be removed with a wrench specially made for the purpose. Female singers also made unprintable comments when the gilt came off on their formal gowns as they swayed back and forth against the piano.[57] Consequently, no fresh gilt was ever applied.

Most of the Steinway family trooped down to Washington for the presentation. Theodore's friend, Josef Hofmann, who had celebrated his golden jubilee in the United States the previous year, played three Chopin works. The eleven-foot piano, two feet longer than the normal concert grand, is kept in the East Room of the White House except during the presidential signing of legislation or special ceremonies, such as when the casket of President John F. Kennedy was placed there on a catafalque before his funeral. Then the piano is removed to the lobby. It is tuned only before a performance because with more than one million people annually touring the House, the doors are constantly open - not the best conditions under which to keep it in tune.

Steinway also provides a piano for the private use of the First Family, in the style of their choice. But, whereas in England firms are permitted to advertise that they have a Royal Warrant, as Theodore's father, William, had done, firms supplying the White House must remain silent about their honor. Not many of the recent First Families have been pianists, although Mamie Eisenhower, Rosalyn Carter, and Presidents Richard Nixon and Harry Truman all played.

One of Truman's friends was Baldwin's vice president of sales, and in 1952 Baldwin presented Truman with a grand that had a handwrought silver eagle sculpted on the fallboard above the keyboard, as well as silver caps over its feet. Truman had this piano placed opposite the Steinway in the East Room. In 1953, Mrs. Eisenhower had the instrument moved to the White House library, where she played it at times. In 1956, the Baldwin was loaned to the State Department, where it remains today. Later, Baldwin donated a twin to this piano to the Truman Library in Independence, Missouri.

As a pre-eighty-fifth birthday gift to Truman, newly elected President Nixon, hitherto no favorite of Truman's, presented the former president in 1969 with a Steinway from the second-floor presidential quarters in the White House for the Truman Library. Nixon played *The Missouri Waltz* for Truman in tribute to the latter's performance of the tune on the piano when he was president.

Perhaps the most famous White House Steinway grand was that used by Margaret Truman. After the piano fell through the rotting floor beams, it was finally decided to renovate the mansion.

Under Theodore, Steinway & Sons had weathered the troubled 1930s during which the American piano business shrank to a skeletal $10 million a year from $104 million before the crash. Many of Steinway & Sons' rivals no longer existed. By 1939, only 20 firms survived of the 250 in existence twelve years earlier when Theodore had become Steinway's president.

As the challenge arose of what to do about Steinway's unique position among pianomakers during World War II, Theodore had little time for self-congratulation. Steinway & Sons alone had the dilemma of owning operations in both allied countries - the United States and England - and in enemy territory - Germany.

## Chapter VI
# *Theodore Edwin: The Later Years*

During the war, it is highly probable that employees from the New York and London operations were fighting those from Hamburg. Moreover, the Hamburg and New York factories were each producing war materiel for the armies of their embattled countries.

Because of the Hamburg factory's extensive lumber holdings, the Nazi government ordered it to participate in glider production. Like German-owned piano manufacturers, the Steinway facility made beds for air-raid shelters, gun butts, and dummy airplanes.

The American government declared that pianos were second among nonessential industries, behind stained-glass windows. However, pianomaking did not stop completely at Steinway. The company sold more than 2,500 uprights, dubbed *GI* pianos, to the government for use in entertaining the troops. When a general complained, "Why are we buying Steinways for our fellows when we don't purchase Rolls Royces to ride around the fields?" the Steinway salesman retorted, "Don't we buy them the best wool socks?"[1]

In addition to the *GI* pianos, the U.S. factory built wings, underbodies, and tail assemblies for the large troop-carrying gliders used by the United States Army Air Forces. Steinway later adapted the glues that the defense department supplied for laminating together piano rim planks. In addition, the government requested the factory to produce caskets for soldiers killed in battle. It was a depressing assignment. Steinway records show that in 1944, for example, casket orders ranged from $9,000 to $19,000.[2]

The United States Army regarded the maze of buildings at the Long Island City factory as so similar to German plants that it used the place as a backdrop for anti-Nazi training films.

Theodore's three oldest sons, then working at the Long Island City factory, enlisted. Theodore Davis ("Teed") who was twenty-eight when the United States entered the war, was assigned to intelligence at General Douglas MacArthur's headquarters where he compiled a dictionary of Philippine dialects and gathered information used in the invasion of Luzon, the largest of the Philippines. Henry, twenty-seven, was assigned to Army Intelligence. He was stationed on Governor's Island just south of Manhattan.

John, twenty-five, served in the Middle East and quickly added to the Steinway legends. One story has him coming to the rescue of the British pianist Ivor Newton who was accompanying several singers and a violinist in the Persian Gulf. Newton later recollected bemoaning the poor condition of the local piano to a young soldier standing nearby. The soldier said he would find a wrench and see if he could help. To Newton's delight, the piano was in perfect condition at concert time. "You've done a wonderful job; this can't be the first piano you've tuned," Newton praised the soldier. "Well, perhaps you know my family," John replied, casually telling Newton his surname.[3]

Another story is that John was asked to fix singer Nelson Eddy's piano after it plunged from the back of a speeding truck en route to a concert for U.S. troops in Egypt. The original draft by NW Ayer, Steinway's advertising agency, had that it was a Steinway piano. John hastened to correct this misconception with a disdainful notation: "It was an English Broadwood. Ours would never have fallen apart."[4]

Immediately after the outbreak of the war, Theodore's oldest brother, Billie, then fifty-eight, returned to New York after thirty years as Steinway's European manager. During World War I, he lived in Germany in order to look after the Hamburg factory. Afterward, he moved to London where he indulged his love for gardening. His rose garden contained more than five hundred bushes of ninety-two varieties, earning him an honorary vice presidency in England's National Rose Society.

In the early 1930s, Billie returned to Hamburg. He left at the beginning of World War II because he had detested having to report as a foreigner to the German police during World War I. He caught the last passenger ship from Genoa to New York. At Steinway Hall, he moved into a corner of the office shared by the two-person concert and artist department and settled into his second career as company goodwill ambassador.

The Hamburg factory, where pianos are made for all Steinway customers outside North America, was damaged severely by an allied bomb. The windows and walls collapsed onto the pianos, and all were damaged. Not that it mattered much - business already had evaporated. Permission to sell pianos had to be obtained from the Nazis, who regarded the Steinway factory as enemy property. The factory managed to export some pianos to Holland until 1941 and to Switzerland and Scandinavia until 1944, but shipments to the London branch halted in 1939 when the British government slapped a ban on German imports.

The skeleton staff that remained at the German operations moved into the Hamburg store, where they sat huddled in their coats around a small stove, rationing out small portions of coal from their meager supply. The factory's safe had been blown apart during the bombing and the staff spent much time separating singed accounting and other records with a fine knife.[5]

Over in England, Steinway-London chafed at the British government's prohibition on German imports. It had thought the closure of German-owned piano companies at the war's outset would provide it with a golden opportunity, as there were no major British pianomakers to take up the slack. For a while it made do with repair business at the workshops, which had opened at the end of World War I in London's north side. But these were demolished during a German blitz. London manager John Eshelby thereupon converted the empty showrooms at the downtown retail store into workshops and gradually built up a healthy secondhand and repair business. Not long after, the store, located in the vicinity of Buckingham Palace, had a lucky escape when a bomb exploded within just a few feet.[6]

Besides repair work, the London branch continued to rent eighteen studios in its building to music teachers and to supply Myra Hess with concert grands for her five-day-a-week morale-boosting luncheon concerts at the National Gallery.[7]

After the war, Steinway resumed piano production in Hamburg. One of the first new instruments was purchased by Queen Elizabeth (now the Queen Mother). Accompanied by Princess Margaret, she purchased a concert grand for a cousin, Lord Elphinstone, who was about to be discharged from the army. He had intended to be a concert performer but had sliced off a finger in a forestry accident.[8]

It took some time, however, until the European operations were back to pre-war strength. The ban on importation of pianos to the United Kingdom from Germany remained in effect for several years; thus Steinway-London continued to rely on the purchase, reconstruction, and sale of used pianos. Exemptions were allowed, though, for the government to import grands for the BBC and the newly constructed Royal Festival Hall in London alongside the Thames. Many performers were Jews who had fled Germany and wished to continue playing the Hamburg Steinway.

Even if there had not been a ban, Hamburg could not have sent more pianos. After the war, it was reduced to 55 workers; it was not until 1951 that it regained its full pre-war strength of 245. To conserve energy, the allied occupation forces shut off electricity and gas at factories for most of the day. All supplies were scarce in Germany, including piano strings, screws, and hammer felt. With the German mark devalued to the extent that one week's salary was equivalent to the price of a pack of cigarettes on the black market, the Hamburg plant, like other factories, bartered for goods.

The factory was in the British sector. Although American-owned, the British Occupation Forces chose to treat it like other German companies. Steinway was forbidden to recommence manufacturing, and all its bank accounts, save that at the post office (Europeans can do consumer banking at the post office) were frozen. From those pianos it had managed to restore after the bomb damage during the war, the factory sought to sell one a month so as to pay workers at least part of their salaries. Other pianos were confiscated by the British, frequently without payment. At such times as they did pay, the sum was a pittance.[9]

Rumors abounded that some English officers, acting on behalf of British pianomakers, were seeking the dismantling of the Hamburg factory. Back in England, Steinway-London was alarmed when it heard that a deputation of United Kingdom pianomakers was headed for Hamburg, partly to get hold of the Hamburg plant's lumber. Neither fate occurred, however. Instead, as American property damaged by allied bombing, the factory received sufficient restitution to rebuild without having to call on Steinway headquarters in New York for financial aid.

While the reconstruction was underway, Hamburg's manager, Walter Günther, had the task of keeping the branch in business when it had virtually no pianos to sell. Fluent in English and French as well as his native German, Günther had joined the company immediately after elementary school as an apprentice in the factory. Soft-spoken and quick-witted, he was also well organized and efficient. As a stop-gap measure, he initiated the sale of sheet music at the Hamburg store. As the company could not afford to pay copyright fees, Günther duplicated classical pieces on which the copyright had expired or surreptitiously photostated music. Inasmuch as Günther's flouting of the law was not exceptional in that grim postwar period in Germany, the British closed their eyes to his illegal printing operation. Indeed, some even gave it respectability by patronizing the Steinway store.[10] Günther's maneuver, born of desperation, later led to his introduction of a concept new to Germany - a full-line music "supermarket" that sells competitive pianos, as well as sheet music, records, and other musical instruments.

As the postwar economic recovery escalated, so did Steinway's prices from the level at which they had been frozen during the depression by Theodore. The baby grand rose from $885 to $985 in 1940, $1,524 in 1945, and $2,585 in 1950. The forty-inch upright increased from $495 in 1940 to $757 in 1945, and $1,475 in 1950.

In his new role as "Uncle Billie," Steinway's ambassador of goodwill, Billie not only acted the part, but looked it, too - lovably stout, one hand holding a cigar or drink, the other clasped on the shoulder of the person to whom he was reciting an anecdote. In 1948, he posed for an advertisement for Webster Cigars, "Executive America's top cigar" (thirty-five cents for the deluxe Directors' length). Every day he would host performers from noon to four-thirty at dining and drinking marathons at the Steinway table in the center of the ground-floor restaurant at the Barbizon Plaza Hotel near Steinway Hall. "Come to lunch at twelve-thirty when we are best-natured and at our thirstiest," he would say. He often joked about his thirst. Once after an operation he said: "They cut out almost everything, but thank heaven, they left me my sense of humor and my thirst."

Another favorite jest concerned the piano-playing abilities of the Steinways. "The only thing the Steinway's don't do is play the piano," he liked to joke. "Why should a two-legged Steinway make a living playing a three-legged one?"[11] Actually, there was a goodly measure of truth behind the humor. Most of the later Steinways do not play and of those who do, several own another make. A few own Steinways received from their parents or from relatives. Except for a brief period early this century when the directors, mostly family, received a 10 percent discount, Steinway has never offered price reductions to members of the family.

Uncle Billie had a gift for setting everyone at ease. Often, when a young Leonard Pennario paid a visit to Steinway Hall, a shoeshine boy would be finishing polishing Uncle Billie's shoes. Billie would put his arm around the pianist's shoulders, saying "Time to have a shine," and pay for Pennario.[12] Job seekers also felt free to approach Uncle Billie. One was Ted Kostakis, who now heads his own piano renovation business in New York.

Back in 1955, Kostakis was a busboy at the Barbizon Plaza. One day as he was clearing dishes, he asked for a job at the Long Island City factory. "Do you mean it?" Billie asked. When Kostakis assured him he was serious, Billie called the maître d'. "Excuse this young man for the rest of the day," he said. Only then did Billie ask Kostakis a pertinent question: "Do you know anything about pianos?" Even though Kostakis confessed he did not, Billie took him to the factory, introduced him to the personnel manager, and asked the manager to check his records for upcoming openings due to pending retirements. When the manager said there would be one in three months, Billie requested that Kostakis be hired as an apprentice during the interim.[13] Kostakis justified Billie's faith in him. Within eleven years, he attained the senior position of an inspector.

The war years and the immediate postwar period were difficult for Theodore as president. What lightened his burden was the support of his wife, Ruth. He was thirty and she twenty-three when they married in 1913, fourteen years before he became president. Theirs was a long, happy marriage of forty-four years. Except for her lack of interest in stamp collecting and his in traveling, they shared common interests. Because he preferred spending holidays at home, Ruth did not begin taking trips until after his death as she did not believe in separate vacations for husbands and wives.[14]

Family and friends describe Ruth, a banker's daughter, as a salt-of-the-earth, dignified, no-nonsense, strong-willed New England Yankee. Tall, slim, with a cropped hairstyle that her daughters Betty and Lydia copied, she had a regal bearing even if she was just wearing a housedress when a performer paid an unexpected visit. Her grandchildren, who called her "Utie," their version of Ruthie, and longstanding and new acquaintances alike all single out her ability to make each of them feel as if whatever he or she had to say was of particular import. Her longtime friend Ruth Loud would fondly say that "You could drop in for tea with her and get your life straightened out."[15]

Like many undemonstrative but loving people, Ruth found it hard to express her emotions, even to her children. In his autobiography published in 1977, her son-in-law, Schuyler Chapin, described some reversals he and his wife Betty, Ruth's eldest daughter, had undergone, capped by his being fired in 1975 as general manager of the New York Metropolitan Opera. Shortly afterward, Ruth, then eighty-seven, was driving Betty to a friend's place to pick blueberries.

As the car sped through the woods, she turned to Betty and said, "I've read Schuyler's book. You haven't had a very easy life." "It's been interesting," Betty replied. "Here, would you like to drive my car?" Ruth asked. To Betty, this showed that Ruth approved of how she had conducted her life. Ruth let Betty drive only to the nearest gas station, then said, "Now I'll drive again."[16]

For many years Ruth's precise age was a matter of conjecture because she did not have a birth certificate. The mystery was resolved only when she started traveling overseas to such places as Timbuktu. Then close to seventy, she applied for her first-ever passport, for which she needed a birth certificate. She had to get someone to swear under oath the date she was born. For help she turned to a maid her mother had had. The woman remembered the occasion well. "I was serving dinner when a messenger came and said you were born. I recall it vividly because there was a terrible typhoon in Samoa that same day,"she told Ruth. All that Ruth had to do was double-check a newspaper for the date and the government accepted what she said.[17]

Both theater buffs, Ruth and Theodore first met at Manhattan's Amateur Comedy Club to which they belonged. Founded in 1884 by a group of New York bluebloods, its productions are considered to be just a notch below professional ones. At one time, the club staged its events in the thousand-seat Carnegie Lyceum, a basement auditorium at Carnegie Hall, conveniently near Theodore's office at Steinway Hall. Ruth and Theodore starred in such plays as *The Amazons*, *The Ghost of Jerry Blunder*, *Foiled Again* (or *The Sob of the Painted Woman*), *The Bathroom Door*, and *Bluebeard in Bologna*.[18]

Ruth also staged shows at the private Cosmopolitan Club, a social club for women in the arts and professions. Her talent was such that the inevitable question was "Do you think we can get Ruth Steinway to be the narrator or leading lady?"[19] They always could.

A civil rights supporter, Ruth convinced the club to admit Jews and once hired black jazz great Count Basie and his orchestra to play there. When other members refused to let the group stay for dinner, Ruth invited Basie and several others to have dinner with her and Theodore at their home. The club's cold shoulder to Basie did not intimidate Ruth from asking black singer Marian Anderson if she would allow Ruth to nominate her for membership so as to break the club's color barrier.[20]

Like her husband, Ruth had a deep interest in music. On New Year's Day, they would have dozens of friends and musicians for afternoon tea. In the early 1930s, Ruth wanted to proselytize those of her acquaintances who were not music lovers. She persuaded a teenage Rosalyn Tureck, already a recognized Bach expert, to give lectures on Bach's cantatas to a group of seventy-five women from the Junior League. The young pianist found Ruth to be "vital and alert with an enquiring mind and a sterling character," and they became close friends.[21]

When their six children were young, Theodore and Ruth permitted them to sit on the stairway and peer down into the dining room when famous pianists came for dinner. When they grew older, their parents included them at tea or dinner with Sergei Rachmaninoff, Josef Hofmann, Artur Rubinstein, and Myra Hess, letting them join in the conversation. Rachmaninoff, afterward, liked to play poker, although he amiably participated with the children in their favorite card game, *Go Fishing*.[22] As with others who knew Rachmaninoff, Theodore and his family were particularly struck by the difference between the composer-pianist's public and private personality. On stage, Rachmaninoff projected severity and glumness. Once when he was especially downcast before a performance, a Steinway employee solicitously inquired whether he was ill. "No, no, I'm all right; I'm just rehearsing my sadness," Rachmaninoff replied.[23] By contrast, offstage, he was jovial.

Ruth had had a traditional education at Brearley, a girl's school started by wealthy New Yorkers who believed the city lacked a good school for young ladies. She hired nurses and governesses for her six children and sent the three eldest - Theodore Davis, Henry, and John to conventional boarding schools. But she decided on a more liberal approach for the three youngest, Frederick called "Fritz," Betty, and Lydia.

Her choice was New York's "progressive" Dalton School, a particularly expensive private school, at which children could be enrolled as young as two and a half years of age. As they got older, the youngsters could arrange their own schedules and were given a month's work at a time with the onus placed on them for how to plan their study of the assignment. Theodore, who had so wanted to attend Yale University but had had to join Steinway at the age of eighteen instead, insisted that all his children obtain a university education.

Summers were spent at Long Pond, a lake on Cape Cod where Ruth's family had a compound. Early in their marriage, Ruth's father casually mentioned at lunch that he would give Theodore some of the land for a vacation retreat.[24] Theodore pounced on the offer instantaneously. "May I see you after lunch, Mr. Davis?" he requested. He received two acres. (According to John Steinway, it was 4 acres and was given directly to Ruth rather than Theodore.) John Steinway owned his parents' former home, and Betty Steinway Chapin and her husband Schuyler have a house next door.

As the children grew up, Theodore and Ruth had the chore of advising them on how to cope with the celebrity attached to the Steinway name. "They told us the name isn't famous, the piano is," Fritz says. "It wasn't too much of a problem."[25] Betty, however, found that "everybody assumed we were very rich which we weren't, so we had to settle that misconception. Next, everyone took for granted we were very musical and could play the piano well, which we couldn't. Or, they would ask if they could have a free piano."[26]

How to handle the famous-name dilemma continues to perplex the current generation of Steinways. Henry, the last Steinway to head the business, gave no specific instructions to his children, and Harry, his youngest son, who bears the same name as the founder, Henry Engelhard, had difficulty learning how to deal with the curious. He, too, had to cope with the assumption that "I am tremendously wealthy. I've never wanted to trumpet the connection and am always reluctant to discuss it when people inquire."[27]

Betty's son, Theodore Steinway Chapin, who handles business matters pertaining to the late Richard Rodgers and Oscar Hammerstein, such as requests to stage their shows, was startled by the reaction of people he had known for years when a newspaper article diclosed his middle name. "They all acted as if I'd been holding out on them," he remarks bemusedly. "I tell everyone that my goal is to make the money everyone assumes we have."[28]

All this emphasis by the Steinways on their lack of wealth should not be interpreted as meaning they are but one step from the poorhouse. Although not in the same league with the Rockefellers, perhaps, their life style is a very comfortable one.

Theodore and Ruth were not strict disciplinarians, but Theodore did warn Betty and Lydia that he would ask three questions of anyone who proposed marriage to them: "Do you love her? Can you support her? Who is her grandmother?" When Schuyler Chapin, who met Betty through Fritz, a school chum, made a formal appointment to ask Theodore for permission to marry Betty, Theodore scheduled the appointment at Steinway Hall and dressed in his best suit for the occasion. Right away, Theodore asked: "Do you love her?" Chapin: "I most certainly do." Theodore: "Can you support her?" Chapin: "I will try to; it will be a little skimpy at first, but hopefully things will move along." Theodore (after a long look at Chapin): "I shall waive my third question since I knew your grandmother."[29]

Eric Cochrane, whom Betty's younger sister Lydia married, escaped the ordeal. She had met him on a postcollege trip to Europe after striking up an acquaintanceship with his parents. All Lydia did was send her father a photograph of Cochrane's feet sticking from beneath a car he was fixing.[30]

After Theodore's death, Ruth spent the last twenty years of her life at Long Pond. She liked the isolation, and when her family worriedly asked what would happen should she injure herself, she replied, "If I break a leg, I'd rather lie there until found than live with somebody boring."[31] When the children fretted that she must be lonely, Ruth assured them that she was content: "There are days when I don't speak to anybody but I'm always happy the next time the telephone rings." To relieve concern about her safety, she got a license for a gun and purchased a .22 caliber pistol, which she kept in her bedside table. But she never used it.

Sadly, Ruth was a victim of the solitude she so treasured. In 1978, when she was eighty-eight years old, she had a cooking accident. According to her death certificate, she suffered fatal second-and-third-degree burns to her face, shoulder, and arms.[32] The family telephoned longtime friend Gary Graffman, then winding up a tour in Japan and Australia, and asked if he would play at her funeral. Graffman, who had spent long weekends every summer at Long Pond, readily agreed and was sent a photostat of an arrangement done by Ruth's friend, Myra Hess, of a Bach choral prelude, *Jesu, Joy of Man's Desiring*, that was a favorite of hers. He had never played it and as a person who "likes to live with a piece for a long time," he practiced as assiduously as for a concert.[33]

Besides entertaining Steinway artists at her home, Ruth played a major role in planning the celebrations for Steinway's 1953 centenary along with Theodore, their son Henry, and Roman de Majewski. Their preparations were marred by behind-the-scenes disagreements with Steinway dealers as to what form the centennial should take. Discontent with what they considered were inadequate plans by Steinway, the dealers formed their own committee and hired a high-powered public relations firm.

Henry reacted with alarm to the agency's hard-sell ideas, vetoing most, especially a suggested paean to the piano as "the last of the handicrafts." Aghast at the implication, Henry snapped, "The emphasis on 'last' is wrong." The dealers also were divided over whether Steinway should produce a special centenary piano and if it were to, whether it should be an upright or a grand. Ultimately the company produced a commemorative contemporary-style grand; it sold poorly and was discontinued.

The highlight of the centenary was a banquet on October 19 for 2,100 guests at the Waldorf-Astoria Hotel, and a concert at Carnegie Hall featuring thirty-four Steinway artists. The sumptuous menu included caviar, oysters, lobster, duck, ham, and lamb. Then came a ten-tiered cake with a miniature Steinway piano on top, Steinway lyre trademark decorations, and one hundred medallions bearing the names of prominent artists. As the cake was wheeled in, everyone sang "Happy Birthday" and toasted the Steinways with champagne.

The Carnegie Hall event was an extravaganza. On arrival, it was obvious to the audience that this concert would be unusual. Instead of a solitary piano in the middle of the otherwise vacant stage, ten grands loomed side by side. The recital began patriotically. Ania Dorfman, Sascha Gorodnitski, Gary Graffman, Skitch Henderson, Constance Keene, Willliam Masselos, Menahem Pressler, Nadia Reisenberg, Franz Rupp, and Gyorgy Sandor marched out and played Josef Hofmann's version of *The Star-Spangled Banner*. Alas, their synchronization did not match their enthusiasm,[34] but the audience disregarded this in its delight at the twenty-hand performance of the national anthem.

The New York Philharmonic then played Wagner's festive *Meistersinger* Prelude and excerpts from Edward MacDowell's *Indian Suite*, a favorite of eighty-four-year-old Julia Steinway, the family matriarch. Following these selections, an eleventh piano was rolled out and the Philharmonic's conductor Dimitri Mitropoulos, sat down and played the finale from Prokofiev's *Piano Concerto No. 3*. After Morton Gould's *Inventions for Four Pianos*, ten more pianists appeared on stage: Ethel Bartlett, Alexander Brailowsky, Gaby Casadesus, Sydney Foster, Rudolph Ganz (who doubled as conductor), Eugene List, Moura Lympany, Guiomar Novaës, Rae Robertson, and Beveridge Webster. In complete unison, unlike the first group, they presented Chopin's *A Major Polonaise,* Opus 40.

The musical smorgasbord proceeded through an orchestral performance of Manuel De Falla's Suite from *The Three-Cornered Hat* and headed into its finale, a spirited rendition by the orchestra and yet another ten pianists of John Philip Sousa's *Stars and Stripes Forever*. This group consisted of Jacques Abram, Ellen Ballon, Erno Balogh, Robert Casadesus, Abram Chasins, Carl Friedberg, Leonid Hambro, Muriel Kerr, Jan Smeterlin, and Alexander Uninsky. The concert concluded at midnight and the partygoers returned to the Waldorf and danced until dawn.

Immediately after the October 19 spectacular, Theodore dispatched his youngest son, John, then thirty-six, and Fritz, thirty-two, on a cross-country promotional tour. In Syracuse, New York, Fritz found himself caught in a battle of egos between the music reviewers of the rival newspapers. "The music editor of the *Syracuse Herald-Journal* has held the position for twenty-five years and everyone is afraid of her," Fritz reported to Theodore. "The music editor of the *Syracuse Post-Standard* has the reputation of being equally difficult to deal with, and there is no love lost between them. You evidently have to deal with one or the other. This, in combination with the fact that both papers have strong 'anti-commercial' policies, accounts for the lack of strong newspaper coverage in Syracuse for our centenary activities."[35]

In Spokane, Washington, he had widely divergent experiences in visiting two purchasers of Steinway pianos. "I went to the home of a good customer, a Mrs. De Neff, and autographed her piano and then visited a Mrs. Hildebrand, who is a weird female with delusions of pianistic grandeur and was unhappy about her *M* grand. There was nothing wrong with her piano that selling her an *L* or *B* would not cure and I told [Carl] Hollenback [the local dealer] so," he wrote his father.[36] The *L* and *B* are larger and more expensive.

The centennial celebration was meant to convey to the world that Steinway was an ongoing success. The company spent $200,000 on the festivities. But, the glitter hid the fact that Steinway & Sons was in trouble. The centennial took place at a time when Steinway was losing money. The reason was that production at its Long Island City factory had been reduced to every other week as a result of the post-Korean War recession.

In addition, Theodore was seventy years old and his attention to the business had begun to slacken. When his young cousin, John Ziegler, joined the factory after college to determine whether he would enjoy working in a family business, he was astonished at the disarray. "The older generation was letting things run by themselves; the president, Theodore, was never at the factory," he says.[37] Based on their findings during their nationwide tours, John and Fritz cautioned their father about problems that increasingly would plague the company - low dealer inventories and complaints by local concert sponsors that dealers were either not servicing their hall's piano or doing a poor job. In turn, the dealers expressed concern about Steinway's constant production backlog. Fritz also emphasized that Hollywood movie studios probably would no longer be major customers because the big musicals were nearing an end.[38]

Even the White House no longer relied on Steinway to arrange the formal entertainment following state dinners. Mamie Eisenhower preferred her staff to do the bookings so as to obtain a broader cross-section of performers. The Kennedys elaborated on this, introducing the still-followed formula of 50 percent classical music and the rest, jazz and western as well as ballets and readings.

Steinway gained access to the Japanese market in 1953. The coup was not of its making. Instead, the initiative came from Hiroshi Matsuo, who had opened a music store after retiring as concert manager of the symphony orchestra of NHK, Japan's leading broadcasting corporation. As the Yamaha was not yet regarded as of concert-stage quality, Matsuo had imported Steinways and Bösendorfers for NHK and wanted to continue his association with Steinway.

Three years later, in 1956, the affiliation was endangered when a Matsuo employee, who wanted to start his own business, came close to convincing Steinway-Hamburg, which handles Steinway's international sales, to deal with him instead. In turn, this man proposed to distribute through Yamaha, which already handled Bechstein Piano sales in Japan. In a passionate letter to Walter Günther, Matsuo warned of the peril of such an alliance, writing:

> Once Yamaha gets the Steinway agency, I am sure it will never be so eager in its handling of Steinway as it says it is now.
> Yamaha's manufacturing capacity is so big, I am confident the time is not far distant when it will face difficulties in clearing its stock. If that happens, it will have to take drastic steps to overcome the difficulties. It is now the sole agent for Bechstein. Steinway is its next mark. If it gains possession of those good famed pianos, it considers that it can act however it likes.[39]

The letter persuaded Günther to make an on-the-spot appraisal. He flew to Japan, where Matsuo repeated his argument. Convinced, Günther awarded him the sole rights to Steinway in Japan. Matsuo fared well in Yamaha's and Kawai's backyard, even though the two Japanese firms prohibit their dealers from carrying Steinways. Officially, Matsuo only sells Steinways at its Tokyo store, a ten-minute walk from the famous Ginza shopping district. Unofficially, Yamaha and Kawai dealers secretly sell Steinways on special orders from customers.

Even Genichi Kawakami, chairman of Yamaha from 1950 to 1992, bought a Steinway. He purchased his 1905 grand through Harrod's in London five years before Yamaha began making grands. Haruki Matsuo, who became president of Matsuo Musical Instruments after his father's death in 1983, proudly maintains that Steinway is the first choice of Japanese concert performers.[40]

But the main issue Theodore wrestled with after the centennial was which of his four sons should succeed him. It was still to be a male domain, although his oldest daughter, Betty, asked if she could join the firm after graduating from college. Even today, so many years later, she remembers the exact words of his shattering response. "Go away, you embarrass me. Even our secretaries are male," her father replied.[41] That was an exaggeration, as by then Steinway did have some female secretaries.[42]

Instead of Teed, the eldest son, then head of engineering at the Long Island factory, Theodore, decided upon Henry, then factory manager, as his successor. Just like when Theodore was made president rather than Billie, the Steinways are tight-lipped as to why Teed was bypassed, but likely it was due to his drinking problem. "He was never out of control in the usual alcoholic sense, but he was easier to talk to earlier in the day than late at night, although his drinking never took the form of verbal or physical abuse," his widow Josephine says.[43]

Teed married Josephine in 1956, one year before his father's death. Steinways had divorced in the past but Teed was the first to marry a divorcée. When he introduced Josephine to the family clan at Long Pond, several fascinated young Steinways asked her, "Are you really, really divorced?" Josephine, an Oklahoman who had two daughters by her first marriage, met Teed at Arthur Murray's Manhattan dance studio where she was an instructor. Because Murray forbade teachers to date students, Josephine and Teed kept their courtship a secret from the studio's manager.

Their marriage took the Steinways by surprise as they had thought Teed was a confirmed bachelor. They erroneously were convinced that his brother, John, who shared an apartment with him and who occasionally had dated Margaret Truman, was far more likely to marry. Instead, it was John who remained single.

Teed dressed conservatively in dark suits and ties and white shirts. When fashion tastes swerved to two-button from three-button suits, he had a tailor add a buttonhole to his off-the-rack clothing. Whereas his father collected books and stamps, Teed, regarded by the family as its "intellectual," filled filing cabinets with material on the western states, colloquialisms that intrigued him, and scrapbooks of newspaper pictures in which the expression on a person's face conflicted with the caption. A fan of Kurt Weill's music, he bought every piece of Weill sheet music and all recordings of his compositions. Like his mother, Ruth, he was interested in turtles, a consequence of the many turtles that regarded Long Pond as home. An expert skier, Teed had contemplated opening a mountain resort for skiers and white-water rafters before he joined Steinway.

As she describes their marriage, it is apparent that Josephine loved Teed deeply. But it is also evident, although she does not say so outright, that life with him was not easy. Besides his drinking, which he did not view as a problem or try to give up, Teed never shook his bachelor habit of eating at restaurants. He often would dine out alone, leaving his wife, the two girls, and a son, Theodore Alexander ("Sascha") born a year after he and Josephine got married, at home.

Just why Teed drank still puzzles Josephine. She speculates the cause was a reluctance to discuss what he considered unpleasant and from suppression of anger, an emotion he despised. Whereas most people are unable to remember week-old arguments, Teed could recount the two or three times in his life that he lost his temper.

On April 8, 1957, Theodore Edwin Steinway died. The dynasty was drawing toward its end. Henry would be the last Steinway to run Steinway & Sons.

## Chapter VII
## *Henry*

Of the six Steinways who headed Steinway & Sons, Henry Engelhard was the founder, William the builder, Charles Herman the expansionist, Frederick the promoter, and Theodore the conserver. The sixth, Henry Ziegler Steinway, is the one who sold the family patrimony to CBS in 1972 both of his own accord and in response to shareholding relatives who were discontent with the low dividends they received.

The man who presided over this wrenching decision, causing a family split that has never fully healed, is tall, slope-shouldered, a wearer of Brooks Brothers' suits and horn-rimmed glasses, soft-spoken, intelligent, articulate, and a nonpianist, unlike his father and grandfather. He is, however, a dedicated concertgoer, whereas his brother, John, so disliked attending concerts that he sometimes fell asleep and ultimately stopped going.

Capable of enormous warmth, Henry ("Hank" to acquaintances) is described as possessing "totally unaffected naturalness and charm" by Carlos Moseley, chairman emeritus and former managing director of the New York Philharmonic. Yet, when annoyed, he can be prickly and bluntly abrupt. Self-described as a "hard-nosed, practical Yankee"[1] in business decisions, he largely delegated the upbringing of his three sons and two daughters to his wife, Polly.[2] The daughter of a co-owner of a shellac business, Polly, an amateur painter, met Henry at Long Pond through her friend and his cousin, Lydia Davis.

A good host and mixer at public events, basically Henry is a loner, with a summer home in Vermont rather than at the Long Pond family compound. Nor does he socialize with performers as did his parents and grandparents. His reason is that "Steinway's function is like that of a tailor providing a suit."[3]

As a "practical Yankee," Henry today owns stock in those competitive pianomakers that are publicly traded because "I'm nosy and can get information from their annual reports." He stresses, though, that he makes no secret of his shareholdings and buys "under my own name and address."[4] He held onto his several hundred Baldwin shares even when they dropped more than $50 in value in the early 1980s. The drop was due to troubles that arose after the 1977 merger of Baldwin with United Corporation, an investment concern based in Baldwin's hometown of Cincinnati. Baldwin-United overextended itself in acquisitions and was forced to declare bankruptcy in 1983. The piano business, however, remained profitable and its two senior executives purchased it in 1984. They relisted the stock in 1987 at around five times the price to which it had plunged so that Henry's tenacity was not in vain.

Henry's impact on Steinway & Sons is rife with contradictions. He receives high praise from former concert and artist manager David Rubin, as "an exceptional man who did a wonderful job and brought the company into the twentieth century."[5] Henry Ziegler, who, while serving on Steinway's board, urged his cousin to sell, says "Henry had a lot of ability and turned the company around."[6]

Yet administrative procedures at the firm remained of Stone Age vintage rather than twentieth-century technology. Performers who had been loyal for years began to drift away, alienated by what they viewed as abrasiveness and haughtiness on the part of David Rubin and a deterioration in the quality of the piano. In addition, although Henry and Walter Günther, the Hamburg manager, were close friends, the New York operation came to regard the German one as a competitor instead of as an associate. The situation worsened when several prominent pianists publicly declared they preferred the Hamburg to the New York Steinway.

In addition to having to deal with this turmoil, Henry had to find a new advertising agency when NW Ayer dropped its sixty-year association to handle Yamaha. During his presidency, too, the long-simmering dispute with Grotrian-Steinweg, the piano firm whose origins dated back to Henry's grand-uncle, Theodor, culminated in a court battle at which Henry was the sole witness against the German company. Unlike his father, Henry had no hobbies outside the office to relieve the tension.

Theodore Edwin never pressured his sons to go into the family company, nor, with the exception of John for one summer, did they work there during school vacations. Nonetheless, they all wound up at the firm. In Henry's case, when he graduated from Harvard University in 1937, the depression had not lifted and jobs were scarce. Thus, he decided to join the family business.

In line with Steinway tradition, the factory manager was a relative - Theodore Cassebeer, a brother of Julia Steinway. As had his forebears, Henry began in the lumberyard, sorting wood, and then progressed through every factory department. Cassebeer died in 1941, shortly before the United States entered the war. In 1943, Henry, then twenty-eight, was made assistant factory manager. After the war he became factory manager and in 1946 was made a company vice president, as well.

During Henry's presidency, his brother Teed was head of engineering and his brother John advertising director, a position to which his father had appointed him after the War. Fritz, the youngest brother, who was six years Henry's junior, broke from tradition.

In 1957, two years after Henry became president, Alexander Greiner retired as C and A manager. The lively, extroverted Fritz, who held both engineering and business administration degrees, coveted the position, and Ruth Steinway asked Henry to give it to him. Henry was in an awkward position. On the one hand, there was an unwritten Steinway tradition that no Steinway would run the C and A department so as to avoid charges of favoritism by Steinway artists. On the other hand, this brief rift between Henry and Fritz and his mother was uncomfortable for the Steinways liked to present an appearance of solidarity and harmony to the outside world.

Also, according to a Steinway executive very closely involved, Henry and Fritz's brother-in-law Schuyler Chapin, then in the publicity department of Columbia Artists, a performers' agency, wanted the job, too. Chapin is two years younger than Fritz. Chapin, however, denies that he ever wanted or vied for the position at that time. But more than thirty years later, in 1991 at the age of sixty-eight, he became Steinway's vice-president of worldwide concert and artist activities following being general manager of the Metropolitan Opera in New York and Dean of the Faculty of Arts at Columbia University. He resigned in 1992 "to pursue other interests."

The situation in 1957, according to the Steinway executive, was further entangled because Fritz and Chapin had been schoolmates at prep school and Fritz's wife, Mary Castle (nicknamed "Cassie"), and Betty Steinway Chapin had been classmates at Radcliffe College. Fritz had introduced Chapin to Betty and Betty had been matchmaker for Fritz and Cassie.

Yet another complication was that there already was somebody qualified to succeed Greiner - his assistant Winston Fitzgerald. Ultimately, Henry decided to break tradition and appointed Fritz to the position.

Fritz's appointment turned out to be a popular choice with performers, who enjoyed his convivial company at Chinese dinners and the movies. Shortly after he became C and A manager, he helped calm a nervous Van Cliburn as the young Texan embarked on a U.S. tour in 1958 after becoming the first American to win the Tchaikovsky piano competition in Moscow. Anxious to live up to his acclaim, Cliburn was extremely concerned that the Steinway piano in each city be in superb condition. He asked his manager, Harry Beall, to telephone Fritz and request him to personally speak to Steinway's dealer in Denver, where the tour was to begin.

It was noon New York time and when Beall was unable to reach Fritz at Steinway Hall, he gambled that Fritz would be at the Steinway table at the Barbizon Plaza Hotel. "I must speak to him," pleaded Beall, who was losing his usual imperturbability under the strain. "I can't interrupt him; he's with guests," responded the headwaiter. "You must, you must," a now desperate Beall implored. In two seconds, unrattled as always, Fritz was at the phone. "What's up?" he calmly asked Beall, who explained the situation, adding that the dealer "will jump higher and more quickly at the Steinway name."[7]

Fritz instantly telephoned the dealer, who assured him all Cliburn's requests would be accommodated. Cliburn's love affair with the Steinway has never abated. He has three Steinway concert grands on the first floor of his Fort Worth home, two on the second, and several uprights. In fact, nearly every room has a Steinway, prompting record producer Jack Pfeiffer to tease him: "Van, you personify Oscar Wilde's quip that nothing succeeds like excess."[8]

No sooner had he dealt with the issue of Fritz's appointment than Henry had to discover a way to simultaneously finance much-needed improvements to both the Long Island City and Hamburg factories. Hamburg's requirement was modest - a $40,000 addition. But the almost ninety-year-old Long Island City factory was in urgent need of a $3 million modernization. At the time, it was the largest capital outlay in the history of the U.S. piano industry.

Just as he had regarding Fritz's appointment, Henry made a hard-nosed decision; it made possible concurrent renovations of the two factories. His conclusion was that the only way to raise the money was to sell Steinway Hall, the company's glamorous flagship store, as well as the office building above it that Steinway also owned. For a buyer, he looked no farther than across the street to the Manhattan Life

Insurance Company. Its president, Thomas Lovejoy, was married to Henry's cousin, Audrey Paige. A model, Audrey was one of the two children of Henry's aunt Maud and Raymond Paige. Lovejoy had been searching for a new location with more space. The sale was completed in 1958, and Steinway was given a twenty-year lease with renewal options for the ground floor, mezzanine and basement. The lease was renewed in 1978. When Manhattan Life moved in, it ordered that the figures sculpted on the façade be covered over with cement, for although they were muses, it was feared that some might take them for angels, and this symbolism would deter the sale of life insurance.

The controversy over Henry's initial decisions as president had just died down when a bizarre lawsuit was filed against Steinway by pianist Glenn Gould, a Steinway artist. It arose from a casual encounter a few weeks before Christmas 1959 between Gould and William Hupfer, Steinway's chief technician. Gould was visiting the concert and artist department at Steinway Hall, when Hupfer, a physically big man, walked in, laid his hand in greeting on Gould's shoulder as Gould refused to risk shaking hands with most people, and asked "How are you?" A year later, Gould alleged in a $300,000 damage suit that Hupfer had injured him at that meeting.

His charge was that Hupfer "recklessly or negligently let both forearms down with considerable force on the plaintiff's neck and left shoulder, driving the plaintiff's left elbow against the arm of the chair on which he was sitting." Gould further claimed that Hupfer had hurt his neck, shoulder, spinal discs, and left hand to such an extent that he had been unable to perform at recitals or record sessions. The pianist went on to say that he had previously complained to Steinway of the "unduly strong handshakes and other demonstrative physical acts of Hupfer."[9]

The principals in the dispute - Gould and Hupfer - were an interesting contrast. The word eccentric could have been coined for the then twenty-seven-year-old Gould, a Canadian-born Bach specialist. His idiosyncracies earned him attention equal to the much-praised quality of his work. He wore gloves, scarves, and overcoats in the summer, lest he catch cold. It was his custom to request Steinway's London store to place a screen around him and light an electric fire so he would be warm.[10]

Gould was famous for keeping his piano stool so low that his shoulders barely reached the keyboard. He drove audiences to distraction with his loud humming and peculiar posture. He would lean flat back and sway his body around as he played. During concerts in which the orchestra performed first, Gould would sip from a glass of water he had placed beside his stool until the start of the piano portion.

His personality was a mixture of thoughtfulness and selfishness. A loyal friend, he continued using Vern Edquist, his favorite tuner, when Edquist left his Toronto department store employer to go into business on his own. Conversely, Gould refused to recognize that others did not share his odd habits. A night owl, he often telephoned Edquist in the middle of the night to discuss music for several hours. Once, during a 2:00 a.m. break in a recording session, when Edquist was doing pushups to stay awake, Gould petulantly snapped at him to stop because "I don't like it."[11]

Gould and Hupfer did not get on well even before the hand-on-the-shoulder incident because Gould's preference for voicing of a piano ran counter to Hupfer's. Hupfer was the second generation of his family to work for Steinway, which, as a family business, encouraged several generations of other families to work for it. William's father had been employed in the factory and his brother, Walter, was an outside tuner. The Hupfers lived in Brooklyn and Walter, especially, had a thick Brooklyn accent. The pianist Wanda Landowska was once offended because she thought Walter had asked if she had made many "insights" in her recordings, when what he really had said was "inserts."[12]

In 1959, William Hupfer was in his forty-second year at Steinway, having joined the company in 1917 at the age of nineteen. His big break had occurred when Alexander Greiner, then concert and artist manager, assigned him as a traveling tuner to Rachmaninoff, who was dissatisfied with the person Greiner had previously appointed. Rachmaninoff was so pleased with Hupfer that from then on he asked that he always accompany him on tours. Hupfer became Steinway's chief technician.[13]

Ultimately, Gould and Steinway settled out of court and Gould continued to play Steinways until he retired from the concert stage. He subsequently bought two Yamaha grands, which he used for most of his recordings. Gould died in 1982; he willed one of the Yamahas to Toronto's new music auditorium, Thomson Hall.

As C and A manager, Fritz played a crucial role in pacifying Gould. But then he himself became the subject of another controversy. This time it was over his decision to quit his job. His departure in 1964 once more set a family precedent as he was the first Steinway to voluntarily leave Steinway & Sons. What prompted his decision was that as with many one-product family businesses, there were not "earthshaking changes" and consequently, insufficient decision making to apportion among the several members involved. With three older brothers and an older cousin, Charles Garland Steinway, in the business, Fritz concluded "there was a lack of advancement opportunity."[14]

Thus, he was delighted when legendary New York concert and artist manager Arthur Judson, then in his eighties and a friend of Fritz's parents, offered him a partnership in a new agency he had started down the street from Steinway Hall. Fritz became the "S" in JOBS, the acronym of Judson O'Neil Beall & Steinway. Pianists Gary Graffman and Christoph Eschenbach, both of them "Steinway artists," as well as the Guarneri String Quartet, were among his clients.

The Beall in the agency was Harry Beall, who had telephoned Fritz so frantically during Van Cliburn's tour. He says "other Steinways were amazed at Fritz's decision to leave the golden apple - the comfort of a family business - for a new firm."[15] However, as Judson was as much a kingpin in concert management as his rival Sol Hurok, Fritz was not acting rashly. Ultimately, JOBS represented one hundred performers.

Concert management largely involves the careful handling of monumental egos, and Fritz normally was skilled at this task. The exception occurred when a prominent conductor strolled in one day without an appointment and demanded to see Judson. Busy with another artist, Judson, who addressed his associates by their surnames, said: " Steinway, you find out what he wants." Fritz chatted amiably with the conductor, delicately probing as to why he had come. Unable to discover the reason, Fritz finally asked him point-blank. "What can I do for you?" The conductor's response stunned him: "I want to be appointed music director of the Cleveland Orchestra when George Szell retires." As a client, the conductor had the right to express his interest, but Fritz was enraged by his audacity. Torn between fury and the need to be courteous to his visitor, Fritz attempted to smile and replied: "I commend you. The line forms to the right." This was not what the conductor had expected and he left angrily. Subsequently, he severed his connection with the agency. [16]

Fritz remained at JOBS until 1973, when the University of Massachusetts at Amherst invited him to become the first executive director of its fine arts center. He made broad use of his entertainment world contacts to book big names for the center, including Cliburn, Graffman, Leontyne Price, Chamber music quartets, and traveling theater and dance troupes. After his retirement, he joined the board of many

Amherst artistic organizations, a step that none of his brothers took with similar groups in New York.

Not long after Fritz left, his cousin Charles Garland Steinway did, too. Charlie had worked in Steinway's wholesale department as an assistant to Roman de Majewski both before and after World War II in which he served in Army Intelligence in Europe. In 1964, when he was fifty, Charlie became head of Wilking Music Company in Indianapolis, one of two music stores that Steinway still owned outside Manhattan (the other was in Cincinnati). The manager, Frank Wilking, was retiring and suggested Charlie as his replacement.

Unfortunately, it soon became apparent that, as Charlie himself admitted, he was not a businessman. A despairing Henry finally dispatched Richard Gigax, an ace salesman in Majewski's department, to correct the situation. Under Gigax, sales bloomed and within two years of his arrival, he had turned what had been a one-store operation into a six-outlet chain. Pleased, Henry appointed Gigax president of Wilking Music and shifted Charlie upstairs as chairman. While Henry's decision naturally rankled, Charlie and his wife, Sally, were realists and conceded Henry was right. "Charlie and Dick were a superb combination; Charlie worked best with the artists and Dick with business details," Sally said.[17] In 1970, when Gigax sought to acquire Wilking Music, Charlie happily loaned him some of the necessary money. Subsequently, he took a post retirement job of tracking down witnesses for the Indianapolis prosecutor's office and became a volunteer at a recovery home for teenage drug addicts.

The most severe problems in Henry's regime can be summarized in three words: "David Rubin" and "Teflon." It is easy to understand why Henry hired Rubin in 1964 to replace Fritz. His appointment signaled that Steinway & Sons had returned to the tradition of non-family as head of the C and A department. Also, Rubin had a distinguished background: years of piano training under well-known instructors, a music history degree from Princeton University, a career as a music teacher, and eight years at Baldwin, Steinway's chief rival.

Ironically, just a few years earlier, the Steinways had lambasted Rubin for his tactics in trying to recruit Steinway artists for Baldwin. Performers are not chained for life to a piano firm; their endorsement of a piano is of their own free will and they can make, break, and remake affiliations. To lure Gary Graffman, Rubin promised he would have Baldwin make a piano similar to Graffman's favorite Steinway concert grand, *CD 199.* What infuriated the Steinways was that Rubin requested that Graffman "surreptitiously" - as Graffman puts it - take a

Baldwin employee to the Steinway Basement to examine the piano. Instead, Graffman informed Fritz, who scolded Rubin.[18] However, by 1964, the ill feelings over this episode had evaporated.

Rubin is a cultured man and capable of courteous flourishes. It was his suggestion that Steinway artists over seventy-five be exempted from charges for cartage and tuning of pianos for concerts. This was a gracious but inexpensive concession as just four people qualified during Rubin's twenty-two-year tenure: Horowitz, Serkin, Rudolph Ganz, and Rosina Lhévinne.

Rubin also was responsible for the selection of Franz Mohr as chief technician when William Hupfer retired in 1970. Mohr, who had studied violin in his youth in his native Germany, had originally worked for Steinway at its franchised dealership in Düsseldorf. On moving to New York in 1962, he was hired by Steinway Hall as a technician for the retail department. Three years later, he was made Hupfer's assistant.

His first assignment had been to go with Artur Rubinstein on a tour. Eager to make the best impression, before Rubinstein arrived Mohr zealously washed the piano keys and they sparkled. He expected Rubinstein to be pleased when he replied "Yes" to Rubinstein's query as to whether he had cleaned the keys. He was devastated when Rubinstein said, "Oh, no. I should have told you never to clean the keys because I then find them too slippery."

The audience already was seated and Mohr was desperate for a solution. "Why don't you use hair spray?" someone suggested. The spray made the keys sticky and a relieved Rubinstein marched on stage.[19] For performers such as Rubinstein and current Steinway artist Eugene Istomin, whose hands perspire heavily, the natural porous quality of ivory keys is insufficient to soak up the sweat.

Another time, as Rubinstein was well into a Haydn sonata, the middle G key, a frequently used note, broke. Forced to stop, Rubinstein waited while Mohr removed the top key on the piano, which is seldom used, and glued it at middle G. Within ten minutes, the glue hardened and Rubinstein continued. On yet another occasion, a string snapped during a Horowitz performance at Carnegie Hall. Horowitz tried to keep playing but the string's buzzing stopped him. As Mohr replaced the string, an unperturbed Horowitz set him at ease by saying, "Don't worry, Franz. Take your time. This removes some of the tension from the concert."[20]

But while Rubin's promotion of Mohr was applauded, unfortunately the performers, dealers, and concert hall managers who came in contact with Rubin found him to be imperious and inflexible for the most part. Stewart Warkow, house manager and then executive director at Carnegie Hall from 1968 until 1982, succinctly summarizes the animosity Rubin aroused in his comment that "When David Rubin was at Steinway, he was regarded as Baldwin's best salesman."[21]

Warkow further criticizes Rubin as "snippy, snooty, and difficult." Warkow was particularly exasperated when Rubin chided him about the composition of a *New York Times* photograph of Warkow and financier James Wolfensohn, then the chairman of Carnegie Hall. (Wolfensohn is now head of the World Bank.) The picture was taken on the hall's stage hours before Frank Sinatra was to perform. Consequently, the musicians' stands had been set up. Also, there was a Bösendorfer piano, which Sinatra had decided to use instead of the house Steinway. "In the photograph the Bösendorfer was a black blob and nobody could have made out what it was," Warkow recalls. "Nobody, that is, except Rubin, who detected it was a Bösendorfer because the curve of the case differed slightly from that of a Steinway. He stormed down Fifty-seventh Street and came into my office to express how upset he was."[22]

Many dealers also disliked him. Paul Murphy, Jr., president of M. Steinert in Boston, says most dealers found Rubin to be "intimidating."[23] Rubin's haughtiness irritated many Steinway performers, too. "The general criticism of his reign was that he did not listen to the artists; his attitude was that Steinway was supreme and nobody should say it wasn't the best," John Browning comments. "For my part, I agreed that Steinway was the best but that didn't mean there wasn't room for improvement."[24]

Performers who appeared on television talk shows, such as Peter Nero, were displeased that Rubin refused to supply pianos free of charge for their appearances. "By contrast, when I telephoned Richard Probst, Rubin's successor, and requested a decent instrument for the Merv Griffin show, he was most obliging," Nero says. "Granted I was only on three minutes, but it was important to sound good in that brief time. In the Rubin era, the thinking was that three minutes weren't worth such an effort."[25]

The edgy relationship between Rubin and the Steinway artists further worsened over two incidents: the Garrick Ohlsson showdown and the recall of pianos on loan to performers. The Ohlsson brouhaha arose at the time of a September 1972 concert he was to play at the Lincoln Center's Alice Tully Hall. A Steinway artist, Ohlsson had booked a Steinway grand. Then, in an interview with *The New York*

*Times* printed the morning of the concert, Ohlsson was quoted as saying the Bösendorfer "is the Rolls Royce of pianos."[26]

Rubin considered Ohlsson's remark outrageous and ignored the pianist's explanation that he used the Rolls Royce comparison because the Bösendorfer "is twice as expensive as other pianos." An incensed Rubin ordered that the Steinway be withdrawn from Alice Tully Hall. "We're not mad at anybody and we're not telling anybody to play our piano, but we consider Mr. Ohlsson's statement an endorsement of, and testimonial to, the Bösendorfer," Rubin declared as the piano was trucked away. "I don't see why, at our expense, we should supply our piano if he says he prefers another."[27]

That left Ohlsson without a piano hours before his performance. His manager hastened next door to Philharmonic Hall and found an available piano. Coincidentally, it was a Bösendorfer. Not surprisingly, considering the preperformance turbulence, Ohlsson, according to the *Times* reviewer, "did not seem at his best in the first half of the program." But the critic deemed the remainder "superb."[28]

The recall of the pianos on loan bruised Rubin's relationship with performers not for what he did, but because of the way he did it. The pianists well understood it was a financial burden on Steinway to provide hundreds of thousands of dollars' worth of pianos on permanent loan for their residences, a practice it had begun years earlier. And Rubin did offer to sell them the pianos at reduced prices. What angered them was that instead of Rubin and others at Steinway outlining their reasons in a personal telephone call or letter, a mimeographed notice was sent.[29]

The Teflon tempest arose from good intentions that went awry and the subsequent stony reluctance of Steinway to admit it had erred. Steinway's introduction of Teflon in 1959 to the piano's heart, its "action," was hailed by the company as typical of its history as an innovator. The action is an extremely complicated mechanism made from simple materials: wood, leather, and felt hinged together with tiny pins. A well-constructed one can last for more than a century.

Traditionally, the metal pins were lined with cloth bushings to eliminate the friction that results from direct contact of wood and metal. The problem with cloth is that because it absorbs moisture readily, it expands in high humidity, causing the action to become stiff or jerky. Also, cloth bushings can be destroyed by moths, insects, or fungus. Accustomed to these drawbacks, pianomakers moisture-stabilize the cloth and apply a graphite coating as a lubricant.

When the engineering department, headed by Teed Steinway, discovered that Teflon, a fluorocarbon invented in 1938, could be substituted for cloth, Steinway believed an alternative approach had been found. In theory, Teflon offered many advantages. Unlike cloth, it did not absorb moisture; therefore, it was not vulnerable to atmospheric changes. Moreover, Teflon could not be eaten away by insects or fungus. Teflon's chief appeal to cooks - the nonstick surface, making pots and pans easier to wash - also caught the attention of Steinway's engineers. They were convinced the slipperiness would enhance the movement of the action and allow three times firmer pinning than with cloth. Hence, they argued, there would be freer movement by the thousands of action parts, which, in turn, would reduce how often pianos had to be tuned.

Unfortunately, what worked in the laboratory did not in the real world. Concert performers complained that if the Teflon bushings were installed too tightly, the action became sluggish; if too loosely, there was a clicking sound. Technicians grumbled that Teflon had to be fitted directly the opposite of cloth and that servicing it in the same manner as cloth led to disastrous results. They justifiably criticized Steinway for not training them during the experimental stages; the program was launched after Teflon's introduction and two years elapsed before it was completed.

But the basic problems of Teflon continued. As time passed and Steinway stubbornly refused to admit its mistake, the company began to shift the blame, maintaining there was no fault in the pianos but that field servicing was inadequate. The technicians were afraid to rebut the claim as they feared what would result if, as one puts it, "we caused waves." Their mutterings that they were not at fault were given weight by the fact that other pianomakers and Steinway's Hamburg branch did not use Teflon.

Steinway dealers also were unhappy. William Mattlin, whose Cleveland firm, Mattlin-Hyde, switched to being a Steinway dealer from a Baldwin one in 1980, says that during this period, "Steinway had terrible relations with its dealers. It was very arrogant. If dealers said they thought anything was wrong, they were treated like idiots. Henry and John Steinway were two of the sweetest individuals who ever walked, but they had managers who were pretty rough. 'You must be kidding' they would say. 'How could there be problems with our pianos?'"[30]

Henry Steinway never retreated from the use of Teflon bushings. Indeed, they prevailed until 1982 when Lloyd Meyer, the last of the four presidents during the time CBS owned Steinway, abolished them from Steinway pianos and restored the use of cloth bushings. However, the use of Teflon did not vanish entirely. Since Meyer's time, the cloth has been impregnated with a liquid Teflon solution that serves as a lubricant. Yamaha applies a similar mixture to the top of its pianos' hammer jacks and repetition levers to eliminate potential friction.

It was during the height of the controversies over Rubin and Teflon that several prominent Steinway artists switched to Baldwin, including André Watts, Byron Janis, Claudio Arrau, Lorin Hollander, and Dave Brubeck. Most left because they believed Steinway's standards for preparation of pianos for concerts had deteriorated. As Janis explains: "The pianos I encountered on tour required a lot of attention but when I asked the work was not done. Steinway's explanation was that it was difficult to make constant changes to meet the wishes of performers because each pianist wanted something different. The policy was that a piano had to serve many artists. But that is impossible because how a piano sounds is a personal thing for each performer. How one tells a technician to voice the instrument can be vastly different from what another wants. Thus, I felt my performances were being hurt. By contrast, Baldwin sent a technician with me on tour."[31]

Baldwin began making inroads against Steinway due to its own initiative, as well. In 1960, Baldwin acquired a controlling interest in Bechstein, the well-regarded European pianomaker. The purchase gave Baldwin access to Bechstein's "scales" (designs), from which it developed the *SD-10*, its answer to Steinway's concert grand. The Bechstein connection also provided Baldwin with indirect entry to Europe's concert stages against Steinway's Hamburg pianos. After a quarter century of absorbing Bechstein's techniques, Baldwin sold the company to German interests in 1986. Baldwin's chairman Richard Harrison says Bechstein was discarded because "it no longer fitted in with our marketing plans. We didn't need it because we believe our concert grand is second to none."[32]

After Baldwin sold the Bechstein line, it airfreighted an *SD-10* to Europe for a twenty-six- city tour by internationally acclaimed pianist Jorge Bolet, who had switched to Baldwin from Steinway years before. He had been introduced to the Baldwin by Serge Koussevitzky. Bolet and the *SD-10* drew rave reviews, enabling Baldwin to gain a foothold in Europe. Subsequently, Bechstein, which produces about 1,000 pianos annually, began limited shipments to the United States.

Baldwin further chipped away at Steinway by hiring as its concert manager the amiable Jack Romann, who was the antithesis of David Rubin. Romann, who had majored in piano at Juilliard and later worked in the record business, assiduously cultivated pianists through not charging for shipment and tuning. Leonard Bernstein, for example, was loaned a half-dozen pianos for his apartment and country house; his sister received one, too. Romann further built up a reputation for helping young pianists get launched professionally. He combed major music schools and domestic competitions for new talent, signing up ten promising people annually.

Romann was extremely popular among performers. Thus, there was a tremendous outcry when he was shunted aside to a different position in 1986 and replaced by Rubin upon the latter's retirement from Steinway. Within weeks, Harrison bowed to the pleas of musicians and reinstated Romann. Rubin was made director of corporate information, a position he carried on from his apartment even though Baldwin's Manhattan office is nearby.

Most of the ex-Steinway performers - but not Brubeck - ultimately returned to the fold when Steinway, shaken by their defection, realized it had to shed its arrogance. Also, Steinway benefited from a lapse in the quality of Baldwin pianos during the settling-in period following the transfer begun in 1958 of Baldwin's operations from Cincinnati to Mississippi and Arkansas.

At the same time that Baldwin was giving Steinway fresh cause for concern, Far Eastern pianomakers began to invade the U.S. market. Henry came to regard Yamaha, the largest Asian pianomaker, as an even tougher competitor than Baldwin becauses of its much lower prices. Yamaha's prices, on average, are half Steinway's, whereas Baldwin's on average, are about one-fifth lower. Henry decided the best defense was to emphasize Steinway's "quality of construction." He requested NW Ayer to devise a new advertising campaign with this theme. Ayer came up with "Only the Steinway sounds like a Steinway" backed up by "The things that money can't buy come into your house with a Steinway."

In a variation of Raymond Rubicam's classic "Instrument of the Immortals" ad, ordinary people, portrayed by staff at the agency, were pictured at Steinways imagining they were "immortals." The copy read: "It sounds immodest, I know, but for a brief moment, I reminded myself of Rubinstein [or Cliburn, etc.]. Was it the Steinway?"

A 1966 ad explained, with tongue-in-cheek, that Shakespeare, "so conscious of beauty around him, never wrote a sonnet to the Instrument of the Immortals because he never heard a Steinway." Its lament aroused the sympathy of Brian Mead of Scarsdale, New York, who promptly filled the void with a laudatory acrostic used by Ayer in its next ad:

> **S**hall I compare thee to a harpsichord?
> **T**hou are more lovely and doth sound more sweet;
> **E**ye hath not seen, nor listening ear hath heard
> **I**n all of Music such true Concord meet.
> **N**ow 'tis the softest whisper that we hear,
> **W**hen pianissimo the score doth say;
> **A**nd if instead it calls for loud and clear,
> **Y**ou know the instrument will sing that way.
> **P**erformers all prefer its matchless tones;
> **I**n its true purity of tone they find it best,
> **A**nd each will strive until at last he owns
> **N**one but a Steinway, scorning all the rest.
> **O**h, none can make such heavenly sounds as Thee;
> **S**urely on this all pianists agree!

Steinway resorted to some third-party tie-in advertising, too. John Steinway appeared in the celebrity campaign of American Express, along with golfer Jack Nicklaus and Jim Henson, creator of the Muppets. He also was featured on his own, saying "At a concert I look to see if my name is on the piano, but the ticket office looks for my American Express card." At the same time, Steinway continued to watch out for tie-in ads that might harm its image. Under U.S. laws, it could not prevent its piano from being photographed as part of an ad for another product; it could only take action when a comparison was made. As the general public was unaware of this distinction, it was Steinway that was attacked when one of its grands appeared in the background of a whiskey ad and when another was used as a resting place for a cigarette package in a tobacco company's promotion. John Steinway pleaded with the firms not to repeat their ads, explaining that "We are getting lots of letters from nonsmokers and from the Bible Belt saying 'How dare you stoop to advertising pianos with whiskey?' "[33]

When, in 1969, Ayer severed its long association with the company, Steinway began the search for a replacement. One day, Richard Lord, chairman of the then two-year-old New York agency of Lord, Geller, Federico, Einstein, Inc. was paid a visit by a stranger. The man introduced himself as F. Kingsland White, a friend of John Steinway and a fellow member of Manhattan's Amateur Comedy Club. In what was then a common practice in the advertising business, White offered to be a liaison between Lord, Geller and John Steinway in return for a "finder's fee." Lord agreed and White introduced him to John.[34]

The Steinways were interested in Lord, Geller because the young firm already had a roster of prestige clients. Since its 1967 beginning with "no business, no clients, no prospects, no promises," Lord, Geller had become the agency for Tiffany's, Elizabeth Arden, *The New Yorker*, and other blue-chip firms. Although Steinway's $200,000 budget was small, compared with the megabucks spent by bigger companies, Lord, Geller was interested as the Steinway name fit with the quality image it was nurturing for itself.

The agency devised sprightly ads with snappy punchlines for Steinway. One showed Steinway's forty-inch-tall upright, its shortest, in a small, empty room, and said, "In situations like this, Steinway stands tall." Another, of a big musical-note, had the slogan, "You'll hear all of it on a Steinway." Also talked about was an ad that referred to Theodore Steinway's rejection during the depression of a million dollars from a refrigerator manufacturer for use of the Steinway name on its product. Underneath a picture of a refrigerator, Lord Geller wrote, "Not for a million dollars," going on to explain why. But its most memorable concoction, headed "The Land of No Steinways," featured penguins at the South Pole and read: "It doesn't happen to be a concert hall or a recording studio or a music composition. But if it were, the Steinway piano would be there, too."

In addition to having to cope with the onslaughts of Baldwin and Yamaha, Henry found himself in court over a dispute for which he had no responsibility. For that matter, his opponents were not directly responsible, either.

The case had its origin in the permission granted by Henry's great-uncle Theodor to his former employees, Grotrian, Helferrich, and Schulz, to include "Successors to Th. Steinweg" in their corporate name when he sold them his Braunschweig business. One of their first customers was Clara Schumann. In 1895, the German firm registered the trademark "Grotrian-Steinweg" in Germany. This registration was canceled after Steinway-Hamburg sued against its use.

In 1918, in the next round of what would turn out to be a seventy-eight-year conflict, the Grotrian family petitioned the Braunschweig government to allow it to change its name to Grotrian-

Steinweg even though the Grotrians and the Steinwegs were never related. The government agreed and the family then adopted the same name for the company.

In the early days of the renamed company, such Steinway luminaries as Bela Bartok, Richard Strauss, and Paderewski played the Grotrian on occasion, as does a current Steinway artist, Alfred Brendel. Actress-singer Julie Andrews owns two Grotrians.

It was under the Grotian-Steinweg name that the company attempted to enter the United States market in 1925 with the establishment of a Delaware corporation for the distribution of its pianos. The instruments were purchased by Wanamaker's, the famous department store, as well as by a small dealer in New York. Steinway protested that Grotrian was infringing on its trademark, but the quarrel was cut short by Grotrian's withdrawal from the United States.

There was a lull, due to an American boycott of German products during World War II. Then, in 1952, Grotrian began exporting to small American dealers, who sold the pianos without advertising. Not many were sold; only 458 between 1952 and 1972, when the trial commenced. Steinway was stymied from preventive action because it could not determine who were the Grotrian dealers since they did not advertise. What brought matters to a head was a deal reached in 1967 by Grotrian with the Wurlitzer Company, which was unaware there was a problem over the Grotrian-Steinweg name. Thus, it agreed to distribute Grotrian pianos through its nationwide chain of stores. When Henry telephoned Wurlitzer's chairman and explained the situation, he instantly tore up the contract.

Grotrian reacted by suing Steinway. Steinway countersued. Henry was the sole witness for Steinway. At one point, the Grotrian side claimed that Uncle Billie's smoking of a cigar back in 1929, when he was European manager, with Grotrian's owner had signified Steinway's capitulation. The Steinway side retorted that Uncle Billie was such a cigar lover he would smoke one whether he was with friend or foe.

In October 1973, after CBS acquired Steinway, the New York District Court decided in favor of Steinway, commenting "It would be difficult to conceive of a more deliberate intent of an infringer to imitate and palm off his product as that of another."[35] As a result, the company can sell its pianos in the United States only under the name "Grotrian." Elsewhere in the world it uses "Grotrian-Steinweg." The same principle applies to how the president signs correspondence: Knut Grotrian for the United States, Knut Grotrian-Steinweg, elsewhere.[36] Ironically, according to Grotrian, Steinway and Grotrian-Steinweg might have become one company, despite the court ruling, if he had accepted a CBS bid to buy it around the time of the Steinway takeover. Instead, he rejected CBS outright.[37]

The Grotrian piano, despite what the court declared, is not an imitation of a Steinway. In fact, it is not even remotely similar in the way it is made. It makes much greater use of mechanization and its construction methods differ radically. Steinway bends the inner and outer rims simultaneously by hand and has a different size press for each model. The bonded-together rim remains in the press all day. Grotrian bends its inner and outer rims at separate times in a hydraulic press that is adaptable to molds of all size pianos. The rims are left in for only one hour.

At Steinway, the case is made first and the mechanism - the action, soundboard, and so on - installed in it. At Grotrian, the mechanism is assembled first and then the case is wrapped around. Steinway maintains its procedure provides a stronger foundation for the soundboard and necessitates a more precise fit of the interior parts, resulting in better projection of the music. Knut Grotrian says Grotrian's technique dictates that the interior be stable since otherwise the instrument would be irreparably damaged when the rim is attached. He goes on to explain that Grotrian's system enables it to better meet customer demands. Whereas Steinway's method requires that it rely on past sales records and advance orders as its yardstick for what models to make for the forthcoming season, Grotrian only needs one week's notice as to the type of case. "Consequently, there is no danger of back orders or surplus inventory," Grotrian says.

By 1972, Henry had served seventeen years as president. While outwardly the company appeared strong, behind-the-scenes arteriosclerosis had afflicted it. There was a constant backlog of orders. Dealers understood the Steinways looked upon the waiting list as a security blanket, but they were equally convinced that the delays of six to nine months were far too long. As one complained, "We keep wondering who's our friend at Steinway who's going to supply us with some pianos." The corollary was that dealers began to emphasize other pianos to the detriment of Steinway sales. To make matters worse, Steinway had not continued Roman de Majewski's organized sales training seminars for either its own Steinway Hall staff or its dealers, as did competitors.

Then, too, there were clashes with John Steinway over Steinway's promotional material, which some dealers believed had become unsatisfactory. A stamp collector like his father, as well as a gourmet cook, John, who died in August 1989, had a toothbrush moustache and gold-rimmed glasses. He wore suspenders with a piano key design, and the hood ornament on his Mercedes was shaped in the style of Steinway's lyre trademark.

There were two distinct sides to John's personality. A member, like his parents, of Manhattan's Amateur Comedy Club, he was a ham actor at heart, as well as a skilled raconteur. This ebullience endeared him to Steinway dealers, as it helped enormously to sell pianos when he went on promotional tours. He also was capable of great kindness. Byron Janis recalls that when he was on tour in Italy some years ago and had trouble locating the prescribed formula for his infant son, John sent over supplies.[38]

But the jovial John Steinway who offered to sit, legs sprawled, on the floor with the salespeople at a local dealer's for a pose that he believed looked more relaxed for a picture could explode in anger even over trivial matters. "He could be stubborn," John Furlong, a longtime factory employee, recalled. "Once, when he was supposed to autograph a piano, he was furious that there was no lacquer available with which to spray his signature so as to protect it. None was available because he autographed a piano just once or twice a year. A can of spray was obtained the next day."[39]

Longtime Steinway dealer and friend Paul Murphy, Jr. of M. Steinert says John "could be very strong when he felt righteous." One such instance occurred in 1986, as John was about to star in a thirty-second commercial being filmed at Steinert for the Steinway piano. The camera was ready to roll, but John did not like the script. "Everyone waited while he made corrections," Murphy recollects.[40] John maintained he improved the script, which was used for some time by the company.

Administrative procedures had also become a serious problem. Record keeping was primitive, done by hand in notebooks rather than computerized.[41] The cost acounting department consisted of one person who had compiled twenty volumes detailing each and every expense in pianomaking. It was a virtual encyclopedia, but wading through it and finding particular information was very time consuming. By contrast, Steinway's competitors had computerized the myriad details of assembly. At Steinway board meetings, considerable time was devoted to discussing which factory workers had the flu and the resultant slowdown in output. Full turnout was crucial to the company's well-being. In most companies absenteeism in general might be raised but not usually on a person-by-person basis.

By 1972, Henry had restored Steinway's balance sheet to the black from the unprofitable state in which he had inherited it. He also had improved the New York and Hamburg factories to some degree. Nonetheless, the painful truth was that Steinway had severe problems. Still it was in no more a precarious position than in the past, if as bad. It had pretty well concealed its troubles from the public eye and retained its illustrious aura. Moreover, there were several younger-generation male Steinways who could continue the dynasty.

Yet, out of the blue, Steinway & Sons was sold.

## Chapter VIII
# *The CBS Years*

It was the third item listed on the shareholders' notice that drew full attendance to the 11:30 a.m. annual meeting of Steinway & Sons on Thursday, April 27, 1972, at the Long Island City factory. (The notice said Wednesday, but the twenty-seventh was on Thursday.) In dry prose it called for the "adoption and approval of the merger of Steinway & Sons with CBS Musical Instruments, a wholly-owned subsidiary of Columbia Broadcasting System(CBS)." By lunchtime, approval had been given for the 119-year-old family business to become just another CBS subsidiary.

Why had it happened? As Robert Campbell, the CBS executive who shepherded the deal, puts it, "Everyone wondered why a grand old company had sold to a nasty New York conglomerate. Everybody thought the Steinway was made by non-money-hungry people and now that it was owned by a dehumanized, big conglomerate, the product would go to hell. The general view was that to own Steinway was to own a national trust."[1]

The decision to put the company up for sale caused the first major schism among the Steinways. Hitherto, through four generations of ownership, the family had prided itself on its private and public harmony and unity. Suddenly, it was a house divided. The split was inevitable because Steinway no longer was a one-man show as it was when Henry's grandfather, William, was in charge and owned the majority interest in the company. The Steinways tend to have large families, and by 1972, the shares were spread among close to eighty cousins.

Those opposed to the sale cast Henry in the role of the villain for throwing away the family heritage and not giving the younger generation, including the women, a chance. Partisans of the sale fell into two groups. The first had an attachment to the business except for annoyance at dividends below the rate of return on a bank account. These cousins saw the CBS bid as a ticket to financial security. The other group believed there was no alternative to the sale because Steinway's financial needs exceeded its funds. These cousins were equally certain the young Steinways were uninterested in the business or were not sufficiently capable.

Convinced that Steinway had to be sold to survive, this camp further believed that if the shareholders were to wait longer, they would not get as good a price and, perhaps, not as prestigious a buyer. At that time, CBS was referred to by investment dealers and broadcasting critics as the "Tiffany" of networks. Whereas Steinway was a closely held stock, with just over 50 percent owned by the family and employees and the rest lightly traded on the over-the-counter market, CBS was a widely traded, popular, blue-chip stock. Thus, these cousins reckoned, CBS shares would be easier to cash in should the need arise for quick money.

Moreover, CBS offered generous terms: a tax-free exchange of 7.1 shares for each of Steinway's. All told, Steinway shareholders received 375,000 CBS shares then worth $20,437,750. The two largest Steinway shareholder groups - the Zieglers, and Henry, his brothers and sisters - each held 15 percent, equal to $3 million under the deal.

Yet another theory for the sale is that Steinway encountered many of the problems that beset a family-run business when it gets fixated on past glories. "Its problems were generic to family businesses. Desire is only one facet of running a company; business skills are also important and nobody in the family at the business had attended business school or law school," says Henry Steinway's cousin, Henry Ziegler, who happens to be a lawyer. "The mind-set was one common to a family business: if our great-grandfather did business a certain way, that was the way to do it. The family as a whole did not understand change, nor how to evaluate other people, because they weren't exposed much to others. On the other hand, the concern was an imported executive wouldn't understand the quality side of the business and how to deal with the artists. It is a very easy company to ruin if changed in the wrong direction. In my opinion, CBS put in whiz kids who interfered just the wrong amount."[2]

The events that led to the sale had begun with a friendly visit to Henry by Robert Campbell, a longtime acquaintance, shortly after Campbell became president of the CBS Musical Instruments division in 1970.[3] Campbell had met Henry, his father, brothers, and Uncle Billie a quarter century earlier when he worked for the Indiana-based Conn Organ Corporation, which Campbell joined following service in World War II. The U.S. music business was then much smaller and people quickly came to know one another. In 1960, Campbell left Conn to become president of Electro Music Company, a California manufacturer of electric organ systems.

At his meeting with Henry, Campbell reviewed how CBS had begun back in 1962 to branch out via acquisitions from broadcasting and record production into educational products, publishing and even major-league baseball with its purchase of the New York Yankees. As part of its expansion drive, CBS had decided the musical instrument business was complementary to its own field and the way to move into it was through buying existing firms. The first, Electro Music, was acquired in 1962. Fender Guitar was added in 1965, and Rogers Drum in 1966. In 1970, a separate musical instruments division was created and Campbell was made president with a green light for more takeovers. Besides the Steinway purchase, he arranged for the acquisitions of Gulbransen Organs, Gemeinhardt Flute, Rodgers Organ, and, in 1977, Lyon & Healy, which both made harps and owned a chain of music stores in the midwest. In Chicago, it was Steinway's dealer. Two years later, CBS closed the stores because profits from the harp business were two times greater. Lyon & Healy produces 90 percent of the harps used worldwide by professional orchestras.

In his pitch to Henry, Campbell stressed that it "is obvious Steinway needs a big infusion of money to modernize and maintain quality." CBS, Campbell added, had that money and was willing "to make the necessary investment for Steinway to grow." He went on to assure Henry that he and his brothers would not be kicked out because "CBS never buys a company without commitments to the existing management that it will stay on."[4]

Steinway had never had written contracts with its executives or employees; CBS gave Henry, John, and Teed guarantees of employment through 1975 with provision for renewal. Campbell also pledged that CBS would continue Steinway's employees' pension plan and increase the payouts, as well as add hospitalization coverage benefits.

Henry was given further assurance by verbal promises of CBS executives from chairman William Paley down that there would be no interference with the quality of the Steinway piano. To underscore his sincerity, Paley told Henry after a tour of the factory, "I want you to remember one thing - we're counting on you to maintain the quality of the Steinway piano; that's our chief concern."[5]

Adhering to the example set by Paley, the CBS people were sensitive to the Steinways' pride in their name and handled Henry with kid gloves. When Henry gibed to Harvey Schein, head of CBS/Columbia Group, the division to which CBS Musical instruments reported, that "I suppose you'll put the Steinway name on the Fender guitar," Schein replied, "You think I'm crazy?" He went on to assure Henry that Steinway would be kept separate from the other CBS companies. On another occasion, then CBS president Arthur Taylor gingerly backed off from a suggestion that Steinway, like all other CBS subsidiaries, state in its letterhead that it was a "division of CBS." "It doesn't add anything to Steinway to say that," Henry objected. "You're right. We'll make an exception," Taylor agreed.[6]

Henry had rejected takeover suitors in the past, and he turned down Campbell's overtures twenty times. But on Campbell's twenty-first try, Henry said yes. He changed his mind because of his own appraisal of Steinway's outlook and in response to pressure from major shareholders. As a "practical, hard-nosed Yankee," Henry was "uncertain Steinway could survive if interest rates were to rise because as a seasonal business it was always in a borrowing position. I kept thinking 'God knows what will happen if interest rates rise.'"[7] Interest rates did skyrocket after Steinway was sold to CBS, and Henry "often thought thank goodness it was sold since the company could not have remained profitable on its own if I had had to borrow at 14 and 15 percent, whereas CBS was cash rich."[8]

Henry further realized that Steinway was trapped by its ethos: its refusal to automate as most of its competitors had. This distinctive characteristic appealed to customers who believed handcraftsmen do superior work to the machine. But it also locked Steinway into limited output in an age of mass production. Moreover, the company could no longer count on a ready supply of skilled workers. The tradition of succeeding generations mastering the trade of their forebears had vanished. The desire of young people for quick money made them impatient at the time and painstaking attention that must be devoted to handiwork. As a result, Steinway's production lagged behind demand not just occasionally, but constantly. Whereas many companies suffer back-order problems from time to time, Steinway "was in this predicament for twenty years," according to Henry Ziegler.[9]

John Phillips, who followed Harvey Schein at CBS/Columbia Group, says Steinway might not have had to sell if it had been willing to take an unpopular step: raise prices. "Steinway was in difficulty because on the one hand, its orders exceeded what it could produce and on the other, its costs had risen," he remarks. "Consequently, it was not making enough money to continue. When CBS took over, it raised prices to no ill effect: instead, sales stood firm."[10] The prices of Steinway pianos climbed an average of 300 percent during the thirteen years CBS owned Steinway, compared with an average of 20 percent over the thirteen years preceding the CBS takeover. The bulk of the increase occurred in the first eight years of CBS's ownership during a period of heavy expenditure to renovate and modernize the Long Island City and Hamburg factories.

Besides his concerns over costs and backlogs of orders, Henry was worried about the inroads of Far Eastern pianomakers and about the future of Steinway-Hamburg. He was convinced - wrongly, as it turned out - "that the German thing would collapse one day due to political reasons."[11] His anxiety deepened when his good friend Walter Günther fell ill. Günther suffered a heart attack during a golf game just before Christmas in 1971. For the next six months Steinway-Hamburg had no manager. Finally, Siegfried Maczijewski, a sales representative who had joined Steinway after being with a competitor, Ibach Pianoforte Fabrikanten, was made acting manager.

Then, too, Henry was well aware that at fifty-seven, he had to think about the question of succession. His eldest son, William, was, at twenty-six, old enough to be in the business. But Bill, a political science major at American University, had been part of the 1960s hippie movement and was repelled by the idea of life in the executive suite. Henry's second son, Daniel, then twenty-five, did not like New York or the idea of putting on a tie and going to work. After graduating from Harvard with a degree in English literature, he moved to Henry's retreat in Vermont, spending his days walking through the nearby woods, observing nature, and doing occasional repair work on the house.

Harry, then twenty, was in his first year at Wesleyan University in Connecticut, studying architecture, after being hospitalized for several months with hepatitis. He had fallen ill while spending a year in Madrid after graduating from Andover Academy, a Massachusetts prep school. Ironically, after the business was sold, both Bill and Harry joined the company. Although some of Henry's nephews and nieces contend they did want to join the business, Henry genuinely believed there "were no prospects of any other members of the family coming in."[12]

An option would have been to retain ownership but leave the daily operations to professional managers in the mode of Louis Renner GmbH, the present German supplier of actions to Steinway and other firms. Renner's ownership is evenly split between Louis Renner's descendants and those of Wilhelm Megenhardt, a friend of Renner.

Although family members are on the board, they take no part in the management but instead pursue other careers. This alternative was summarily dismissed by those Steinways who pushed the sale. They rationalized that either the salary of an imported executive would not be justified by the size of the business or that in his eagerness to prove himself, he would ruin the company through unwarranted diversification and acquisitions.

In listening to Bob Campbell's siren song on behalf of CBS, Henry was also bowing to the wishes of key shareholders - the Zieglers and William Rosenwald. The latter's father was Julius Rosenwald, a Chicago clothier who acquired control of Sears, Roebuck in 1908 when founder Richard Sears voluntarily sold his portion of the business to him. (Previously Sears had bought out Alva Roebuck's one-third interest and Rosenwald had held some shares.) When Sears lost $16 million in 1921, Rosenwald bailed it out from his personal fortune. He also became one of the world's leading philanthropists and is credited with making possible Chicago's Museum of Science and Industry. William Rosenwald owned about 5 percent of Steinway & Sons, purchased due to his longstanding interest in classical music. He had met the Steinways throught Henry's aunt Julia, a fellow trustee of the New York Philharmonic.

Henry and his cousin Henry Ziegler had healed the rift that had existed between their branches of the family ever since Henry Ziegler's grandfather was given the bonds by Henry's grandfather, William. The Zieglers' position had so rankled Henry's father, Theodore, that he excluded John Ziegler, Henry Ziegler's brother, from a Steinway centennial picture of members of the family working at the company. John was in the factory at the time. The Zieglers believed that Theodore felt his branch contained the "real Steinways" because they bore the surname and the Zieglers were just "second fiddles."[13]

The two Henrys, however, respected each other. Henry Ziegler, who had become a member of Steinway's board in 1968 following the death of his father, Frederick Jacob, considered his cousin "very able and a very good executive." For his part, Henry Steinway regarded Henry Ziegler as "very bright." Ziegler is the first lawyer in the Steinway family. Born in 1933, he is eighteen years younger than his cousin. Since 1958, he has been at the large, prestigious New York law firm of Shearman Sterling. In 1983, he became head of the "individual clients' department" dealing with the superrich worth $5 million or more.

He takes a keen interest in music and encouraged each of his three children to learn a different instrument so that he and they could form a quartet. He became a board member of the Lincoln Center Chamber Music Society in 1973 and its president ten years later. The presidency rotates every few years, so Ziegler no longer holds the position but he is still on the board.

Charles Wadsworth, the founding artistic director of the society, describes Ziegler as a "gifted, serious amateur pianist who loves playing in chamber groups." Wadsworth also has high praise for his fundraising efforts on behalf of the nonprofit society, as well as for his diplomatic skills. "He easily grasped the complex finances and also is willing to ask people to raise money or raise it himself," Wadsworth says. "Further, his enormous tact smooths ruffled feelings and gets people to see both sides of an issue."[14]

It was Ziegler who instituted regular lunches between performers and management to nurture rapport. As it happens, the society's house piano is a Steinway, but Wadsworth stresses that Ziegler played no role in that decision and, indeed, on occasion performers request a different make.

When Henry Steinway told Ziegler about the CBS offer, Ziegler found it attractive because "There is nobody on the horizon who could be the next chief executive officer. Neither your brothers, children, nor the people in the business have the sophistication to run it."[15] According to Henry Steinway, he also "quite properly and nicely pointed out that we were not getting a suitable return on our investment and leaned on me in a very nice way as to what I was going to do about it."[16] William Rosenwald, too, kept asking Henry,"What are your plans, where are we going?"[17] Both men urged Henry to accept the CBS offer.

Henry's immediate family largely supported him. He sympathized with how his eighty-two-year-old mother, Ruth, was "emotionally torn because my father had spent his life in the business." "Are you sure you're doing the right thing, throwing away 119 years of a family company?" she asked Henry. On the other hand, she respected his business acumen. "She blew hot and cold about the sale but she was a Yankee and saw the logic of it and so voted in favor," Henry says.[18]

Of Henry's siblings, all but Betty supported his reasoning, although with considerable sadness. Lydia Steinway Cochrane, the youngest, summarizes their feelings on that April 27 and afterward when she comments, "It was a logical and practical necessity. The optimum size for a business changes throughout history and Steinway, independently, was too small. It had fought valiantly for some years but the world was getting too big for it. Moreover, there was the question of succession, as none of the young people were preparing for the business."[19]

Lydia is a person who is "impatient with Monday morning quarterbacking." Thus, when her sons, fifteen and thirteen in 1972, and her nieces and nephews talk regretfully about the missed opportunity of being in the business, her rejoinder is: "What did you do to prepare for it?"[20] As it happened, two of Lydia's nephews, Betty's twin sons, Ted and Sam, who were twenty-two at the time of the sale to CBS, believed that Henry deliberately discouraged their interest in the business. (Their elder brother, Hank, like Henry's sons Bill and Daniel and many other young people in the 1960s, was a non-conformist.)

Both Ted and Sam had worked at the Long Island City factory. They say they were "apprentices" but according to John Steinway "they just had summer jobs." The twins believed Henry would never allow them to run Steinway & Sons because "the tradition was that those whose surname was Steinway came first and therefore, Henry felt his children came before us, even though Ted could have used his full name of Theodore Steinway Chapin." They found it impossible to convince their uncle Henry otherwise since, says Ted, "he is not a confrontational person. His attitude was 'I have the responsibility and you will have to like it or lump it.'" [21]

Ted and Sam decided to present their views to all Steinway's shareholders in a letter sent April 7, twenty days before the shareholders' meeting and two months after Henry's notification of the CBS bid. The letter said:

> In the summer of 1969 I, Ted, worked in the stockroom of the Astoria factory. During the several weeks of my work I tried to talk to the workers so I could get their honest opinions about the company. There appeared to be a kind of reverence for the family but an exasperation and distaste for the way the factory was being run, with complaints about a lack of communication between the management and themselves. John was concerned and helpful, stopping by to see how things were going several times, but Henry, on the other hand, remained unenthusiastic and disinterested to a point of discouragement. He made me feel as if I was taking unfair advantage of my family position.
>
> I, Sam, worked during the summer of 1967 attempting to create order out of the archives of the

family and company. I was fascinated by the employees of Steinway, factory and office alike, who would come in and look at old photographs, documents, letters, concert programs, advertisements and the like and speak with affection of former family they had known. They conveyed to me their pride of and love for the traditions of the family and business.

The president in his letter implied that there are no more Steinways interested in the business. It has been our experience that against the traditions of Steinway and Sons the present administration has been, at times, discouraging to the "next generation." There are Steinway men and women of our generation who have not committed themselves to other vocational interests. Moreover, the Steinway men currently working in the company are not the only ones of their generation who could be a part of the company's future.

We know that after a similar acquisition by CBS of Fender Guitar the quality of that instrument deteriorated markedly and sales declined sharply. The CBS/Columbia Group feels certain they have learned from their errors and are proud to have Steinway and Sons as part of their corporation. But whatever verbal assurances they may make about maintaining the present quality, they will soon own the company and will therefore have the power to do with it what they will. The Steinway name will live on if the merger is approved, but no one can be sure it will be affixed to a product equalling the quality of the piano on which the Steinway tradition has been built.

We feel certain that the proposed merger is not really necessary at this time. If you care about Steinway and Sons, we urge you to attend the Stockholders Meeting on April 27 in New York and let your opinions be known to the management.

Sincerely yours,

Samuel Chapin, Theodore Steinway Chapin

A copy of the letter found its way to Harvey Schein, the CBS negotiator. He was not happy with its contents and decided to confront Ted and Sam. A CBS limousine took him the sixteen blocks north from

CBS headquarters to the Chapins' apartment and waited outside during his visit. Schein and the twins' father, Schuyler, were longtime acquaintances, and Schein at first addressed his remarks to him. Chapin quickly stopped him: "Harvey, don't talk to me. My sons are highly independent and you should discuss this with them." Schein persuaded the twins that for them to speak out at the April 27 meeting would be like a "harangue;" thus, they remained silent.[22]

Following the sale, Ruth moved quickly to close the family ranks and end the rancor among her children. She had them all to dinner and told them that now the sale had gone through, she expected them to be as affectionate as before to one another. The occasion reminded her children of how seven years earlier she had invited them for supper at the Cosmopolitan Club, divulged the contents of her will, and asked for their opinions. Three of them had told her they were pleased; the other three had disagreed. She was equally firm after the sale that her children, then in their late forties to late fifties, behave as she ordered.[23]

The general public impression is that the CBS years were disastrous for Steinway because CBS did not have a clue as to how to run a leisurely paced factory where, under the paternalistic Steinway management, everyone had addressed the president by his first name, prefixed on occasion by "Mister." According to this scenario, the quality of Steinway pianos dipped considerably during the CBS era.

The real story is not a clear-cut case of the good guys (the Steinways) versus big, bad CBS. On financial matters, CBS scrupulously honored its commitment to be generous, and then some, as exemplified by Campbell saying "The expenditures needed far exceeded our projections for retooling and modernizing in New York and Hamburg. Steinway's budgets were very lengthy because a lot of the capital expenses were considerably overdue."[24] Henry candidly agrees with that assessment, saying he had "held back on improvements. CBS was willing to spend, too, on items such as $1 million for a new power plant in Hamburg that didn't add one dollar to the bottom line."[25] All told, CBS spent several million dollars on the factories, as well as for new premises for the London branch after its lease expired on its original building and Sotheby's moved in. By contrast, the average annual expenditures under the family's ownership never topped $150,000.

CBS's heavy outlay on Steinway prompts high praise from Ed Hendricks, Steinway's Chicago dealer for many years. "CBS's ownership was the best thing that ever happened to Steinway," he states emphatically. "If it weren't for CBS, Steinway would not exist today in virtually its original image. CBS was willing to spend the money necessary to save Steinway. For a business to thrive, its owners must put money back into it and the Steinways were not doing this. Henry Steinway was honorable and capable but he did not own enough of the company to override those in the family interested only in dividends. By contrast, CBS knew what was required in capital expenditures and did it."[26]

Where CBS stumbled - and badly - was in people relations, not just with the Steinways, but also with the presidents it appointed. Between 1853 and 1972, almost one and a quarter centuries, Steinway had had just six presidents; in only thirteen years, between 1972 and 1985, when CBS sold Steinway, there were four. The first, Henry, was eased out; the second, Robert Bull, was fired; the third, Peter Perez, was forced to resign in a power struggle; the fourth, Lloyd Meyer, barely into his job, was ousted by the Birminghams, the new owners, when CBS sold the company to them. While presidents were coming and going at Steinway, CBS itself sank into turmoil as Paley sacked president after president, not only of the parent corporation, but also of CBS/Columbia Group to which Steinway reported. CBS/Columbia Group covered a wide miscellany of activities ranging from musical instruments to toy manufacturing, video games, electronic watches and calculators, telephone answering machines, home security devices, and Pacific Stereo, a retailer of home electronic entertainment products. There were five changes in the corporate presidency and six at CBS/Columbia Group while CBS owned Steinway.

In addition, the presidents CBS appointed to Steinway were enmeshed in power politics battles with the executives over them at the parent company. CBS had selected presidents who were knowledgeable about pianos and cared deeply about the Steinway reputation. But their position was undermined by CBS's tendency to hire manufacturing consultants who did not understand pianomaking. To speed up production levels and lower order backlogs, for instance, these consultants suggested using wood with fewer rings of growth - a violation of a basic piano construction rule to use thick wood for stability and vibrancy.

Also, as is often the case when family businesses are sold, the Steinways found it hard to accept they were no longer the owners and often flexed their muscles against the new presidents. The upshot was that during the CBS years Steinway was rife with dissension. What made it all so sad was that those at loggerheads were intelligent and committed to quality; unfortunately, their ambitions and personality clashes either at Steinway or with the head office obscured their commonality of purpose. This dark period is aptly characterized by Robert Bull as one with "many elements of Greek tragedy and comedy."[27]

The comedy stemmed from the majestic style in which CBS corporate executives conducted themselves. Both London and Hamburg were deluged with managers not only from the musical instruments division but also from accounting, records, and publishing who wanted to tour CBS's latest acquisition, especially the overseas parts. "CBS whiz kids would drive up in a limousine, tell the driver to leave the motor running, and dash through on a quick tour," London's Robert Glazebrook recalls, shaking his head in astonishment at the memory of the hello-goodbye visits.

Glazebrook realized the extent of the gap between the rush-rush world of CBS and the more leisurely pace of piano dealers when "a computer whiz kid in one of the delegations asked how many sales we made in a day and why we let a customer leave without a purchase. In vain, I explained to him that apart from a house, a piano is the most expensive item many people buy and therefore, it is natural for them to make three to four visits to the store before making a decision. He thought about what I said for some time and then told me he still could not understand."[28]

Over in Hamburg, the factory's employees were flabbergasted by what one describes as the "movie star" visit of John Backe, one of the many CBS presidents appointed and fired by Paley during the late 1970s and into the 1980s. Backe arrived in Hamburg by private jet and went by limousine to the factory. The Hamburg people strove to be courteous to the many other CBS executives who flocked over in his wake but grew weary of all asking the same questions.

Some comic relief also was provided by a couple of farcical occurrences involving Steinway artists. The first involved Claudio Arrau early in the CBS era when he was on tour in the state of Washington. It had always been Steinway's custom to supply traveling performers with practice pianos for their hotel suite, and this was done for Arrau. Unfortunately, the instructions were misunderstood as to what date the piano should be retrieved. Thus, as Arrau was blissfully soaking in the bathtub, the movers, unaware he was still there, took the piano away. Distressed, to put it mildly, Arrau telephoned his manager who telephoned Steinway-New York's concert and artist department, which telephoned the local dealer who in turn told the movers to take the piano back to Arrau[29].

Not long afterward, Leonard Pennario faced an unusual predicament moments before he was to play at a Los Angeles auditorium. The three movers, whom he describes "as looking like they were ninety years old," dropped the piano so hard on the stage that a pedal and leg fell off. Nonetheless, Pennario remained calm. The conductor offered to cancel the concert, but Pennario believes in the show business maxim that the show must go on no matter what the disaster. "Why don't you put me on after the intermission, instead of before, as scheduled, so we can use the time to get the piano fixed?" he suggested. This was done and the best tradition of show biz was upheld.[30]

The tragic part of the CBS era was the turnover in presidents. True to its word, CBS began by retaining Henry as president. But it did decide to bring in an outsider as manufacturing manager of the Long Island City factory when Frank Walsh, a fifty-year employee, retired from the position in August 1972 shortly after the sale. The new man, Ron Davis, was no stranger to the piano industry; he had worked at the Wurlitzer Company for eighteen years and was a vice president as well as manager of its Logan, Utah, plant.

Accustomed to making investment decisions on his own, Henry found it hard to adjust to the bureaucracy of a huge corporation, especially as "empire building occurred in the musical instrument group and CBS as a whole became encrusted with more and more layers of management." When Steinway was an independent family business, it had had one accountant. Suddenly, Henry had to cope with three levels of reporting: Steinway's accountant and those at the musical instruments division and headquarters of CBS. Not surprisingly, he chafed at their demands "to break this down, break that down" and exasperatedly complained, "I could spend all my time doing this."[31]

Knowing that his refusal "to do what I was told was not in conformity with the policies necessary in any big company," Henry waited for the inevitable showdown. It finally came in May 1977, two years after the expiration of CBS's guarantee of employment to him and his brothers. CBS said it wanted to bring in its own man. "Fine, it's okay with me, I'll retire," Henry, who was sixty-two, answered. "No, no, stay on as chairman," CBS asked. "All right, it's fine with me. I'll bring the body in for three more years," Henry said with a sigh.

Nevertheless, he did not regret selling Steinway - only the unexpected problems that ensued. "It was just too bad that CBS began having problems shortly after we sold," he comments. "There were always new people and naturally they paid more attention to the most important businesses. The musical instruments group was always over in a corner. It never had the attention of the top management at CBS."

But while Henry admits that his disdain of CBS procedures led to his ouster, he found it difficult to reconcile himself to the fact that he no longer ran Steinway & Sons. Thus, it would have been hard for anyone who succeeded him to make him happy. It was Bob Bull's misfortune to be the first to replace Henry and to have a forceful personality that rubbed many the wrong way. "Keep in mind his surname: he was a strong-minded character," says Bob Campbell, who appointed Bull to the position.[32]

Campbell's choice of the fifty-year-old Bull was logical: he came from a piano family who had known the Steinways for fifty years and he had an excellent business record. Bull's maternal great-grandfather, Hampton Story, was the Story in Story & Clark Piano Company of Chicago, established in 1869. Story is also well known as the cofounder, along with Elisha Babcock, of the showplace resort Hotel del Coronado near San Diego. Completed in 1888, the Victorian-style hotel is believed to have been the inspiration for the Emerald City where the Wizard dwelled in L. Frank Baum's *The Wizard of Oz*. Baum lived nearby while writing the book.

Bull's father, who was president of the family firm when Bull graduated from college, was opposed to nepotism. Although Bull had worked in the factory during summer vacations, his father believed he lacked sufficient experience and should gain that knowledge elsewhere. So Bull worked for a New Orleans piano dealer for two years. By then Story & Clark had lost three key salespeople and was having difficulty filling the positions. Bull's father still did not want to hire him, but Bull's uncle on his mother's side, who was in charge of the sales force, persuaded his father to relent.

When he was in New Orleans, Bull had noticed that customers preferred the forty and forty-two-inch-tall console pianos to the thirty-six and thirty-seven-inch-high spinet. He convinced his father to concentrate on the production of console pianos, and by the 1960s, Story & Clark was the world's foremost manufacturer of such instruments. Ultimately Bull became president, and he retained that position for five years after Story & Clark was purchased by Chicago Musical Instruments in the late 1960s. He left in 1970 when Chicago Musical Instruments was acquired by Norlin Corporation, a manufacturer of organs and guitars as well as a printing company, because he disagreed with Norlin's business appoach. (After a decade of heavy financial losses, Norlin went out of business in 1985.)

Bull's career then took a detour from music. He was co-owner with his father-in-law of a resort in Utah and decided to become its manager. Soon afterward, Bob Campbell asked Bull to become the head of Fender Guitar. Fender was in the red when Bull arrived in 1972. It was to this sorry state that the Chapin twins had referred in their letter of opposition to Steinway's sale. Indeed, CBS had declared it would do "something drastic" if Fender did not recover.

Bull succeeded in restoring Fender to profitability, although he refuses to take all the credit, saying "I arrived at the right time; the right people were there, and the product was improving."[33] By early 1977, Fender was responsible for 80 percent of the profitability of the musical instruments group. CBS Chairman William Paley singled Bull out for congratulations and Bob Campbell, who, according to Bull, had previously tried to persuade him to take over the management of Steinway, asked him again.

Bull had said no in the past because he did not want to move to New York from California where Fender was based. This time Campbell made Bull an offer he found he could not refuse: a maximum posting of three years in New York. Knowing firsthand how it feels to lose control of a family company, Bull sympathized with Henry Steinway's awkward situation. But he believed all would be fine because Henry flew to California and encouraged him to accept the position.

They spoke frankly and at one point, as Bull recalls, he told Henry, "I may have to do some things you won't like" to which Henry gave a startling, unexpected reply: "I don't care if you have to fire my son." When this actually came to pass, Henry denied having made this remark.[34]

On his arrival at Steinway in May 1977, Bull found what he describes as "a very, very bad situation. Theoretically, the Steinways were still running the business; in actuality, they no longer had their hearts in it as CBS had interfered by sending in so called manufacturing experts who did not understand pianomaking." The Steinways resented these uninformed, extremely self-assured people telling them how to run the factory and, says Bull, "They folded their tents and waited for their contracts to expire."[35]

Bull says he found the condition of the Steinway pianos "so bad that I wouldn't have shipped them out as average pianos, leave alone Steinways. The pianos being shipped out had pockmarks, dampers that were not aligned, and poor voicing."[36] However, Ron Davis, the factory manager then, maintains "It is overstating to say everything was in a mess."[37] Bull had been given carte blanche by Campbell to fix Steinway no matter what the cost, and he acted accordingly. "I had to do a lot of tough things and many thought I did them brutally and ruthlessly - a valid criticism," he concedes.[38]

The "tough thing" that particularly rocked Steinway's employees was Bull's decision shortly after his arrival to close down new production at the Long Island City factory for six months so as to overhaul the place and to rebuild approximately one thousand pianos he had rejected as unsuitable for shipment. To shut down for such a reason was unprecedented in the pianomaking industry. What made it even more amazing was that Steinway had always promoted its pianos as unrivaled in excellence. While Henry had spent on machinery, Bull believed the workplace still needed improvement.

He had the factory's interior painted, dirty windows washed and "dozens" with rotting casements or missing glass, replaced. Cracks and gouges in the floors were repaired and an area set aside as a lunchroom. Hitherto, workers often sprawled on parts of the piano to rest during lunch breaks, a habit that the new facilities did not end. Indeed, the custom still persists.

Bull and Davis also reorganized the factory's layout. In modern piano factories there is only one floor, enabling a smooth, time efficient traffic flow. Steinway, however, consists of several multistory buildings. Manny Monti, personnel manager then, calculates that formerly a Steinway piano traveled three miles from the start of its construction to when it was packed for shipment.[39] The realignment shortened the excursion by placing one stage of production adjacent to the next.

While the closure did lead to an improvement of the factory and the pianos, it had a devastating effect on the workplace. Bull says only employees in the initial stages of piano construction, such as woodcutting, were laid off for the duration, whereas others farther along in the production process were recalled to work on their specialties as required. He states he made an effort to recall as many as possible for enough time for them to qualify for unemployment insurance for those weeks there was no need for them. But Monti says the workers were angered that management continued to receive full salary.

There were other debilitating results: the withholding of pianos slated for shipment so as to rid them of defects caused inventories to swell alarmingly and back orders, always a problem, piled up even more. Not surprisingly. Steinway-New York lost money.

But CBS was supportive and so were Steinway's dealers. "They screamed they were not getting enough pianos, but their anger was offset by their agreeing the quality had deteriorated," Bull says. The dealers had frequently complained the pianos arrived in such poor shape that they had to spend up to $1,000 to correct the faults. A Southeast dealer joked to Bull that he "had put three furniture refinishers out of business" through his improvements.[40]

While the dealers appreciated what Bull had accomplished, many disliked his abrasiveness. "He is highly intelligent with terrific drive and an uncompromising personality," says Ed Hendricks, who had been hired by Henry Steinway in 1975 to be Steinway's director of marketing, the new name for the dealer relations department. "Bob was not very tolerant of the capability of dealers in handling problems. At Story & Clark, he had done business with dealers who shared his belief that the customer is always right. But by the time he became president of Steinway, the maxim no longer was practiced by business in general. It had become tough to get capable salespeople and good technicians."[41]

After disrupting the factory, Bull applied his unorthodox style to Steinway's marketing department. In January 1978, Hendricks departed. Some Steinway insiders claim Bull fired him, since he wanted people loyal to himself rather than to Henry. But Hendricks maintains he resigned "because I had lost my enthusiasm. I was tired of the job and the glamour had gone."[42] To the amazement of Steinway workers, Bull decided to serve as marketing director as well as president. When he had worked at Fender there were four product lines, and he felt he lacked a full workload at Steinway even though he started his workday at 6:45 a.m. Bull's explanation to Henry that he had "the extra time" did not go over well. Henry urged Bull to relinquish the job and let him hire somebody exclusively for the position.

When Bull not only said no but then hired an assistant of his own, his relationship with Henry became decidedly frosty. Bull's choice, Littlepaige Wemple, was known to Henry but her selection was a radical departure for the company, which hitherto had only had male senior executives. Wemple had met Henry many years earlier when, as a piano student, she attended a Columbia University music seminar and was introduced by the professor. Before Bull hired her, she had been a piano instructor at the University of Hawaii and had run a teaching studio for a Hawaiian dealer. She looked much younger than her thirty-five years when she joined Steinway and to force the employees to treat her as a grownup, she willingly divulged her age, doing so on her thirty-sixth birthday.[43]

Since in Bull's view, John Steinway, still nominally in charge of advertising, was "just sitting there," one of the responsibilities he assigned Wemple was to send out publicity material to dealers. The dealers had been annoyed that John had refused to update the illustrations of shoppers to current fashions and hairstyles in a pamphlet he had written some years before on the "Reasons Why" to buy a Steinway. "There was a lot of inertia then at Steinway," Wemple recalls. "For example, the covering form letter for a publicity packet was outdated in that certain titles and booklets it mentioned were not in the packet. When I suggested to John's secretary that the letter be changed, she said that since the material was out of print, there was no need to change the letter.

"She told me: 'John has decided not to reprint the out-of-stock information, but we're still using the letter because we have lots left. I've worked for Steinway for twenty-five years and that's the way we've always done it.'" Wemple discovered that "in fact, there were about fifteen hundred letters left."[44]

The earthquake reverberations of the Bull regime were not confined to Steinway-New York. Bull left Steinway-London alone but cracked down on Steinway-Hamburg because he was convinced "it was not doing all it could. Granted its product was much better than New York's and its factory clean and bright, but it was too satisfied with itself and I didn't believe it should be. Instead, I thought it could improve its scheduling so that machinery would not lie idle, awaiting more material. I also felt its dealer relationships could be improved."[45]

To Bull, the solution was to rein in Hamburg by making it report more to U.S. headquarters rather than have a free hand, as Henry had given it. Although Henry and he were not on cordial terms, Henry agreed to accompany him on his trips to Hamburg and to back him up. "Hamburg adored Henry and when he told the staff to cut out their obfuscation, they listened," Bull recalls.[46]

When production resumed early in 1978 at the Long Island City factory, Steinway-New York quickly returned to profitability. An uneasy calm descended on the entire company even though Henry persisted in ignoring corporate reporting channels, going over Bull's and Campbell's heads by writing directly to their superiors, including Paley. But it was only the lull before the storms that led to Bull's departure on December 7, 1978, a day that young Harry Steinway wryly describes as symbolic because it was the anniversary of another bombing, that of Pearl Harbor.[47] The first storm occurred when Bull fired Bill Steinway; the second when he became embroiled in a losing battle with John Phillips, to whom the musical instruments division reported.

Bill had started working in the factory in 1973, after the sale to CBS. He had told his father he preferred manual labor to an office job. By 1978, he was in the engineering department, then still headed by his uncle Teed. In 1977, Bill's brother Harry also joined the company; his first job was in payroll and cost accounting. He did most of the transferring onto computer tapes of Steinway's twenty looseleaf binders on how to make pianos.

The employees regarded Bill and Harry as being as different as salt and pepper. Monti says Bill "acted as if he were the crown prince; he was arrogant and did not relate well to people."[48] Bull says Bill "was very talented and smart, but insisted on being treated differently from others of his rank. As a Steinway, he thought he deserved special privileges, such as coming in an hour late. He became a disruptive force." By contrast, Bull "liked Harry. He had a lot of ability and I hoped he would be the next generation to head the company."[49]

Bull held several private luncheon meetings with Bill to try to ease the tension. He told Bill that he understood the unique strain on sons of bosses because of his similar situation at Story & Clark. "I told him that I knew how this circumstance puts all sorts of pressures on a person such as not to take advantage of his position and to be better than everybody else," Bull says. "But Bill never really trusted, believed, or respected me."[50]

Bill Steinway refuses to discuss his days at Steinway. His brother, Harry, comments that Bill considered Bull "power-mad and regarded the conflict as if it were a personal combat."[51] What brought the animosity to a head was Bull's discovery that Bill was job-hunting at competitors. He charged that Bill had intimated he would divulge Steinway secrets.

Harry says it is correct that Bill had "talked to a couple of competitors but whether he actually considered joining is another matter."[52] Whatever Bill's true intentions were, Bull thought he should be fired. He did so, bearing in mind his recollection of Henry saying at their initial meeting, "I don't care if you have to fire my son."

As it turned out, Henry did care. Livid with rage, he immediately telephoned Bob Campbell's office. As Campbell was away for the day, Henry spoke to Peter Perez, executive vice president of CBS Musical Instruments and ultimately Bull's successor. Perez could tell instantly that something was wrong because uncharacteristically, Henry's voice was filled with anger. Also, Henry, who uses the occasional "hell" and "damn," startled Perez by employing much stronger language. "Peter,

I was trying to get Bob Campbell; you're second-in-command, so I'll speak to you," Henry began. "That bastard Bob Bull just fired my son Bill. I won't rest until I get rid of him."[53]

But it was not Henry who got rid of Bull. Bill was fired late in the summer of 1978 and Bull was still at Steinway in December of that year. Although it was widely believed he was booted out to mollify Henry, what really did Bull in was his clash with John Phillips.

Phillips lacked Bull's background in the music industry. Until he became president of CBS/Columbia Group in 1973, his entire career had been in nonmusic consumer products, including stints at Armour & Company, American Home Company, and R.J. Reynolds Foods, Inc. Nonetheless, William Paley and Arthur Taylor, the chairman and then president of CBS, personally hired him, and he says that he brought to the position his experience "in marketing and cause and effect in management."[54]

It is putting it mildly to say that Bull detested Phillips. "I consider John Phillips one of the most incompetent men I've ever met," Bull says. It was not unusual for him to engage in toe-to-toe shouting matches with Phillips. He believed that Phillips regarded him as a threat to his own career aspirations. His suspicions were fueled since "Phillips was very supportive when Steinway lost money during the time I shut down new production, but not when Steinway recovered."[55]

For his part, Phillips says he found Bull to be "very independent-minded. I was concerned that he was not as sensitive as he should have been in a delicate situation regarding his dealings with the Steinways. They needed understanding and respect."[56] The upshot was that Phillips fired Bull who was then halfway through the three years he had promised Campbell he would stay at Steinway. Ironically, shortly afterward, according to Campbell, Phillips was reassigned at CBS due to disagreements with fellow managers. It is Phillips's recollection that he continued as president of CBS/Columbia Group until he left in 1983, but CBS annual reports do not bear this out.

> Postscript on the Robert Bull era:
> Bull: I was very fond of Henry Steinway and used as tender a touch with him as possible.
> Henry: Bob Bull was a bright, outstanding, strong executive, but I disagreed with a lot he did.

After Bull was ousted, CBS temporarily reinstated Henry as president. Then Bob Campbell asked Peter Perez to take the job. For the thirty-eight-year-old Perez, it seemed the pinnacle in an already meteoric career. Five days after graduating from Yale, he joined Conn Organ Corporation where Campbell had once worked. Perez married the daughter of Conn's president but did not leapfrog over his fellow employees to head the company. Instead, he worked his way up over a period of ten years, becoming president in 1974, five years after Macmillan Inc. had purchased Conn. At thirty-four, he was the youngest president in Conn's history.

Under Perez, Conn diversified from organs into a variety of instruments made at sixteen plants and had sales of $60 million. The head office was in Chicago, as was that of CBS Musical Instruments. In mid-1977, Bob Campbell contacted Perez and offered him the position of executive vice president at CBS Musical Instruments, by then the largest company in its field in the United States and third in size in the world. Perez delightedly accepted the position. However, as executive vice president, he was "not on the firing line, as at Conn, but simply a liaison" with the division's subsidiaries, and he yearned to once again run the daily operations of a business.

Nonetheless, when Campbell approached him about becoming president of Steinway, Perez hesitated.[57] He was torn between the lure of running a firm "regarded as being at the top of the heap in the music industry" and his knowledge of Steinway's recent stormy history. Still uncommitted, within days of Bull's firing, he attended Steinway's traditional year-end luncheon for employees at which, at the instigation of Henry Steinway, he was the featured guest.

Afterward Henry took Perez on a three-hour factory tour. Perez found Henry to be "a consummate diplomat and gentleman with strong views. He said a lot of supportive things about my coming but he was still hurt by the decision to bring in Bull and a little bit disdainful of CBS management." Feeling that their meeting had gone well, Perez drove back in the snow to La Guardia Airport for his flight back to Chicago, reflecting that he had an "opportunity one seldom gets; to have somebody entrust you with the management of an international treasure." By year-end he had accepted the position.

The general view among Steinway employees is that Perez worked wonders in restoring good will within the factory and with dealers, was a "personable gentleman," but "not a good businessman." Campbell says "he was not the right man to have appointed." Bob Bull, who could not be expected to like Perez, dismisses him as a "Caspar Milquetoast."[58] But Perez has his fans. Not suprisingly, one is Catherine Bielefeldt, whom he appointed director of Steinway Hall in 1980, the first time in Steinway's existence that a woman filled the position. She describes Perez as "fantastic to work with. He was young with a modern way of thinking and an understanding of why and how people do things as well as the best communicator I've ever met."[59] Pianist Rosalyn Tureck enthuses that he was "extremely sympathetic to performers' needs and competent."[60] London's Robert Glazebrook comments that Perez's "problem was that he was too nice a guy."[61]

In terms of hours at work, Perez was as committed as Bull. He left his New Canaan, Connecticut home, about forty miles from the plant, at 5:30 a.m. and, because he frequently attended performances of Steinway artists, often did not get back until midnight. Sympathetic to such a schedule, Henry sponsored him for membership in the New York Athletic Club where he could shower and change before concerts.[62]

It is a nonpublic concert by Vladimir Horowitz, however, that remains especially vivid in Perez's mind. With his wife, Carroll, Perez had taken a dealer and Wanda Horowitz to New York's 21 Club for dinner. On their return to the Horowitzes' home, Wanda invited them in for champagne with her and her husband who had stayed home for the evening. To their disappointment, Horowitz did not volunteer to play for them, but on their way out, as they descended the spiral staircase from the second-floor living room where he kept his piano, he surprised them by performing some études. They sat on the steps and listened, then silently left.[63]

Perez considered as his priority the elimination of the hurt and anger that had characterized the Bull era. He regards himself as a "strong people person with the ability to motivate and communicate with everyone from a floor sweeper to a sophisticated concert artist." To obtain "a sense of the pulse of the factory" and emphasize his commitment to quality, he spent much of his time on the factory floor. He also involved the workers in financial planning so that "instead of budgets being set on high, each department proposed its own." He followed up on this innovation with monthly lunch meetings of ham sandwiches and potato chips at which management informed the foremen and superintendents about the company's status.

Another new procedure was the introduction of an employee handbook on rules and regulations, printed in both English and Spanish as by then Steinway had many Hispanic workers. Perez further began a formal "buddy" system, an elaboration of Steinway's tradition of veterans helping out newcomers, and he asked John Steinway to record an audio-visual presentation on the factory and its history to show these employees.

Perez also sought to convince the Steinways they were still important to the business. Shortly after he became president, he rehired Bill Steinway and appointed him director of engineering when Bill's uncle, Teed Steinway, retired early in 1979. He also pulled Harry Steinway out of the clerical jobs in payroll and cost accounting that Harry had come to find "boring" and promoted him to the marketing department. It could be construed that Perez's reemployment of Bill was a "tradeoff" for his appointment to Steinway's presidency, but he stresses that this was not the case and that, in fact, Bill was "ambivalent" about returning. [64]

Once again, Bill's presence proved a source of dissension. This time the crisis erupted over Bill's ambition to become manager of the Long Island City factory. Ron Davis left in 1979 to become plant manager for Merillat Industries, the largest U.S. manufacturer of modular kitchen cabinets. He got the position by chance. A Chicago recruiter, to whom Davis had turned for assistance in obtaining engineers for Steinway, called him one day about the Merillat job. Perez believed Davis should be replaced by his assistant, Joseph Pramberger, an engineering graduate who had joined Steinway in the 1960s, well before Bill's arrival. Moreover, Pramberger also had strong familial ties to Steinway: four of his relatives, including his father, had worked for the firm. His aspirations thwarted, Bill resigned in the fall of 1981.

Like Bull, Perez had expectations that one day Harry would become president of Steinway & Sons. But Harry had grown discontented, too. At first he enjoyed working in the marketing department, answering consumers' queries about the history of their piano or about technical matters, getting to know dealers, attending trade shows, and helping institutional buyers and the occasional individual client select pianos at the factory's showroom. To him the position offered the best of two opportunities: "The chance to get involved in the world outside the factory while learning more about the place and how pianos were made."[65]

On the other hand, he came to resent that his boss, Dick Gigax, the man to whom Henry's cousin Charles Garland Steinway had sold Steinway's Indianapolis operations in 1970, did not move to New York from Indianapolis. "I'm more emotional than my father and Bill and I thought if Dick were truly committed, he should live in New York," Harry explains.[66] Harry was also less than thrilled at having to pick up

Gigax on Mondays at La Guardia Airport, located very close to the Long Island City factory, and drive him back on Fridays. This assignment, however, was less demanding than Gigax's daily chauffeuring of his boss Roman de Majewski in the days when Gigax was in Harry's junior position.

Perez had appointed Gigax marketing director shortly after he had become president. About the commuting and the attendant expense of hotel accommodation four days a week for him in New York, Gigax says he had made it plain from the outset that he did not wish to transfer to New York. He further points out that other CBS employees had similar arrangements. Perez considered the extra cost of Gigax's airplane and hotel bills as warranted because Gigax's return to Steinway signaled that Steinway intended, as Gigax says, "to be more sensitive and responsive to its dealers' problems."[67]

Gigax expanded Steinway's dealer network by thirty to an all-time high of 140. He also reemphasized the field training workshops, Majewski's concept, and flattered the representatives by putting more dealers' pictures in Steinway's newsletter. He regarded Harry Steinway as "a marvelous addition whom the dealers liked very much."[68]

But Harry began to fret that he had no future at Steinway. Although Perez says his plan was to groom Harry for the presidency, starting with appointing him as Gigax's successor, Harry doubted whether "real career progress or power could ever be in my grasp. I had the feeling that the people at CBS regarded me as useful because my name was Steinway but that basically, they were always suspicious of the Steinways' motives. My goal was to eventually run the company and when I didn't see it in the cards I left in 1980, but without closing the door on my possibly returning."[69]

Thereupon Harry spent four months job-hunting and discovered that "my experience at Steinway was not translatable into other businesses." To rectify this drawback he enrolled in Columbia University's Business School. He urged his brother Bill to get a business administration degree, too, but Bill was not interested. Upon graduating, Harry spoke to Perez about rejoining Steinway but within weeks of their discussion, Perez was forced to resign.

Harry then joined the investment firm of Dean Witter Reynolds Inc., ultimately becoming an assistant vice president responsible for the firm's communications system with its several hundred branches. During this time, he approached Lloyd Meyer, Perez's successor, about returning but this probe, too, was foiled as CBS sold Steinway & Sons shortly afterward.

In addition to his internal public relations campaign to improve employee and dealer relations, Perez expanded Steinway's promotional efforts. John Steinway's "Reasons Why" brochure, the one that had annoyed dealers because it was outdated, was revised. Perez encouraged John to provide anecdotes about Steinway artists on a radio program featuring the recordings of many. A booklet was compiled with the performers' views on the piano and distributed to music teachers and institutions, as well as potential Steinway customers.

One outfit that Perez could seldom persuade to use Steinway pianos was the CBS television network. Bending over backward to avoid charges of favoritism, the network so rarely rented Steinways that Perez and Steinway's concert and artist manager David Rubin joked that ABC was a better customer. CBS Chairman William Paley did not play the piano. But Thomas Wyman, CBS president during Perez's sojourn at Steinway, had a Steinway upright in his office in line with CBS's policy of displaying its products in its executives' suites.

Perez's appointment of Catherine Bielefeldt as director of Steinway Hall was a significant blow against the male chauvinism of the piano industry at that time. She had been hired early in 1978 by Bull to be Steinway's eastern district sales manager. That, too, was a breakthrough for women since besides Steinway, only Kawai had a female traveling salesperson. Bielefeldt previously was a consultant to Lyon & Healy, Steinway's Chicago dealer, which CBS acquired in 1977.

At Steinway, she emphasized product knowledge education through regional seminars for local piano technicians and music teachers. She also turned an upstairs showroom into a museum in which she placed early historic Steinway pianos. Unsentimentally, Henry had had them shoved into a storeroom along with old tools. It took some time for Henry and John to adjust to a woman as Steinway Hall director, but they eventually did so. It was much harder for her to get along with David Rubin. "Has anybody said it wasn't difficult dealing with David Rubin?" she asks rhetorically.[70] According to Ed Hendricks, at whose company she subsequently became a vice president, Bielefeldt was handicapped by a lack of firm backing from Perez, who was "distracted by the many other matters with which he had to deal."[71]

Uppermost in Perez's mind was survival in his job. Similar to what had happened to Bull, Perez's downfall came when everything seemed much rosier. In his case, he could point to a steady increase in output by the Long Island City factory and to the fact that Steinway contributed $52.6 million of the $76.2 million in revenue made by

CBS Musical Instruments in 1981 and $6.8 million of its $9.2 million pretax profit. Unfortunately, the financial results were insufficient to win him good marks. Like Bull, he had antagonized the Steinways and a powerful CBS executive.

Perez and Henry were scarcely on speaking terms after Bill and Harry left the business. Perez says his relationship remained cordial with John Steinway, who had succeeded his brother as chairman early in 1980 when Henry turned sixty-five. But John was just a figurehead in that, according to associates of him and Henry, he always deferred to what his older brother deemed best for the business.

Perez was also encountering problems with John McLaren, who had succeeded Bob Campbell as president of CBS Musical Instruments after Campbell's retirement in 1980. McLaren was no stranger to Steinway - he had been a salesman at Steinway Hall after emigrating from England. Later, he became general manager of Yamaha's United States piano division, and from there he went to CBS. McLaren declines to discuss his days at CBS.

According to Perez, McLaren was too busy at first with CBS's other musical subsidiaries, most of which were marginally profitable at best, to cross swords with him. Moreover, they rarely ran into each other because McLaren had convinced CBS to transfer the instruments division's headquarters from Chicago to Los Angeles where he lived. He rarely traveled east to "Black Rock," the nickname for CBS's New York head office.

Their showdown came over Perez's opposition to McLaren's plan to merge Steinway's sales force with that of Gulbransen Organs, one of the organ manufacturers CBS also owned.[72] Gulbransen was losing money and was topheavy with sales personnel. Perez reacted with fury, accusing McLaren that "You want to merge Steinway's profits with Gulbransen's losses. What you propose will irreparably damage Steinway." His outburst placed him on a collision course with McLaren.

On May 15, 1982, the disagreement reached its climax. McLaren summoned Perez to Black Rock and demanded his resignation. Should he refuse, McLaren said he would fire him. Incensed, Perez marched out of McLaren's office and burst in on CBS president Thomas Wyman. He pleaded his case for thirty minutes, backing it up by supporting documents. "My performance has been in line with company requirements; I have delivered profits, the piano is better, and the dealer organization bigger," he told Wyman. "Yes," Wyman agreed, "your performance has been in line with expectations. It's a political thing. John wants his own team." Realizing McLaren was the winner, Perez asked Wyman to act as a reference for him, and Wyman said he would. But not long afterward, Wyman was fired as part of Paley's serial axing of one president after another. McLaren did not oustay Perez for long. He was ousted a year and a half after he forced Perez to leave.

Perez drove to New Canaan to tell his wife in person about his expulsion. But when he arrived, she already knew; a friend had telephoned to express anger and sympathy over what had happened, unaware that Perez had not yet spoken to her. As soon as Dick Gigax heard the news, he submitted his resignation. McLaren asked him to stay, but Gigax said he believed McLaren had treated Perez unfairly and that out of loyalty to Perez, he could not remain. By 4:00 p.m. on the day Perez was pressured out, Gigax had departed, too.

Steinway dealers were shocked at Perez's virtual dismissal. "He had been a welcome relief from Bull and was regarded as an ideal choice because of his background, manner, and appreciation of the product," Ed Hendricks sums up. Several dealers publicly criticized McLaren, who called each one in an effort to pacify them. Then he appointed Gulbransen's president, Lloyd Meyer, as president of Steinway and Meyer absorbed Gulbransen's six-person sales force into Steinway's.

In retrospect, Dick Gigax scornfully dismisses McLaren's strategy of merging the Steinway sales force with Gulbransen's as "the worst possible idea, as silly as saying that golf balls and tennis balls are alike. Pianos and organs are different animals and therefore, are sold differently. Very few Steinway or Gulbransen dealers were interested in carrying both products."[73]

> Postscript on the Perez era:
> Perez: I still feel affection for the company.
> Henry: Peter Perez had a pleasing personality, but he lacked Bob Bull's ability. He was dumped unceremoniously by CBS.

Lloyd Meyer's connection to the music industry had begun in his college days when, to pay for his tuition in music education, he sold musical instruments at the Dayton-Hudson department store in Minneapolis. After graduating, he taught, worked at Northwest Organ in Minneapolis, and then joined Chicago Musical Instruments, coincidentally, the company to which Bob Bull's firm of Story & Clark was sold. In his tenth year at CMI, Meyer was invited to join CBS Musical Instruments, where he became a senior vice president and subsequently president of Gulbransen. He was forty-three when he became president at Steinway.

Meyer initially was wary of Henry because of his role in the ousting of Bull and Perez. Wondering whether the impasse between Henry and his predecessors was "because Henry wanted more control," he confronted the issue head-on by asking if Henry's real motivation was that "he regretted the sale to CBS." "No, I don't regret it, but I want the company run right," Henry answered.[74] Henry and Meyer did get on cordially. Henry accompanied Meyer, who speaks German, on trips to Germany and helped him when problems arose with dealers. In addition, Meyer found that John Steinway was a tremendous asset in dealer promotions.

On the surface, Meyer's appointment to Steinway made no sense: It seemed ridiculous that CBS would place someone who had been president of a money-losing operation in charge of a profitable one. But Meyer's background actually was appropriate. He was the musical instruments division's chief troubleshooter and had been placed in charge of Gulbransen at a time when most organ manufacturers were in bad shape due to a steep decline in demand. CBS reckoned his experience there would be an asset at Steinway because the combined sales of all American-made pianos also had plunged drastically.

They had fallen from 240,000 in 1978, the highest in twelve years, to 162,000 in 1982, and this trend appeared likely to continue. By contrast, imports were gaining market share by leaps and bounds. In 1980, 30,000 were sold; by 1982, 37,000; and projections indicated that by 1986, the total would reach 70,000, a 133 percent increase in just six years. The shaky outlook for U.S. pianomakers combined with the turbulence of the last decade at Steinway placed Meyer in an unenviable position. "He had the toughest tenure of the trio appointed president by CBS," Ed Hendricks comments. "Moreover, shortly after he began, he was relegated to a lame-duck existence because CBS had decided to sell Steinway."[75] Harry Steinway bestows undiluted praise on Meyer as "the first smart choice by CBS for president of Steinway. He had a sense of mission, a definite strategy, and an emotional commitment to the company."[76]

Steinway's branches in London and Hamburg were less enchanted. London's Bob Glazebrook was outraged when Meyer ordered him to fire his secretary. Meyer considered her personality was too retiring, but Glazebrook regarded her as highly efficient and suitably reserved in her demeanor. "Pay her off and get a new secretary," Meyer instructed Glazebrook who irately retorted, "You can't treat people that way." The secretary remained.[77]

To Glazebrook, Meyer's demand typified the "much more aggressive American management style," which he finds distasteful. "In the United States, it's no disgrace to be fired - indeed, people there often regard it as a merit badge - but in the United Kingdom it is still regarded as shameful," he stresses.[78] Over in Hamburg, Max Matthias, a piano construction expert whom Meyer had promoted to manager in 1983, was uncomfortable with what he viewed as Meyer's manipulation to get him to do something without giving a direct order. Matthias saw it as Meyer's way of dodging responsibility,[79] but it is conceivable that his only motive was to avoid offending Matthias by seemingly infringing on his authority.

Meyer did accomplish a lot in his brief two and a half years at Steinway. He realized that although Steinway made only one product - pianos - and was not a huge conglomerate like CBS, "it was still a complex company to run with its operations in New York and Germany, complicated manufacturing process, and very demanding artists. There also was the challenge of keeping the plant running at full employment. If not, skilled labor would drift away. Conversely, the danger was that the inventories would get out of control. It was necessary to maintain a steady balance between production and sales."[80]

Meyer took over at the height of the controversy over whether the American or Hamburg Steinway was superior. On the one hand, Steinway executives insisted the American and Hamburg Steinways were as alike as peas in a pod. On the other, Steinway-New York maintained the Hamburg Steinway could not withstand the U.S. climate, which is dryer than Europe's. Steinway-Hamburg just as adamantly declared its pianos were perfectly capable of survival in North America.

Steinway-New York went to extraordinary lengths to keep the Hamburg Steinway out of the United States. On one occasion, the Chicago Symphony was unable to prevail upon Steinway's local dealer to deliver a Hamburg instrument shipped over at the request of pianist Maurizio Pollini for a recording session. When the symphony later bought the piano, it received scant cooperation regarding servicing.

Significantly, the controversy erupted as many Steinway oldtimers at the Long Island City factory either retired or died. In Europe, apprenticeship training still is the custom, and the Hamburg factory had - and has - a formal program. At one time, even its secretaries served apprenticeships. The Long Island City plant, however, had - and has - no such program, relying instead on veterans teaching novices on the job. Consequently, when the number of longtime employees shrank sharply in the 1960s, Steinway had to scramble for recruits.

Those it got were not always satisfactory. As one senior factory supervisor of those bleak days recounts: "People were hired off the street who had no knowledge of pianos, were not handy with tools, and were unwilling to learn. Many left for higher-paying jobs in other industries. The result was that the quality of the pianos suffered. Because Steinway has a sophisticated clientele - professionals who can readily detect changes - they realized immediately that the Steinway-New York piano had declined."

Perez had sought to improve the American Steinway by having Bob Glazebrook, London's sales manager and senior concert technician, fly over ten times a year for two-week stays to help voice the American Steinways. Glazebrook became manager in London about the time when Meyer took over at Steinway, so Meyer instead brought over Glazebrook's brother, Michael, also an expert tuner. Meyer also brought over Max Matthias from Hamburg, then both a technical consultant and a European sales representative, to serve as director of research and development in New York.

The degree to which CBS restored the Steinway to its original quality largely is due to Matthias. He was regarded as one of Europe's leading authorities on piano construction and had served as a consultant to all the leading European pianomakers. He also had been managing director of Bechstein and technical director at Baldwin prior to joining Steinway in 1975. Meyer fired Siegfried Maczijewski as Hamburg manager and gave the job to Matthias because he felt the Hamburg piano also had deteriorated and that Maczijewski was not cooperating sufficiently with the rest of the company. Unlike Matthias, Maczijewski was a salesman by training.

In New York, Matthias made major modifications to the American Steinway. He changed the dimension of the ribs on the grand soundboards and altered the length and the thickness of the strings in the Model $K$ vertical, the biggest upright, so as to improve the resonance. He also successfully urged Meyer to dump Steinway-New York's keyboard supplier, Pratt, Read Corporation, because he believed there was no difference between the quality of keyboard Pratt, Read made for Steinway and lesser pianos.

Matthias convinced Meyer to import keyboards from Kluge, a German firm that is regarded as the foremost in the world in its field and which had been supplying Steinway-Hamburg for years. The principal distinction between Pratt, Read and Kluge keyboards was in the type of wood. Pratt, Read still used sugar pine, the original type of wood employed. Matthias believed sugar pine no longer was as strong because it had come to be used more commercially, resulting in a deterioration in quality. By contrast, Kluge's material is spruce, one of the most resonant of woods.

Meyer also began buying a main part of the action, known as the *wippen*, from Louis Renner of Stuttgart. (The wippen, a mechanism of underlevers, controls the jacks that push the hammers up to the strings.) Established in 1882, Renner is regarded as the world's leading producers of actions and already was supplying Steinway-Hamburg. Its other clients include Baldwin, even though Baldwin first established a joint venture with Pratt, Read in 1985 and then bought it out in 1986. Bösendorfer and Korea's Young Chang, Samick, and Daewoo are customers, too, along with Germany's other pianomakers and about fifty more foreign firms.

Meyer started by buying actions for the concert grand *D* and the next largest, the *B,* and was on the verge of proceeding with other models when CBS sold Steinway & Sons. The company continued to purchase the wippen for the two grands from Renner, and in 1987, it also turned to Renner for the wippen for Steinway-New York's uprights. Steinway-New York still makes its own hammers and the shanks to which hammers are attached.

Uncomfortable as he is at the question, Renner's managing director Robert Lins concedes there is little contrast between pianomakers' actions. Steinway does specify that aluminum is to be used for upright rails to which parts are attached, whereas other companies prefer wood. Steinway also calls for more notches on flanges and buys the actions disassembled, whereas most companies buy them assembled. Lins says these differences are irrelevant "because the quality is the same." He adds that Steinway assembled its actions "to keep its workers occupied and to obtain a slightly lower price."[81] Renner does not use a Teflon solution on the action bushings; Steinway-New York does.

No one should jump to the conclusion that because actions are basically alike from firm to firm there is no distinction between makes of pianos. Pianos sound different because each firm has its own "scale" (layout of the strings) and construction methods.

It was also Meyer who unhesitatingly got rid of Teflon bushings, a step from which both Bull and Perez had shied away. It was Meyer, too, who reinstated the use of ivory keys on the New York concert grand. In the 1960s, Henry had decreed that Steinway-New York switch to plastic as the cost of raw ivory had risen substantially due to restrictions on the use of elephant tusks for ivory under the Convention on International Trade in Endangered Species. Concert pianists prefer ivory because it absorbs perspiration, whereas plastic does not and, therefore, becomes slippery.

Subsequently, Meyer stepped up Perez's modest sale of Hamburg Steinways in the United States. He imported two hundred, which he distributed to twenty major markets to prove that "A Steinway is a Steinway is a Steinway." He ordered that they be sold side by side with the New York pianos "so as to end the mystique in the United States that the Hamburg Steinway was better. I felt that Steinway's previous tactics of making it impossible for the German piano to get into the United States and of inventing stories that it fell apart were self-defeating."[82]

So that the Long Island workers would still feel important, Meyer selected an "employee of the month" whose picture he pinned on a soundboard used as a bulletin board. He also hosted weekly "President's Lunches" to which he invited workers from every department, but not their supervisors. He considered the relaxed atmosphere to be more conducive to a frank discussion of any concerns the workers had.

In response to dealers' complaints that they had to spend far too much time "prepping" new Steinways because the voicing was not to their satisfaction, Meyer partitioned part of a floor at the Long Island City factory into soundproof rooms. Hitherto, perfect voicing was impossible since the work was done in the midst of construction noise.

He went on to muzzle David Rubin, the bête noire of many performers and dealers, by hiring Richard Probst as Rubin's heir apparent. Music was part of Probst's upbringing; he started taking piano lessons at the age of six and began singing in choirs at a young age, too. However, he decided he preferred a career in the music industry to one on the concert stage. For ten years he worked in France at Buffet-Crampon, a woodwind manufacturer whose roots date back to 1831, two decades before the establishment of Steinway. At Buffet-Crampon his responsibilities included helping performers select instruments. On his return to the United States, Probst was contacted by Steinway which had heard of him through mutual acquaintances in the music industry.

Probst says his experience made him "understand how very gruelling on the nerves piano concerts can be and, therefore, how important it is for concert pianos to be in first rate order." He continues: "It was obvious when I came that there was a need for a greater emphasis to the dealers on how important the concert artist activity is to Steinway. I discovered that the dealer network was not completely sensitized to the need for good relations with pianists." In what he describes as "almost a laying-on of hands to transmit my missionary zeal," Probst deluged the dealers with letters, telephone calls, and meetings. His theme was that neglect of a piano was "like locking a racehorse in the barn until the day of the Kentucky Derby and then expecting it to perform."[83]

Over in Hamburg, which Meyer visited every six to eight weeks, he encouraged Matthias to hire for the first time in Hamburg's long history an advertising agency and in-house public relations person, as well as to add two more dealers in Western Europe, one for Eastern Europe, and a network of agents in Asia and South America. Matthias also established a spare parts and service department and worldwide training seminars for technicians.

In marketing Steinways, Meyer opened Hamburg's "Secrets of a Steinway," a display of parts, and launched a "factory selection" promotion. Under Meyer's campaign, up to seventy grands were sent from the factory to a dealer who would advertise the shipment as a "Factory Selection." Actually, all pianos go straight to the dealers from Steinway's factory; the only difference was the quantity sent for the event. Meyer was confident the label "Factory Selection" would appeal to most shoppers' idea that they can get a better choice at the manufacturer than at the retailer. In addition, monthly sales seminars were run for dealers and the number of district sales managers was increased. Further, a separate department was set up to develop contacts at and provide service to music schools.

Meyer's two-and-a-half year presidency and CBS's thirteen years of ownership of Steinway limped to a close in 1985, when the Birminghams acquired the company.

> Postscript on the Lloyd Meyer era:
> Meyer: I'm very fond of Henry Steinway.
> Henry: Lloyd Meyer was an able executive. He was just getting his hands around the business when it was sold to the Birminghams and they replaced him.

The CBS years had had a devastating human toll. Able, intelligent people who had thought their careers were securely mapped out suddenly were cast adrift. Few of them remained in the music industry, a tragic loss of talent to the business.

Bill Steinway moved to Los Angeles and became an artist, specializing in abstract paintings.

Harry Steinway left Dean Witter in the summer of 1986 for Equitable Life Assurance where he remained for a year and was involved in the computerization of the firm's agency offices. Then he resumed studying architecture.

Bob Bull did freelance consulting, then retired early and moved to Florida where he became a champion bridge player.

John Phillips, after leaving CBS in 1983, became vice chairman of the National Executive Service Corps, an organization of retired executives who do consulting on a volunteer basis.

Peter Perez bought, in late 1983, ailing Aeolian Pianos, Inc., of Memphis, maker of the Chickering, Knabe, and Mason & Hamlin pianos with a $10 million loan from Citicorp. In less than a year he restored the company to profitability. Unfortunately for him and for Aeolian, 1984 was a pathetic year for the United States piano industry. Domestic shipments fell by 20,000 units from 1983. As Aeolian slid back into the red, Citicorp seized its assets, rejecting a bid by Perez in conjunction with Lowrey Pianos and Organs to purchase the firm. Because Aeolian was a major employer in Memphis with five hundred workers, Perez received pledges of financial assistance from six Memphis banks and from city hall. The mayor and other officials accompanied him to Citicorp's headquarters in New York in an effort to save the company. Citicorp, however, decided to sell Aeolian's assets to the Chicago-based Wurlitzer Company.

Perez subsequently became the president of a Memphis eye-care products firm and a management consultant with diverse clients, ranging from a retirement housing builder to a woodworking equipment manufacturer.

John McLaren became chairman of an Orange County, California firm that makes signal processors for stereo and audio equipment.

Lloyd Meyer became the co-owner of Camilleri Pianoworks Ltd., a New York restorer of antique and modern pianos. His partner, Robert Philbin, was a factory superintendent at Steinway for sixteen years until 1980, two years before Meyer became president. In 1988,

Meyer guided Seattle investor Bernard (Bud) Greer, an avid pianist, in his acquisition of Mason & Hamlin and subsequently was named president. Established in 1854, a year after Steinway, Mason & Hamlin had been in financial difficulty for some years when Greer bought it. Under him and Meyer the firm did become marginally profitable, but it remained starved for capital and in January 1995 it ceased production.

Only Henry and John Steinway remained at Steinway & Sons, retained by the Birminghams on yearly contracts for the public relations value. A large showroom with a fireplace was set aside for their use. But they could no longer flex their muscles as they had during the CBS years, when their calls and letters were put straight through to William Paley. The Birminghams left them in their gilded cage, but as utterly powerless bystanders except for occasional promotional appearances, primarily by John until his death, and from time to time by Henry.

The Steinway name remains on the company - but not on England's Royal Warrant. From the time of Henry's and John's grandfather, William, the warrant had been held in the name of a Steinway. But when John retired as chairman concurrent with the Birminghams'arrival, Steinway-London worried it would lose the distinction because no Steinways were officers of the company and transfer of the warrant is not automatic.

Executives of the Warrant Association subjected Steinway-London manager Robert Glazebrook to a strict interview and then solemnly departed, leaving him fearing the worst. Some weeks later, the association's members informed him they had granted him the warrant in his name, adding that "We're glad it's no longer held by people outside the country."[84]

Steinway & Sons probably would not have survived without the substantial investment and overhaul by CBS. Consequently, the new owners, the Birminghams, would have a much easier reign.

**Above :** Henry Ziegler's "Woodmere" estate, Long Island, N.Y. (courtesy of Eleanor Ziegler Lodge)

**Silhouettes:** Theodore Edwin Steinway (1883-1957) and his future wife Ruth Gardner Davis in "The Amazons" a performance by the Manhattan Amateur Comedy Club. (courtesy of Carnegie Hall)

**Below :** Eleanor and Frederick Ziegler (standing right) with Theodore Edwin and his brother Bill (Billie) at "Belle Haven," Greenwich, Conn., 1900.

**Above :** Eleanor and Frederick Ziegler with "Harry" (their horse), 1900.

**Above :** John Howland Steinway (courtesy: Sherman Clay & Company).

**Above :** Centaur Sculpture by Frederick Jacob Ziegler (courtesy of Henry Steinway Ziegler)

**Left :** Steinway Mausoleum in Green-Wood Cemetery, Brooklyn, N.Y. Capacity 200. (Photo by Author)

**Right :** Theodore ("Teed") and Josephine Steinway with her daughters, by a previous marriage, 1957. (courtesy of Josephine Steinway

**Below :** Steinway - Concert Grand Piano Model D-274 (courtesy of Steinway-Hamburg)

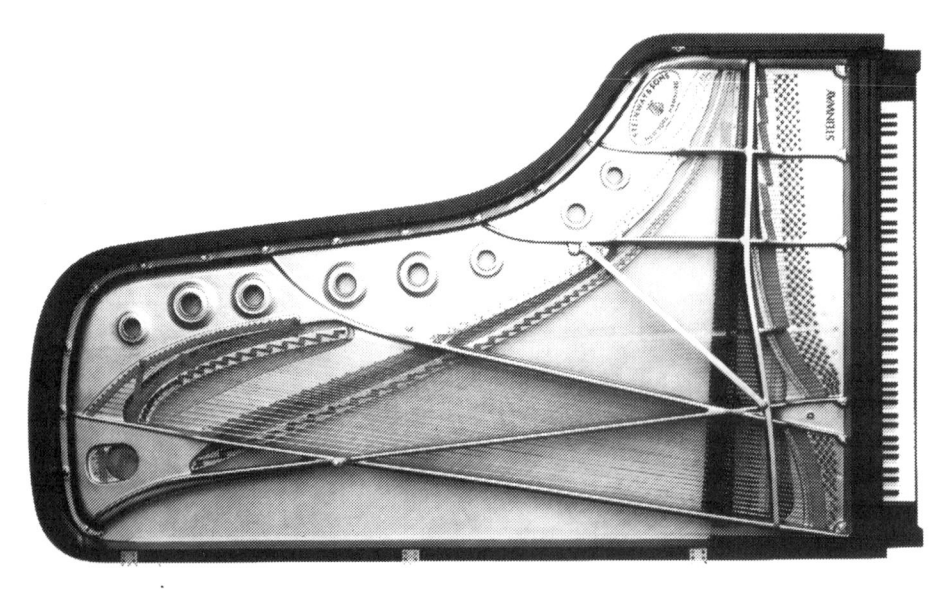

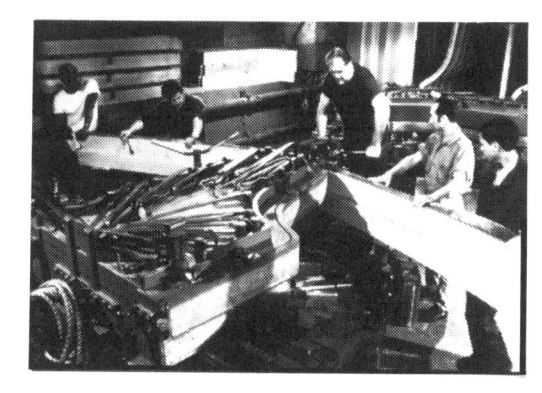

**Left :** Rim bending

**Below :** Cutting the veneers

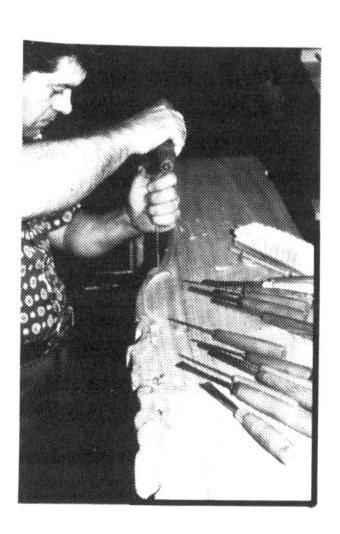

**Above :** Hand carving

**Right :** Closeup of keys and soundboard

**Left :** White satin finish with gilt carvings, Louis XV style. (courtesy of Steinway-Hamburg).

**Right :** The Hidden Features. (courtesy : Steinway-Hamburg) [reading vertically]

1. Tubular Metallic Action Frame
2. Quality Control
3. Voicing the Hammer
4. Grand Leg Assembly
5. Action Regulating
6. Drilling Hammers
7. Continuous Bent Rim
8. Measuring Bridge Bearing
9. Cutting Bridge Notches
10. Blind Doweling
11. Accelerated Action
12. The Duplex Scale

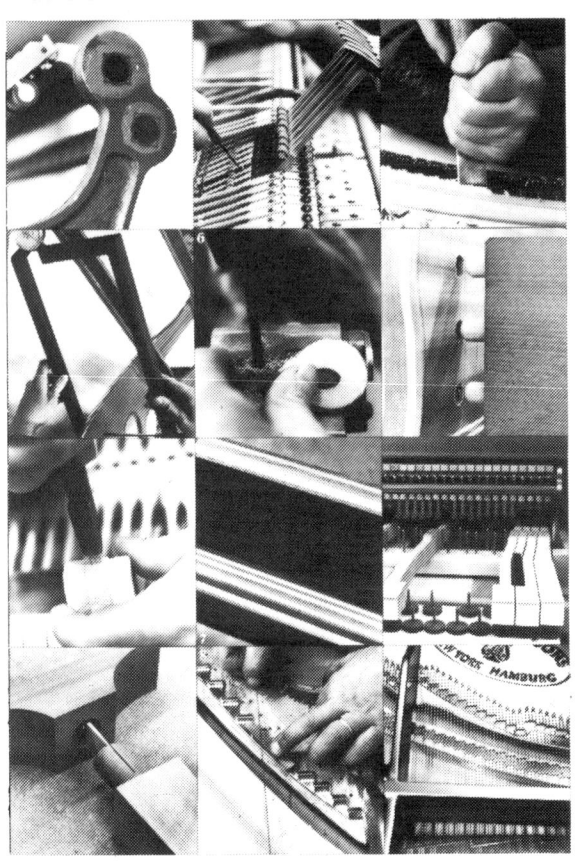

## Chapter IX
# *The Owners After CBS*

By 1984, Steinway & Sons was running smoothly. Not only was it bucking the slump in the piano industry in the United States, but it was enjoying its best year ever. Production at the Long Island City plant was up 20 percent over 1979, compared to an overall decline of 78 percent among American pianomakers. It was one of the few bright spots in the dismal performance of CBS's non-broadcasting ventures in musical instruments, toys, video discs, and theatrical films. In 1983, while all these divisions as a whole lost money, Steinway made a pretax profit of close to $7 million.

Nevertheless, CBS was determined to sell Steinway as part of its retreat from its disastrous diversification. It had come to the conclusion that it should stick to what it knew best: its core businesses of radio and television. In December 1984, the musical instruments division was one of the first it put up for sale. Over the next nine months, all but four of the eight companies left in the division were sold. (The ninth, Electro Music, had been sold in 1981 to the Hammond Organ Company.)

The four remaining were Steinway, Gemeinhardt Flute, Rodgers Organ, and Lyon & Healy Harps. CBS decided the best way to dispose of the latter three was to make them part of a package deal with Steinway as the bait. It was the crown jewel of the foursome because its 1983 performance far exceeded Gemeinhardt's pretax income of $1.8 million, Lyon & Healy's $300,000, and Rodgers's loss of $700,000.

Rumors were rampant as to who would buy Steinway. The most farfetched one was that Yoko Ono, the widow of "Beatle" John Lennon, was interested. Ted Turner, the Atlanta sports and broadcasting mogul who sought to buy CBS in 1985, was not similarly tempted to try to acquire Steinway. Many potential bidders were put off by CBS's all-or-nothing terms. Ultimately, there were eighteen bids. Noticeably absent was any buyback attempt by the Steinways. Harry Steinway did propose to his father and brother Bill that they try to arrange a leveraged buyout. Bill was uninterested and Henry was not keen either, telling Harry that "It is best for others to acquire the firm because we don't have the resources to do so."[1]

Besides the Birminghams, the finalists included Sherman Clay, Steinway's foremost West Coast dealer. Sherman Clay was a formidable opponent. Founded in 1870 by Leander Sherman (C.C. Clay, a retired army major became his partner in 1876), the firm had grown to more than fifty stores, making it the largest retailer of pianos and organs in the United States. It already was a major shareholder in the Wurlitzer Company. Moreover, since its acquisition in 1960 by the Schwartz family of San Francisco, it had become a broadly diversified company also involved in shopping center and office building developments, as well as paper manufacturing.

Unlike the Birminghams, the Schwartzes had longstanding ties with the Steinways. They treasured Charles Herman Steinway's gracious gesture of shipping a dozen pianos free of charge to Sherman Clay's San Francisco store after the 1906 earthquake. In 1961, the Schwartzes had come up with one of Steinway's best promotions: the suggestion that Steinway designate an entire month as "Steinway Month." During that time, Henry or John would visit the dealers' stores, autograph pianos, meet local piano teachers, and be interviewed by every radio and television station and newspaper in the area.

It was also the Schwartzes' idea to set aside a large room in some stores as a recital auditorium, which they call "Steinway Hall." On a personal level, the Schwartz children called John "Uncle," and one of the company' s computers is affectionately nicknamed "Steinway."[2]

Sherman Clay's retail division president Eric Schwartz says that a mixture of business and emotional motives prompted the bid for Steinway. He explains: "As Steinway's largest dealer, our company accounts for 15 percent of the U.S. sales of Steinway pianos. Thus, we felt we brought our retailing ability to the deal. We knew about the manufacturing side because of our stake in Wurlitzer. We felt a close kinship to the Steinways and wanted to protect the prestige of the Steinway name. And from a business strategy viewpoint, it fit in with our constant search for new investment opportunities."[3]

For reasons that Sherman Clay believed were never made sufficiently clear, CBS did not want to sell to people already in the music industry. Thus, it had quickly rejected a bid by Baldwin. Sherman Clay had survived the initial winnowing because it presented itself as an "investor." But ultimately CBS rejected it, too. Schwartz speculates CBS preferred "nonindustry people whom it thought would pay more because the ephemeral value of the Steinway name would blind them to the decline in the piano industry."

CBS's disqualification of Sherman Clay left the Birminghams, the mystery figures in the contest, as the forerunners. Steinway's availability had been brought to their attention by Paul Murphy Jr. of M. Steinert, Steinway's Boston dealer. He had known both Robert and John Birmingham since childhood, as they lived in the same district and he and Bob were classmates[4]. Murphy and the Schwartzes, on their own initiative, gave the Birminghams a complete portrait of Steinway so they would have a fuller perspective than the pretty picture painted by CBS. Henry and John also talked with them.

Eric Schwartz says Sherman Clay's magnanimity was due to the desire "to forge a good relationship with the Birminghams and help make Steinway a better supplier. Because the piano industry is small, there is a symbiotic relationship between manufacturer and buyer."[5] The Schwartzes pointed out the overall poor state of the piano industry. They also cautioned the Birminghams to make certain the paintings at Steinway Hall were included in the sale. Intending to transfer the art to Black Rock, CBS executives had omitted it from the list of contents, arguing there was no book value. The Schwartzes explained that their intrinsic worth was much more important, stressing that "the pictures add to the success of Steinway Hall since, having read about them in guidebooks on New York, people are attracted to the place."[6] Once in the door, the Schwartzes implied, these visitors might very well buy a piano.

The briefings enabled the Birminghams to strike a good deal with CBS, paying far below the $59 million combined net value of Steinway and the other three music companies. As it was a private transaction, the price was not disclosed, but the Birminghams stated it was below the rumored $48 million. The deal was done in the form of a leveraged buyout. Steinway's net worth at the time was $39 million. The Birminghams continued the pension and hospitalization benefits introduced by CBS.

When the papers were signed in September 1985, Steinway & Sons once again became a privately owned family-controlled enterprise, this time under the umbrella of a holding company called Steinway Musical Properties, Inc., encompassing Gemeinhardt Flute, Rodgers Organ, and Lyon & Healy. The Birminghams sold Lyon & Healy in 1987 and subsequently sold Rodgers Organ and Gemeinhardt Flute.

John Birmingham was forty-four when the deal was finalized and his brother Bob, forty. They are low profile, intensely private people who preferred to largely stay in the background during the decade they owned Steinway and leave the daily operations to their hand-picked professional managers. Few dealers or performers knew them, although they did attend dealer associations' conventions and concerts.

Both are well over six feet in height, big-framed, and prematurely gray, looking older than their ages. Neither became chairman; they explained that they felt more comfortable in the role of directors. Besides, only one could be chairman and the Birminghams prefer to work on an equal footing. Jack is the spokesman, but each often completes a sentence of the other. Soft-voiced, they joke in a deadpan delivery. For example, shortly after they bought the company:

> Jack: Shall we talk about our plans for pink keys?
> Bob: What about your idea for a Steinway T-shirt?
> Bob: We're not going to send knock-down pianos through the mail.
> John: Or put one on the back of an elephant.

The Birminghams' wealth largely comes from their father's ownership of White Fuel Company, the largest oil distributor in New England. It was sold to Texaco in the 1960s. In 1977, Texaco purchased another Birmingham concern, General Automatic Heating, a major Boston-based retailer of heating oil. Jack's first career was as a trial lawyer, specializing in securities cases, at the leading Boston law firm of Levin, Cohen, Ferris, Glovsky & Popeo. Bob ran General Automatic Heating until its sale, then turned to management of private investments, including mail-order marketing.

Although comfortably settled, Jack decided he wanted to own a business. "When you grow up with somebody like our father who was a very successful businessman, it gets into your blood," he explains. "There is a great deal of excitement in seeing a business grow. I loved practicing law but I had an itch to do the other. I thought I could have the best of both worlds, but I found I couldn't do both and had to make a choice."[7]

His choice was business. To find one to buy, he turned to James Stone. They had been friends since both served in the Army Intelligence corps after college. Stone had become senior vice president of The Boston Company, an investment counseling firm. He was in charge of the institutional pension division, an operation with five hundred employees and more than $5 billion in assets under management. In 1981, when he was offered the opportunity to buy Robert Williams, Inc., a Massachusetts-based manufacturer of plastic film products for the packaging industry such as plastic windows for envelopes, Stone invited Jack Birmingham in on the deal. To run the company they hired Bruce Stevens, formerly a senior executive at Polaroid Corporation. Stevens also was made a shareholder.

The Birminghams chose to headquarter Steinway Musical Properties in the same building as Robert Williams, Inc., in Newton, Massachusetts, about a twenty-minute drive from Boston and eight minutes from Jack's and Bob's homes. All told, the two companies had a staff of about thirty, including the owners. They shared the same lawyer and chief accountant.

Jack and Bob do not play the piano, but then, neither did John and Henry Steinway. Their younger brother, Mark, who works in a recording studio in Los Angeles, played professionally - on a Steinway. Their mother played, too. "We always had a Steinway grand as we grew up," Jack says. His children do not play. Bob's do.[8]

By 1984, when CBS put Steinway up for sale, Robert Williams had expanded to about $50 million in size, close to Steinway's revenue at the time. Content with Robert Williams' performance, Jack, along with Bob, began to search for another acquisition. Discounting the premise that they have "an overall investment strategy," Jack states that their basic requirement was a manufacturing firm. "When Steinway came on the market, it was almost unbelievable to us," he reflects. "We felt very lucky to be able to pursue it and entered our bid within days after CBS made the announcement. It fit our qualifications as to size and price, was profitable, and had a good product, too. Also, we felt it was a firm to which we could contribute a little bit in terms of our ability to manage and also, that we could bring a little bit more invigoration into what was a fairly old company. We further thought private ownership would be good for it because more energy is possible when you don't have to wait three years for a decision, as often happens in a big corporation."[9]

As soon as they became the new owners, the Birminghams told Steinway's management, "Forget about CBS. You're now dealing with a small group."[10] But while CBS's bureaucracy vanished, much of its philosophy remained. CBS followed modern business administration practices such as sales targets, constant tracking of turnover, and firm budgets. So did the Birminghams. "They didn't know anything about the business when they bought it, but they learned quickly and turned out to be much more aggressive than I expected," Steinway-London's manager Bob Glazebrook discovered.[11]

"The Steinways are marvelous people but they don't have much of a brain for business. During their time, if one piano was sold a week, they thought it was great stuff. They didn't push regarding targets and in this age, if you sit back you won't survive. Under the Birminghams, as under CBS, we were under pressure to reach certain goals and I think that's good because it encouraged initiative, efficiency, and a fighting spirit."

As soon as they became the new owners, the Birminghams tried to allay the uncertainty aroused by the ten months CBS took to conclude the sale. "It was tough on the employees because they were in limbo and especially hurt in distribution since the dealers wondered what would happen," Bruce Stevens recollects. "The music industry is very small and the competition did a great job of fanning fears that the Steinway Musical Properties firms would go out of business. Rodgers in particular was harmed; a classic church organ costs $100,000 and church committees, concerned about Rodgers's future, held back on purchases. The same thing happened to a lesser degree with Steinway. The result was that Steinway had surplus inventory. It was a very painful period."[12]

To quell the concerns, the Birminghams dispatched Stevens on a grueling cross-country tour to the factories of the four Steinway Musical Properties companies, as well as to their dealers. Additionally, they immediately steeped themselves in an immersion program about pianomaking. They invited Steinway's key technical employees to accompany them to a resort in New Hampshire where for three days they asked question after question about the production process and any problems or bottlenecks that needed attention. "The underlying principles of pricing, packaging, distribution, and management apply to all businesses; what is unique is the product and how it is made and we wanted to impress upon the employees that we were eager to learn as much as possible about how a piano is constructed," Bob stresses.[13]

The brothers, however, steered clear of contacting the performers. They considered sending a letter of introduction but decided against it because, as Jack explains, "A Steinway artist is not a paid endorser of Steinway pianos as a baseball player is for promoting a bat, or a professional golfer is for advertising a set of golf clubs. They're playing Steinways because they want to, so we figured that unlike the new owner of a baseball or football team, there was no need to call them in for a formal announcement."[14]

Behind the Birminghams' soft-spoken amiability is a steellike nature. With none of the fireworks that characterized the CBS years, they were equally, if not more, unflinching in putting their stamp on the company. Naturally, they retained the name because it is universally famous, but otherwise Steinway & Sons became Birmingham & Birmingham. They changed or modified every aspect of the company from management to production and marketing - with mixed results.

Revenue nearly doubled to $101 million during their ten-year ownership, but some of that was due to price hikes rather than a climb in unit sales. For example, the suggested retail price of Steinway's cheapest grand - the *S* - was $13,900 in 1984; in 1995, it was $26,400, an almost 100 percent increase. Over and above the huge price hikes, Steinway's sales revenue climb was helped in recent years by the Birminghams' introduction in 1992 of a mid-priced piano called the *Boston.* Its eight models of vertical and grand pianos ranged in price from $6,395 to $29,990 in 1995. By comparison, the price for Steinway's most expensive grand - the concert model - was $75,800. Sales revenue from the *Boston* jumped sixfold to $16.9 million in the twelve months ended March 31, 1995 from $2.7 million in 1992. But in terms of units sold, the *Boston* has a very small portion of the U.S. market - 2,300 out of the 94,793 "acoustic" (non-electronic) pianos sold in 1994.

In addition, the long-running controversy over whether the quality of Steinway pianos had declined, dating back to Henry Steinway's regime, intensified under the Birminghams. It was inflamed by the well-publicized departure of pianist André Watts to Yamaha, a lawsuit between Steinway and one of its biggest dealers, and an investigation by the Federal Trade Commission of Steinway's manufacturing, dealership, and warranty practices. All told, while the Birminghams themselves stayed out of the public eye, theirs was a period of considerable turmoil at Steinway.

The Birminghams kept hardly any of the senior executives who were there when they bought the company. They started at the top in installing their own team. Lloyd Meyer was replaced by Stevens as president at Steinway, whereas the presidents of Gemeinhardt, Rodgers, and Lyon & Healy were retained. The Birminghams wanted Stevens to double as president of Steinway Musical Properties and Steinway & Sons since the latter contributed the lion's share of revenue and profits and hence required about 75 percent of the attention for the four firms.

Bruce Stevens was born on a farm in Shenandoah, Iowa, which as he grew up had a population of fifteen hundred. His father died shortly after he entered Iowa State University, and at the end of his second year, his sister, who had graduated from a New York City college, persuaded him to apply to the Wharton School of Business at the University of Pennsylvania. After graduating, he worked for eighteen months for Armstrong World Industries, Inc., the tile and carpet manufacturer. Armstrong assigned him to Boston, where he met his wife and was hired by Polaroid.

He was at Polaroid for seventeen and a half years, starting as a traveling salesman and subsequently becoming national account manager, mid-Atlantic manager, and manager of distribution to food stores. Polaroid was having trouble selling to supermarkets because its packs were more cumbersome to display than Kodak's conventional rolls of film. Also, pilferage was a serious problem; since it cost more than a roll of film, the loss of a pack was more damaging to Polaroid. Stevens redesigned the display racks for increased customer awareness and theft prevention.

He went on to become eastern regional manager, followed by a posting from 1980 until 1983 at Polaroid's Japanese subsidiary with responsibility also for Australia, New Zealand, Hong Kong, and Singapore. The Japanese had high regard for the creativity of Polaroid's founder, Edwin Land, and appreciated his establishment of a branch in their country in 1960, well before it was fashionable for foreigners to have operations there. The goodwill helped Stevens boost Polaroid's sales past the $100 million mark at a time when the company was encountering difficulties elsewhere.

Stevens next became director of marketing for Polaroid's European operations. He was on the verge of becoming international marketing director and facing the prospect of further glory when he bumped into two casual acquaintances at a Christmas party: the Birminghams. As the three men chatted, Jack Birmingham suddenly offered Stevens the presidency of Robert Williams. The offer threw Stevens into an unexpected career crisis. He had believed his entire working life would be at Polaroid and had "never looked for a job at another firm or even had a curriculum vitae."[15]

The more he thought about Birmingham's proposal, however, the more appealing it seemed. He was attracted by the "entrepreneurial flair and the opportunity to be a little closer to the action and to be more accountable."[16] By the time of his last day at Polaroid, he had undergone "the pain and anguish of withdrawal which most people experience after they leave a longtime employer. I've never thought 'What if?' since that final day."[17]

Within a year, Stevens was made an equity partner in Robert Williams. A year later, when the Birminghams bought Steinway and its sister companies from CBS, they once again made Stevens a partner. In 1986, he relinquished the presidency of Robert Williams so as to devote full time to Steinway Musical Properties.

Initially, Steinway's dealers were concerned that Stevens was not a full-time president, but Stevens countered that responsible people were in the principal positions and the decentralization was in line with his desire "to instill a spirit of accountability, and credibility, rather than perpetuate the bureaucracy of the past. God forbid if somebody under the CBS regime bought a light bulb without forty-three signatures of approval! I prefer to give people the flexibility to study a problem and to make their own decision."[18]

Besides bringing in a new president, the Birminghams also replaced the senior executives in the concert and artist department and at the Long Island factory. In the concert and artist department, the Birminghams replaced David Rubin with Richard Probst, although Rubin, who had reached sixty-five, had expressed interest in remaining seeing that Steinway had no mandatory retirement age.

Subsequently, Probst resigned in 1988 and was replaced by two people: Steinway relative Schuyler Chapin as vice-president of worldwide concert and artist activities and Peter Goodrich as director of concert and artist activities. Chapin previously was general manager of the Metropolitan Opera in New York and Dean of the Faculty of Arts and Science at Columbia University. He was sixty-five - the age Rubin was at the time he was replaced - when he was hired by the Birminghams. Goodrich joined Steinway in 1975 as a salesman at Steinway Hall, the Steinway-owned retail store in Manhattan. He went on to become manager of the rental department, co-ordinator of on-tour activities for the concert and artist department, institutional sales development manager, and then customer services director responsible for the administration of warranties and the sale of replacement parts to technicians and dealers. When Chapin resigned in 1992, Goodrich succeeded him as vice-president of worldwide concert and artist activities.

At the Long Island factory, Joseph Pramberger, the manager since 1979 and a Steinway employee since the 1960s, was supplanted in early 1987 by Daniel Koenig, a former General Electric employee. As a result, for the first time in the history of Steinway & Sons, both the president and the New York factory manager had no background in the piano industry. (This is still true.) A clash was inevitable between the Birminghams, with their belief that all businesses are alike in their basics, and Pramberger, with his belief in the unique nature of pianomaking.

Pramberger was not fired; rather, he was shunted aside to become head of a fifteen-person service center the Birminghams established on Long Island at a separate location from the factory. But he was apprehensive about what would happen to the quality of Steinway pianos. He said: "There is always concern that new owners might be misled by the surface appearance that the business is easy to run. The danger with people unfamiliar with a business is that they can make honest decisions that have serious repercussions.

"Even with seasoned managers in place, changes create anxieties. Steinway requires hands-on control and the directors of marketing, advertising, and manufacturing, as well as the owners, are new. When I was manager, I had to tread a thin line between maintaining the integrity of the Steinway system and keeping pace with technological innovation. Nor could the need for cost control interfere with that integrity. I've been teaching the new owners about the Steinway system to get them to understand how sensitive a product the Steinway piano is."[19]

The edgy relationship between Pramberger and the Birminghams was destined to lead to a split. It came early in 1988 when after close to a year as head of the service center, Pramberger left Steinway. He now has his own piano reconditioning business on Long Island.

Daniel Koenig, Pramberger's successor, previously was a troubleshooting expert at General Electric. As manager of industrial engineering applications, he was in charge of twenty senior engineers who served as in-house consultants on questions ranging from employee efficiency to production layout and the flow of materials. His projects included upgrading the efficiency of GE's appliance division in Louisville, Kentucky, designing the layout of its jet engine plant in Lynn, Massachusetts, and developing a computer-aided production system for its aerospace components facilities in Philadelphia, Syracuse and Binghamton, New York. He is a strong advocate of computer-aided design and computer-aided manufacturing (CAD/CAM) as a way to reduce labor, overhead, and material costs as well as to improve productivity. Another GE alumnus, Sanford Wilson, was hired in 1991 as vice president for operations. He was manager of strategic planning and development at GE and later general manager of the furnace induction division at Asea Brown Boveri, a Swiss-Swedish multinational corporation. Like Koenig, Wilson had no background in pianomaking.

When he was contacted in early 1987 by an executive headhunter on behalf of the Birminghams, Koenig was tempted because GE's disposal of its consumer electronic business "meant people with my type of background no longer were as valuable to the company."[20] He was convinced the relatively old-fashioned world of pianomaking offered greater opportunity to practice his theories than GE's futuristic environment of aerospace equipment.

Koenig was not a pioneer in CAD/CAM in the piano industry. Many of Steinway's competitors, including Baldwin, have used CAD/CAM for years, but the background of their senior production executives is in pianomaking, unlike at Steinway now.

Koenig's language normally contains such modern business buzzwords as productivity gains, process control, and efficient processes. He describes the piano as being "as modern as any device today, even though its main material - wood - has remained basically the same throughout all the years. The ingenuity of the action is superb and I believe the elegant shape of the grand piano is an art form."[21]

The objective of the Birminghams and Koenig was to increase the use of modern production methods and hence output to some extent, while retaining some traditional hand-done time-consuming processes such as the strenuous initial steps in rim-bending. They repeatedly pledged that their intentions were honorable and Koenig stressed that Steinway would not become a mass producer. "Anything we do to improve productivity will not be at the expense of the quality and image of the piano," he said.[22]

Nevertheless, it was this intention to wed Steinway & Sons' tradition of hand craftsmanship with today's high technology that brought the controversy surrounding the company to a head under the Birminghams. Steinway's principal appeal to piano buyers has always been that its instruments are superior because they are hand-built by master craftsmen with years of knowledge. It is this perception that enabled the Birminghams to hike prices.

The guild hall image which Steinway cultivates, no longer exists in reality. Under the guild system, apprentice and journeymen craftsmen learned from more experienced workers and after a long period of time reached the master craftsman level. Today, the process has disappeared at Steinway's Long Island factory, although it is still followed at its Hamburg factory due to apprenticeship training still being practiced in general in the trades in Germany.

Further, in view of its competitors modernizing their manufacturing methods much earlier, the company had to accept the twentieth-century in some measure in order to survive. And indeed a number of Birmingham-inspired mechanization changes already were standard procedure in pianomaking.

Soon after their purchase of Steinway, the Birminghams installed a device that automatically drills the holes for the 245 tuning pins, an arduous task to perform manually. Also, because of the sheer number of holes, hand-drilling can result in inaccuracies and even the slightest inaccuracy can affect a pin's stability. Other pianomakers had introduced this equipment prior to Steinway.

Fitting the soundboard to the rim also was mechanized. "In the days when skilled craftsmen were readily available, Steinway could rely on these people just looking at the soundboard to determine if it was a close fit and if not, shaving it with a razor blade to the precise measurement," Koenig explained. "Today, it is hard to obtain such well-trained people. Moreover, there is machinery that helps guarantee no voids between the rim and the soundboard. Computer-controlled devices cut the soundboard to the identical shape of the inner rim and sonic devices detect better than the human ear whether the fit is exact."[23]

It should be borne in mind, however, that both these procedures involve the fitting together of parts and not the parts themselves. It is over allegations of a record number of Steinway pianos having soundboard cracks that much of the recent controversy arose. In that the soundboard amplifies the volume of a piano's strings, it is as critical to a piano's quality as a solid foundation to a house.

There is no precise rule regarding at what stage a cracked soundboard becomes a problem. It is difficult to devise a set definition because a crack may not be apparent until some time after a piano is purchased and because a small crack may or may not spread. Furthermore, such cracks are not uncommon since the soundboard is made of solid spruce, a wood that is vulnerable to temperature and humidity changes. Constant shifts in a piano's position, as happens on concert stages, can cause cracks, too. Still, spruce continues to be used, rather than plywood which does not split, because spruce transmits sound best.

An example of a soundboard crack not necessarily harming the sound was a venerable Carnegie Hall Steinway concert grand, numbered *CD18*, which was retired in the early 1980s after lengthy service. It had a large devoted following among performers despite its crack.

Steinway management maintains that thin cracks and ridges are to be expected as a normal response by the soundboard to humidity changes, and that they do not harm the sound or the value of the piano.

But bad cracks can make a piano sound harsh, shorten sustaining tones, and create tuning instability. At their worst, when they run across the entire soundboard, they can cause the ribs on the soundboard's underside to separate. The ribs' purpose is to increase the amplification. Consequently, in addition to sound deterioration, the piano's value plummets. Since the popular conception is that a properly maintained old Steinway is better than a new one, Steinway purchasers expect their purchase to be as good as, if not better than an investment in gold. Often, an old Steinway, which cost much less than today's model, can fetch as much money on the resale market as a new one, thereby yielding owners a hefty profit.

The cracked soundboard issue eventually led to a two-year investigation by the Federal Trade Commission and subsequent appeals over several years of its decision to close its investigation. The issue was brought to a head by A. Michael's Piano of Waterford, Connecticut, a Steinway dealer from 1982 to 1987. A. Michael's was started in 1973 by J. Michael Yeager on his graduation from university. He had earned his tuition by repairing pianos. He chose the name A. Michael's in order to obtain the first listing in the telephone yellow pages under pianos.

Yeager began as a dealer for Mason & Hamlin. He switched to Steinway in 1982 when Mason & Hamlin began to decline financially. Soon, Yeager was Steinway's largest single-location dealer in the United States. His success was largely due to his charging less than Steinway's "suggested" retail prices.[24] While pleased with his sales record, Steinway pressed him to adhere to its suggested prices. This difference of opinion culminated in late 1987 when Steinway proposed a new dealership contract and Yeager rejected it. Steinway thereafter refused to ship new pianos to A. Michael's Piano.

Yeager continued to sell new Steinways out of his inventory from 1987 to 1989 and to service those his store had already sold. In the course of servicing these pianos, he said he noticed a marked increase in the number of cracked soundboards and separation of the soundboards from the ribs that hold them in place from the time the Birminghams bought Steinway in 1985. Of the 173 pianos that he alleged were defective, he said 64 percent had occurred after 1985. Of the 173, he said 117 had cracked soundboards and 27 of these also had suffered rib separation.

In 1989, as Yeager was compiling his statistics, he was not the only person concerned about the upsurge in cracked soundboards. On February 9, 1989, Frank Mazurco, Steinway's marketing vice president and the executive in charge of dealer relations, wrote Steinway's president Bruce Stevens on the same issue. The memo revolved around product quality problems reported by Steinert, Steinway's Boston dealer as well as one of its largest. Its complaints had special significance because Steinert had been a Steinway dealer since 1869 and current president Paul Murphy Jr. had informed the Birminghams, acquaintances of his since childhood, of CBS's intention to sell Steinway.

Mazurco wrote Stevens: "I think it's important for everyone to know that this particular dealer has really been experiencing some of our shortcomings in product quality. Notice this piano, 503678, with a cracked soundboard. In addition, I have raised concerns in the recent past about the numerous cracked soundboard reports. We must look more carefully at this matter. I believe we have never had this many cracked soundboard problems in the past. I believe our records would provide proof of this."

When this memo became public knowledge, Daniel Koenig, head of the Long Island factory, tried to downplay it. He said: "Frank has to be manufacturing's severest critic. Every time he sees a speck of dust on a piano, he's got to complain about it. And that's who we want him to be." Mazurco, however, knows much more about pianos than whether they need dusting. He holds a performance degree in both the piano and the organ, sold Steinway pianos in Cincinnati for years, joined Steinway's head office in 1981 as a dealer liaison, and was appointed vice president of marketing by the Birminghams, one of the few holdovers from the CBS era. Mazurco was not punished by the Birminghams for being outspoken; instead, he was later promoted to executive vice president in 1995.

Exactly why the incidence of cracked soundboards grew is hard to pinpoint. Yeager contended that the Birminghams were rushing production by drying soundboard wood "at a super high level in the kiln so they could build pianos more quickly." Wood drying is one of the most important steps in pianomaking. The wood is first air-dried and then kiln-dried with the objective of reducing the moisture content in order to minimize the possibility of changes in dimension.

However, if the moisture level is too low, the wood cannot contract and expand in response to normal humidity changes. This creates tension and the tension causes cracks. Yeager hired a number of piano technicians and wood experts to examine his pianos. He says their concerted opinion was that the problems "indicated inadequate or improper controls over wood moisture content during various stages of manufacture."

Production of pianos at Steinway's Long Island factory did increase considerably under the Birminghams to 2,172 in 1990 from 1,321 in 1985. But whereas Yeager attributed this 64 percent increase to rushed production, the Birminghams said it instead was due to the addition of twenty people to the factory's workforce.

In 1990, sixty A. Michael's customers complained to the State of Connecticut's Attorney General's office about problems they were experiencing with Steinway pianos. They charged that Steinway had failed to honor warranties, particularly those dealing with cracks and other alleged flaws in the soundboards. The Connecticut Attorney General forwarded a number of the complaints to the Federal Trade Commission which launched an investigation in late 1990 to determine whether it should take legal action against Steinway for violation of federal laws regarding warranties.

While the investigation was underway, Dan Lofing, a Sacramento, California piano accompanist and teacher, filed a $385,000 lawsuit alleging breach of warranty concerning a Steinway *B* - Steinway's second largest grand - he had bought in 1984 for $24,300. He stopped making instalment payments in 1986, claiming dissatisfaction with the piano and was sued for failure to pay. He then countersued. He won - but it was a Pyrrhic victory. While the jury agreed the piano was defective, it also concluded there was no breach of warranty because Steinway had offered to repair or replace the piano, including an invitation to fly him across the country to its Long Island factory to personally select the replacement. Lofing had refused. The jury awarded Lofing $24,300 in damages - reimbursing him for the cost of the piano - but it also said he must pay the balance he owed of $23,875, netting him all of $425 before court costs.

In January 1992, as the Lofing case neared a decision, the FTC closed its investigation into the complaints from A. Michael's Piano. Subsequently, A. Michael's filed a request under the Freedom of Information Act for access to all the letters and documents gathered by the FTC during its investigation. The FTC had interviewed six Steinway competitors regarding their manufacturing, dealership and warranty practices for comparison with Steinway's. It also had an outside expert inspect a number of Steinway pianos. The FTC refused, maintaining that as permitted under law the documents were exempt from disclosure. Yeager appealed the decision to the United States Court of

Appeals in August 1993. The court ruled against him in March 1994 on the grounds that the documents were part of attorney-client "Work product privilege" - that is, confidentiality of information.

Dana Messina, one of the controlling shareholders of Steinway since April 1995, says he and his associate Kyle Kirkland "investigated the Yeager issue before we bought the company and found that while a lot of press was created, Yeager was not very credible. For example, he said he sold more pianos than anybody in the universe - not on this planet, but the universe! Also, the FTC cleared Steinway and there have been no other complaints regarding cracked soundboards. We regarded it as a vendetta."[25] That the FTC documents are sealed is unfortunate in that it is impossible to know why the agency closed the investigation.

Koenig was succeeded in 1995 by Roy Chesseri who also has no background in pianomaking. He previously was a vice-president of manufacturing at Wallace & Tiernan, a New Jersey manufacturer of chemical machinery and industrial process flow instruments. Prior to that, he was at the management consulting firm of Coopers & Lybrand.

The Birminghams' most dramatic departure from Steinway tradition was their introduction in 1992 of the lower-priced *Boston* made by Kawai in Japan. Originally, the Birminghams planned to call this line *Waltham,* after the Boston-area headquarters of the family's former oil heating business, but they discovered *Waltham* had already been used as the name of a low-priced watch. The *Boston* sells for 20 percent more than mass-produced, mid-priced Japanese pianos. Although best known for its mid-priced lines, Kawai is making inroads in the concert market. In 1994, both the first and second place winners in the International Tchaikovsky Competition in Moscow chose Kawai pianos.

Steinway was a latecomer to the mid-priced pianomaking field. Baldwin had introduced the *Howard* made for it by Samick of South Korea in the 1980s. Moreover, Steinway faced stiff competition from the lower-priced pianos of Far Eastern firms.

Two apprehensions were expressed when the Birminghams introduced the *Boston*. There was concern that Steinway, like other manufacturers, would go on to sell "stencil pianos," generic instruments built by one manufacturer, but sold by a better-known company which merely stencils its name on the pianos. So far, that has not happened. Further, Steinway dealers who also sell Kawai and other mid-priced Far Eastern imports were perturbed that the *Boston* would clash with their sale. Consequently, it has taken considerable time for

Steinway to persuade its dealers to also carry the *Boston*. By 1995, three years after its introduction, twenty percent of Steinway dealers still were not selling it.[26]

The Birminghams left Steinway-London's and Steinway-Hamburg's management untouched. London manager Bob Glazebrook was fifty-five when the Birminghams bought Steinway, and Hamburg manager Max Matthias was fifty-six. Glazebrook's splendid connections and Matthias's technical expertise were assets to Steinway. Glazebrook personally supervised the tuning of the pianos used at the annual winter music series held by the Earl of Harewood, a cousin of the Queen, at his estate in the north of England. He did the same for the musical society supported by the Duchess of Hambledon, the Queen's representative in Scotland, and for that of the Countess of Aberdeen in northern Scotland. He also took care of the two Steinways owned by former Prime Minister Edward Heath, a talented pianist.

He tuned the Steinway Princess Margaret plays at Balmoral Castle, the Queen's residence in Scotland. His brother, Michael, tuned the two Steinways owned by Princess Alexandra, a cousin of the Queen. From time to time, the Sultan of Brunei sent for Glazebrook to tune the white-and-gold Louis XV style piano that Glazebrook sold him. Thanks to Glazebrook - and his predecessors - the BBC purchased seventy Steinways for live broadcasts from its studios around Britain. London's Royal Festival Hall bought a dozen. Glazebrook and many Steinway artists became close friends; they were impressed by his study of composers and also of their own personalities so as to best meet their needs in voicing their pianos.

Artur Rubinstein, Claudio Arrau, and Cifford Curzon had insisted that Glazebrook, in his premanagement days as a technician, accompany them on their United Kingdom tours. His career had received a tremendous boost from his ability to satisfy a hard-to-please Rosalyn Tureck. In London in 1955 to record the *Bach-Goldberg Variations,* she was enormously unhappy with both the Steinway grand and the concert technician assigned her. Glazebrook was dispatched to mollify her. The task was daunting, "as she had an awesome reputation for being difficult. She had already threatened to fly back to the United States without doing the recording because she so disliked the piano."

On his arrival, Glazebrook's nervousness escalated as he beheld a furious Tureck pacing up and down the studio and the disconsolate record producer holding his head in his hands. The pianist calmed down slightly when Glazebrook agreed that the piano sounded terrible. He suggested she take an afternoon rest while he worked on the instrument. At 6:00 p.m., when she returned, he expected her to "condemn" the piano. Instead, she smiled, which caused the producer to also smile, albeit wanly, and the recording session proceeded. Over the next three months Glazebrook arrived at the studio at 7:00 a.m., two hours before Tureck, and prepared the piano note by note. "How's our baby?"[27] he would ask her.

The two formed a mutual admiration society. "She taught me a valuable lesson as to what the artist wants," Glazebrook reflects. "Although she could be very, very difficult, she was not demanding when the piano was all right." As for Tureck, she praises Glazebrook for his appreciation that a piano "becomes something that you love, nourish, nurture, worry over, and get angry with."

Matthias, a good friend of pianist André Watts, once lent the pianist his formal attire for a Sunday morning concert Watts was giving in Frankfurt with humorous results. Usually performers wear pinstripe suits at this time of day, but this particular occasion called for tails and starched shirt. Watts is shorter than Matthias, so the cuffs had to be hastily shortened. But as Watts passionately played a Liszt encore, the stitching unraveled and the cuffs began sliding down farther and farther, until it became a contest as to whether the cuffs would cover his hands before he could finish. Determined to prevail, Watts sped on to the conclusion, striking the last note just in the nick of time.[28]

Besides expanding Hamburg's promotion and distribution in its traditional markets, Matthias made several trips to China to establish contacts there. He rearranged the factory layout so that at certain production steps, a person could work on two pianos, one after the other, instead of waiting for the second one to be pushed to his workplace. Hamburg also preceded New York in the installation of a machine to fit the soundboard into place, rather than manual positioning.

The Birminghams placed heavy emphasis on merchandising from the start of their ownership. One of their first instructions was for "Steinway & Sons" to be applied to the side of the piano facing the audience, as well as above the keyboard, a throwback to the last century when pianomakers used this tactic as an advertising gimmick. The Birminghams were not alone in this return to blatant commercialism; Baldwin, Yamaha, and Bösendorfer are doing likewise and, in fact, preceded the Birminghams' action. Actually, the name is not stenciled on; rather, it is mounted in brass letters on plastic with an adhesive back that is then peeled off. Then the letters are sprayed with clear lacquer and the surrounding area is sanded repeatedly with increasingly fine paper and then handrubbed for an inlaid effect.

Another Birmingham advertising promotion failed. In 1987, in conjunction with the Cunard shipping line, Steinway organized a "Steinway Piano Festival-at-Sea" aboard Cunard's *Queen Elizabeth II*. During a five-day crossing from New York to England, on a rotating basis of one per evening, five Steinway artists performed classical, jazz, and popular music on Steinway pianos and answered questions about their careers and the music. The festival necessitated a quick shuffle in the ship's complement of eight pianos as not all were Steinways. John Steinway described the Festival-at-Sea as a "dismal failure" and it has not been repeated.

Steinway is proud of Theodore Edwin Steinway's refusal to let the Steinway name be used on a refrigerator during the depression. But it has participated from time to time in associated advertising whereby another product's quality is described as comparable to that of a Steinway piano. The Birminghams did this for awhile to extend the company's advertising budget, that is, with no financial outlay on Steinway's part. Steinway does not charge for the use of its name if the other firm's advertising campaign reaches a larger audience than Steinway could afford.

This was the case with two such promotions in the spring of 1988. Ryder System, a large U.S. transportation company, illustrated a full-page advertisement in *The Wall Street Journal* with Henry Engelhard Steinway's picture rather than one of Ryder's founder, current chief executive, or vehicles, and compared Ryder's policies to Henry Engelhard's emphasis on its core business. In a television commercial for its Dr. Ballard's Fancy Feast Cat Food, Nestlé Enterprises showed a white cat walking along the keyboard of a Steinway, then past a Stradivarius violin, while the announcer said, "The piano is a Steinway, the violin is a Stradivarius, and the cat food is Fancy Feast."

Flowing from Bob Birmingham's past investment in mail order marketing, a direct mail program was introduced. It was one reason why the Birminghams switched their advertising plus public relations accounts to Ingalls, Quinn & Johnson, an affiliate of the big advertising firm of BBDO(Batten Barton Dustine & Osborne). Another reason was that the agency was based in Boston, the Birminghams' base. Ingalls, Quinn & Johnson replaced Steinway's previous New York-based advertising agency of Lord, Geller, Federico, Einstein and public relations firm, Manning, Selvage & Lee.

Ingalls, Quinn & Johnson conducted a telephone sampling of three hundred Steinway customers as to what magazines they read, television and radio programs they enjoyed, type of cars they owned, and musical skill or interest. The information was fed into a computer so as to better place Steinway's advertisements and pinpoint on whom to concentrate direct mail campaigns.

The emphasis on promotion also was evident in the design of the five hundred thousandth Steinway piano unveiled at a gala Carnegie Hall concert in June 1988 to mark the company's 135th anniversary. The first two commemorative pianos - the one hundred thousandth built in 1903 and the three hundred thousandth built in 1938 - which were presented to the White House bore decorations honoring U.S. history. But the five hundred thousandth honored Steinway in that it bore the signatures of all nine hundred current Steinway artists. By contrast, the promotional brochures of Steinway performers list the four hundred best known around the world. Two dozen Steinway "artists" played at the concert, but only one used the new piano.

In conjunction with the concert, the Birminghams launched the Steinway Foundation, a non-profit organization to assist up-and-coming pianists and composers. The Birminghams provided some of the seed money and were the trustees, along with Bruce Stevens; the Steinway family also were initial donors. But whereas foundations are usually funded primarily by a family or a corporation, most of the early Steinway Foundation money came from the public. Proceeds from the ticket sales for the June 1988 concert went to it, as did the money from the two-year North American, European, and Asian road tour of the five hundred thousandth piano.

What has not changed over the years since Steinway's ownership switched from the Steinway family is the often almost mystical manner in which concert pianists choose grands for performances. For the pianos in The Basement, Steinway uses a shorthand code of *CD, CB, CL,* etc., with the *C* denoting "concert" and the *D, B,* and *L* the size of the piano and then two or three numbers plucked out of thin air. The *D* is Steinway's biggest piano followed in size by the *B* and the *L*. Like men about town squirrelling away telephone numbers of favorite girls, many performers record in a little black book the numbers of pianos they adore and pass on their rating system to one another.

By contrast, Leonard Pennario will play almost anything. His equanimity stems from his experiences during World War II when, along with singer Tony Martin and actor Melvyn Douglas, he entertained troops in India and Burma. "After playing in the jungle on little uprights and having as my main concern not if they were in tune, which they weren't, but if they worked at all, I feel I could play anything now," he avows.[29]

However, unlike what occurred in the era of Alexander Greiner, most of today's concert pianists cannot afford to send their pianos to wherever they perform due to prohibitive cartage rates, which are now in the thousands of dollars. Only Vladimir Horowitz took his piano around the world on his concert tours. Horowitz also frequently requested that Steinway permit its chief technician, Franz Mohr, to accompany him. For Horowitz's 1987 trip to Russia, Mohr took two bags containing thirty tools each and replacement parts as a precaution against the lack of such equipment there or the loss of one of his cases.

Mohr also had to pay extra close attention to climatic conditions. In winter, with the heat on, pianos tend to sound flat; by contrast, in summer, air conditioning causes sharpness. To test the strength of the keys and strings, Mohr would strike a note with three or four fingers, equivalent to the force applied with one finger by performers.[30]

Horowitz had the negotiating clout to pass on the costs of cartage and Mohr's services to the sponsors of his concerts even for overseas tours. Rudolf Serkin did the same. However, other Steinway artists who travel to Europe can dip into Steinway's minibanks at its London and Hamburg stores. London has seventeen concert grands for touring artists, and Hamburg, ten.

Although concert hall managers insist their house pianos are in first-class condition, many performers spurn them as if they had come from the wrong side of the tracks. They prefer that the local Steinway dealer provide a concert grand from those assigned to it out of Steinway's piano bank. Even Carnegie Hall management finds that performers sometimes reject its Steinways in favor of others requested from The Basement one block away.

It is the practice of Byron Janis, for instance, to request that a Steinway dealer in one city send a piano that Janis likes to a city where the piano does not suit him. "If I am playing Prokofiev, I want a piano with tremendous sound and brilliance, but if I am playing Beethoven's *Fifth*, my preference is one that is not super brilliant," he explains. Janis also points out that there is "nothing wrong in admitting that pianos are different as long as they are of good quality." He compares the fastidiousness of some performers in piano selection to the preference of one violinist for a Stradivarius and another for a Guarnerius, or to the difficulty a prize Thoroughbred horse may have on certain tracks.[31]

Peter Nero is the happy owner of a Steinway that became temperamental at a concert. This piano is one of a set formerly owned by the University of California and dubbed "Adam" and "Eve." When a key on one - Nero does not know whether it was Adam or Eve - malfunctioned during a concert, the UCLA concert manager blamed himself and had nightmares of the angry piano chasing him down the hall. Finally, to get some sleep, he decided to get rid of the piano. When Nero tried it out and fell in love with it, the manager was so thrilled he quoted Nero a rock-bottom price.[32]

Concert artists remain choosy, too, in the selection of their home and practice pianos. Shura Cherkassky, who specialized in the romantic style of playing, requested Steinway's London branch to regulate the baby grand he had at home so it was enormously heavy in the touch and extremely soft in sound. He believed his muscle control was enhanced as a result. Then, for concerts, he asked for the exact opposite - a big, bold, brassy piano - confident that from his practice piano he had achieved the requisite control.[33] Rudolf Serkin was known to hitch a ride with a dealer's truck driver back to the store to rehearse on its piano when dissatisfied with the practice piano delivered to his hotel suite.[34]

Performers say that on what they sit is as important as on what they play. Peter Nero's advice is based on painful experience. "There is an addendum in every artist's contract regarding requirements about lighting, sound, and dressing rooms. There also should be explicit addendums about the piano and the bench. You ask for a concert grand in fine condition and assume a bench will come with it. You think you are being clear but something new arises every time. Your definition of what is fine condition and the concert hall's may not coincide. The piano may not have been tuned or, if it was, the work was done so poorly that the instrument is out of tune again after five minutes. If you do not specify that you want a tufted, adjustable Steinway bench, you may get one into which you sink as if it were a waterbed."[35]

The ways in which a bench can be uncomfortable are endless. It can be so hard that hemorrhoid sufferers want to scream from pain. The only solution is to tape on sheets or blankets. The legs may be so long that tall performers have to chop off a few inches. Or they may be too short and the bench must be artificially raised by placing it on a platform or, under desperate circumstances where one is unavailable, on sheets or blankets. Sometimes the bench may squeak or rattle until the legs are tightened. Little wonder then that at one time Nero hauled around his own bench. The legs were detachable and he would crate up the works and sent it as cargo when he traveled by plane. Bella Davidovich circumvents the bench predicament by using a chair because she likes the support. During those passages when the orchestra plays alone, she uses the opportunity to sit back and rest.[36]

Steinway continues to rely heavily on the world's finest pianists playing Steinways at concerts as its most potent promotion technique. In 1995, for example, Steinway user Van Cliburn spoke effusively about the Steinway piano to Steinway's dealers during the annual Steinway & Sons' breakfast at the National Association of Music Manufacturers. "Steinway is a true classic and when you deal in the classics, you are always safe," he said.[37] Steinway's favorite advertisement still is the scoreboard, showing how many piano soloists play a Steinway while performing with major orchestras in North America - 93 percent in the 1994-95 season, according to its tabulation.[38]

That is an impressive percentage - but it is down from the 98 percent that the company boasted of in its heyday. Thus, it is crucial to Steinway's perpetuation of its piano's image as the "instrument of the immortals" that further slippage not occur. It is this concern that has led to a battle between Steinway and Yamaha that is reminiscent of the rivalries between piano manufacturers during William Steinway's presidency. The warfare stems from Yamaha's decision to launch a concert and artist program in 1987 to boost sales of its concert grand, the *CF-III* introduced five years earlier. In 1986 Steinway had sold 120 of the 270 concert grands sold that year in the United States. Its nearest rival was Baldwin which sold forty. Yamaha had sold merely eight.[39]

Yamaha made inroads with concert artists by not charging them for delivery of the piano and for in-hall tuning, as did Steinway. For popular artists, who play close to 150 or so concerts a year, the Yamaha affiliation yielded savings of $80,000 to $100,000 a year - an attractive incentive.[40]

The Steinway-Yamaha conflict burst into public view in January 1988 when André Watts played the *CF-III* at a televised Lincoln Center performance commemorating the twenty-fifth anniversary of his debut with the New York Philharmonic. Watts has a reputation for being finicky in his selection of pianos and earlier in his career had switched from Steinway to Baldwin and back. His decision to use the Yamaha at the Lincoln Center concert was made just days before the performance. Reportedly displeased with the condition of Steinway's piano bank and with what he regarded as a lack of response to his concerns, he terminated his relationship with Steinway on January 1, became associated with Yamaha on January 5, and played January 15. At the time it was alleged that Watts switched because he had been paying around $90,000 a year to Steinway for cartage and tuning expenses and Yamaha had offered to waive those fees. Yamaha said no financial incentives were involved, while Watts praised the Yamaha's sound and the company's "sense of obligation and willingness to be embarrassed if something goes wrong." Watts declined to specifically discuss his reason for making the change. As of 1995, he was once again playing Steinways, but not as a "Steinway artist" - official endorser of the piano.

In any event, as Steinway - and its rivals - stress that pianists are free to play the piano of their choice, the Watts defection was not something about which Steinway could publicly complain. Where the company did decide to act was at the dealer level to prevent the participation of Steinway-Yamaha dealers in Yamaha's concert and artist program. A Steinway dealer has exclusivity in a city, whereas Yamaha appoints several per community. As a result, in 1987 it had 365 U.S. dealers - more than triple Steinway's total.[41]

In 1987, forty of Steinway's then 110 dealers also sold Yamaha pianos. The situation came to a head that fall when Yamaha asked seven of the forty Steinway-Yamaha dealers to become involved in its new concert and artist program. Of the seven, only one immediately agreed - Hendricks Music Company of Chicago. Yamaha runs its C and A program itself in New York, where it opened a showroom in early 1988 on the same block as Steinway, and Los Angeles, the two largest U.S. markets. But it decided not to in Chicago, the third in size. Thus, who it chose for this responsibility in Chicago was of paramount importance to its success. The selection of Hendricks, from among Yamaha's six dealers in the city, was logical in that Hendricks with four stores, was the foremost dealer.

Hendricks Music's Yamaha connection predated its Steinway one by five years. President Ed Hendricks became a Yamaha dealer in 1974 after ten years as piano merchandising manager at Lyon & Healy, the Steinway franchisee in Chicago. One year later, Henry

Steinway asked him to become director of marketing at Steinway. Yamaha had no objections to what could be a conflict of interest; instead, it allowed Hendricks Music, which Hendricks placed under the management of his son-in-law, William Jenkins, to continue to sell Yamahas. Henry Steinway, moreover, did not request that Hendricks Music relinquish the Yamaha connection.[42]

When Robert Bull succeeded Henry as president, he lifted the longstanding prohibition against Steinway dealers selling competitive makes of pianos. Hendricks says this made his job as marketing director "so much better" because he was able to expand Steinway's dealer network to many places where previously there had been no Steinway coverage.[43]

Yamaha was equally understanding in 1979 when Hendricks himself became one of the combination Yamaha-Steinway dealers after his return to his company. He became Steinway's Chicago franchisee after Lyon & Healy's stores were closed by CBS. Nor did Yamaha object to Hendricks's participation in Steinway's concert and artist program. According to Hendricks, 40 percent of the revenue made by his Chicago stores came from Steinway sales before the controversy erupted between him and Steinway. In 1987, a few months before the altercation, Hendricks opened three stores in Minneapolis with some financial assistance from Yamaha. At these, he sold Yamahas, but not Steinways because Schmitt Music Centers was Steinway's dealer there.

Whereas Henry Steinway did not see a conflict of interest in Hendricks's double affiliation, the Birminghams objected to his decision to become involved in Yamaha's C and A program. In their opinion, it was all right for a Steinway dealer to sell more than one make of piano, but they drew the line at that dealer's promoting another pianomaker's C and A program as well as Steinway's. As they saw it, this unfairly enabled Yamaha to capitalize on the goodwill that Steinway's C and A activities had built up throughout the years. Thus, when Hendricks agreed in the fall of 1987 to participate in Yamaha's C and A program, the Birminghams retaliated by revoking his franchise. In addition, on the eve of Yamaha's dealers' meeting at which Yamaha announced its C and A program, letters stating that Steinway expected "exclusive support" of its C and A activities were sent to all other joint Steinway-Yamaha dealers.

Hendricks sued Steinway, alleging anti-trust violation, but Northern Illinois District Judge William Hart ruled in 1988 in Steinway's favor, saying "It is perfectly legitimate and procompetitive for manufacturers to insist that their dealers devote their undivided loyalty to their products."[44] Hendricks filed an appeal but withdrew it a few months later. In place of Steinways he began to carry more large Yamahas and added Bösendorfers.

As yet, no similar controversy has arisen at joint Baldwin-Yamaha dealerships which constitute 10 percent of Baldwin dealers. Baldwin executives say they have no objection to these franchisees participating in both their C and A program and that of Yamaha. Nor has the Steinway-Yamaha situation been paralleled in the competition between Steinway, Baldwin, and Kimball, the manufacturer of the Bösendorfer, since with the exception of a few Steinway-Bösendorfer stores, there are no crossovers in dealerships among them.

Over and above the rivalry from competitors for concert performers, the Birminghams continued to be harassed by the long-running controversy over whether Steinway's American or Hamburg piano was superior.

While the firm claimed only about 5 to 8 percent of Steinway artists categorically insisted on the Hamburg Steinway, there still was no consensus of opinion among performers about the two Steinways. Vladimir Ashkenazy continued to prefer the Hamburg version because "there is more variety and depth to the sound. Sometimes, I do play the U.S. Steinway in New York because its brilliance and incisiveness is suited for huge halls."[45]

Bella Davidovich, like Ashkenazy, a native of Russia, the cradle of romantic, soulful playing, said she wished the American Steinway had "more of the warm sound of the Hamburg one. I find the American a little metallic."[46] John Browning remained fond of the Hamburg $C$, which New York discontinued during the depression. At seven-feet-five-inches, it is six inches longer than the $B$, which both New York and Hamburg make. "The $C$ has a better bass sound because its strings are longer," he said. "But I also love the U.S. piano if it's in good shape."[47]

By contrast, Byron Janis continued to be an all-out American Steinway enthusiast. "If pianists are looking for a piano that has the dynamic range for all repertoires, the American Steinway is the answer," he stated. "The European Steinway is more limited in its sonority. The U.S. Steinway is built for enormous halls; the European for smaller ones."[48] For his part, Peter Nero found the Hamburg piano "very Teutonic and very heavy and monochromatic."[49]

When the Birminghams bought Steinway, they insisted it was a "long-term investment."[50] Long-term lasted ten years. In April 1995, they sold Steinway to the Selmer Company, a major manufacturer of woodwind, brass, percussion, and stringed instruments used by student and professional bands. It was a merger of two companies close in size in terms of revenue, net income, and number of employees. In 1994 Selmer had sales of $101.1 million, net income of $16.6 million, and 1,014 employees. Steinway had sales of $101.9 million, net income of $13.1 million, and 923 employees(478 in the United States and 445 in Europe).[51] In terms of sales, the Selmer-Steinway combination would have ranked fourth in the musical instruments industry in 1994 as compared to tenth and eleventh respectively.[52] Their combined total of $203 million would have been well ahead of Steinway's longtime chief U.S. piano rival, Baldwin Piano & Organ(1994 sales: $123.1 million). Japanese-owned Yamaha Corporation of America, which makes a wide range of musical instruments besides pianos, ranked first with sales of $600 million.

Selmer's acquisition of Steinway came less than two years after it emerged from protracted turbulence. It had been a subsidiary of the North American Phillips Company from1975 until February1989 when it was bought by Integrated Resources, a highly leveraged financial services company. Six months later, Integrated Resources filed for Bankruptcy Court protection. It put Selmer up for sale in 1991 but it was not until August 1993 that it was acquired by a group of purchasers led by two thirty-one-year-old California investment bankers - Kyle Kirkland and Dana Messina.

Kirkland and Messina had met at the investment dealer firm of Drexel Burnham Lambert. Messina joined Drexel's High Yield bond("junk bond") department's Beverly Hills, California office in 1987, and Kirkland, the following year. After Drexel's early 1990 collapse, Messina became a senior vice president later that year and Kirkland in 1991 at Dabney/Resnick, a Beverly Hills investment firm. There, they specialized in junk bond deals of $10 to $20 million. In March 1994 they formed their own investment banking firm of Kirkland Messina based in Los Angeles.

While both were at Drexel, they had put together the financing for Integrated Resources to buy Selmer. Over the following years they became familiar with Selmer's management team and products. According to Messina, they concluded that although Selmer's sales dropped from $86 million in 1989 to $80 million in 1990, "unlike Integrated Resources, Selmer was not in desperate trouble. It had strong brand names and market shares."[53] Selmer's sales revived to $83 million in 1991 and $86 million in1992. Its brand names include *Selmer* saxophones, *Bach* trumpets and trombones, and *Ludwig* drums. It has a 34 percent market share in the United States in student band instruments and a 45 percent one in professional quality band instruments.[54] Moreover, the outlook for future sales is promising since sales of Selmer's products tend to tally with trends in student enrollment and the U.S. Department of Education has forecast a steady increase in elementary and secondary school population throughout the 1990s and beyond.

Thus, when Selmer was put up for sale, Kirkland and Messina decided to grab the opportunity. "We did it with hard work and wit," Messina recalls with a laugh of exuberant pleasure.[55] The group they convinced to invest consisted of three large insurance companies - Sun Life Assurance, John Hancock Mutual Life Insurance, and a subsdiary of Equitable Life Assurance. Kirkland and Messina are the controlling shareholders with 90 percent of the voting stock. Both are executive vice presidents and directors of Selmer. Messina says he and Kirkland persuaded the insurance companies to invest based on the "forty to fifty times" return investors had made in other companies in which they had been the investment advisors.

After acquiring Selmer, the two young men looked around for another music company to buy. They considered buying Baldwin but decided not to "because while we liked the managers, we believed Baldwin was positioned in the market too close to Yamaha and Kawai," Messina explains.[56] They wanted a company facing less direct competition. "We concluded that if we did enter the piano business, it would be through buying Steinway," Messina continues. "It makes a great product, and its brand name is recognized worldwide." Coincidentally, Kyle Kirkland plays the piano daily - all types of music. Before the Steinway purchase, he owned a Kawai piano. Subsequently, he donated it to a university's music department and now owns a Steinway. Messina does not play. He is from Boston, but did not know the Boston-based Birminghams before the sale discussions.

Kirkland and Messina approached the Birminghams about buying Steinway shortly after acquiring Selmer, but at that time Steinway was not for sale. Then in 1995 "for personal reasons" the Birminghams changed their minds. They received eleven bids which they narrowed down to four, including Kirkland Messina via Selmer as well as the family that owns the controlling interest in BMW, the German luxury car manufacturer. Although Selmer's bid of $101.5 million, a leveraged transaction financed through a bond issue, was $8 to $9 million less than the highest bid,[57] the Birminghams chose Selmer because of its long-term commitment and Kirkland Messina's accomplishments at Selmer. In the first half of 1995 they increased profits by 50 percent and sales by 11 percent over the corresponding period in 1994. Messina attributes the improvement to the replacement of some managers in manufacturing and sales, cutting production costs, and "incentivizing" senior management by allowing them to own shares in the company.

Kirkland and Messina have become the newest Steinway owners at a time when the outlook is mixed for Steinway and the piano industry as a whole. Excluding its new *Boston* line, Steinway derives about 90 percent of its revenue from grand piano sales which have plunged since 1991. Steinway's thirty-year average, 1965 to 1994, of grand piano sales was 3,015 with the peak from 1972 to 1990. Sales in 1990 were a record 3,576 but dropped markedly in 1991 to 2,988, in 1992 to 2,261 (a thirty-year low) and then rose marginally in 1993 to 2,518 and in 1994 to 2,698.[58]

Steinway attributed the 1992 decline to overall poor economic conditions, and to the 20 percent rise in 1992 of the Deutsche mark against other European currencies which adversely affected the sales of Steinway-Hamburg. But as the U.S. economy recovered, Steinway's unit sales continued below traditional levels. Its woes were typical of the U.S. piano industry. U.S. piano sales shrank from 175,142 units in 1988 to 94,793 in 1994.[59] Today's most popular instrument is the acoustic(non-electronic) guitar; 556,000 were sold in 1994[60] - close to six times the number of pianos.

The piano industry's major problem is that the piano no longer is essential for a family's home entertainment or important in a child's upbringing. Children now have less opportunity to learn music at school because such programs have been the victims of budget cuts. Hard pressed for funds, schools place music low on their list of basics for education. Also, today's generation prefers computer-equipped pianos that can record and play performances using floppy disks and the "silent" piano on which the hammers can be electronically sensed to allow listening through headphones. Furthermore, in that Steinway grands range in price from $26,400 to $75,800(U.S.), middle income people who used to buy pianos now prefer to buy a house, make a down payment on one, or purchase a car.

Nevertheless, Kirkland and Messina believe Steinway has many strengths. "We love it when people say an industry is having difficulty because they're not really looking at what is happening," Messina says,[61] referring to the tendency of people to focus on overall woes rather than individual exceptions. While Steinway's famous name is a major asset, in Kirkland Messina's view there are additional strong features. Despite the 1991-94 slump in its grand piano sales, Steinway continues to hold a 9.2 percent market share[62] in this high price/high profit segment of the U.S. piano industry, well ahead of its overall U.S. market share of around 3 percent. Moreover, individual buyers of Steinway pianos tend to be recession-proof. With incomes averaging more than $100,000 per year, they can afford expensive grand pianos. A large number of purchasers are Asian-Americans and people over forty-five years old - demographic sectors which are growing at a faster rate than the general U.S. population.[63] Over and above, Steinway does a steady business with concert halls, conservatories, universities, and music schools.

Messina says Steinway was run well, but that he and Kyle Kirkland believed it "could do better on the marketing side."[64] At the time of purchase, the firm had dealers in forty-five states, but derived 30 percent of its U.S. sales from two: New York and California. Kirkland and Messina think there are further growth opportunities in California, particularly among its affluent Asian-American community of which a high proportion buy pianos. Chicago, Houston, Miami and Philadelphia also are being targeted for greater sales.

Steinway is expanding its dealerships in Latin America and has plans for greater activity in Asia as well. Korea, China and Japan are the three largest piano markets in the world in terms of units sold. Japan is the biggest Asian market, but a mere 4.8 percent of the 99,778 pianos sold there in 1994 were imports. Only 0.5 percent were from the United States.[65]

Steinway sells an average of 200 pianos a year in Japan through Matsuo, its exclusive dealer since 1953, but recently Japan's Fair Trade Commission charged it with blocking imports of Steinway pianos through other channels. Matsuo vehemently denied the allegation and Steinway president Bruce Stevens said it was motivated by a "special agenda" of Japanese retailers whom Steinway had tried to prevent from using its trademark in advertising and sales displays because they are not its authorized dealer. Third party sales of Steinways in Japan have increased in recent years in response to the appreciation of the yen versus the U.S. dollar; Japanese retailers find it cheaper to buy in the United States or Canada rather than from Matsuo.

By contrast, Asian pianomakers have a large portion of the U.S. musicial instrument market. Yamaha Corporation of America, the top seller in 1994, had a 7.5 percent share - higher than that of all imported pianos into Japan.[66]

Also in marketing, Kirkland and Messina intend to "aggressively pursue" business in the restoration of used pianos, a thriving market previously little tapped by Steinway. "On average, a Steinway piano lasts sixty to eighty years; also, for every new one sold, four to five older ones are," Messina explains.[67] Thus, a facility has been opened at Steinway's Long Island factory for the restoration of older pianos. It faces stiff competition from local piano tuners but Messina argues "they do not all use Steinway parts and the factory can provide better quality than the local tuners." Even if Steinway owners agree, they must take into consideration the cost of shipping their piano but Messina has an answer for that, too: the cost is minuscule compared to the value of the piano which restoration would further enhance.

On the manufacturing side, complaints about the Steinway have faded, but it would seem from their actions that Kirkland and Messina believed improvements were still needed in the final stages of manufacture. They have taken steps to halve the amount of time dealers spend on tuning pianos when they receive them from an average of twenty to ten hours. Dealers must still do some work because the tuning has to be adjusted to varying temperatures and humidity across the country and because government environmental regulations regarding what lacquers can be used on the piano's case vary from state to state. Dealers also have to attach the legs to grand pianos since putting them on prior to shipment would make crating very difficult.

Kirkland and Messina will keep Selmer and Steinway separate even though both make musical instruments. "The typical Steinway owner is forty-five years old; the typical Selmer one is ten years old," Messina says.[68]

As at Selmer, Kirkland Messina has "incentivized" senior Steinway management by allowing them to own shares in the combined Selmer-Steinway company. Steinway's executives own a total of 5 percent and Selmer's, 9 percent. Kirkland and Messina keep track at their ten-person Los Angeles office through daily faxes covering such matters as the number of orders and shipments, sales to date for the year, sales targets, and budgets. They also spend a lot of time travelling to

Steinway, Selmer, their prior investments in a food, a beer, a textile, and a paper company, as well as to their most recent acquisition, a violin company.

Steinway is a survivor. When Henry Engelhard Steinway founded the company in 1853, there were twenty-five American pianomakers. Today, there are just three major domestic firms - Steinway, Baldwin, and Kimball. It is unfortunate when a beloved product, such as the Steinway piano, slips from its glorious pinnacle into controversy. It is not possible to coast along in perpetuity on a product's historical glamour, social status, and acclaim. Eventually, the public becomes disenchanted. Love of dividends dislodged the Steinway family's pride and responsibility. The onus is on Steinway's newest owners to retain the abundant affection for the Steinway piano.

# *BIBLIOGRAPHY*

<u>Archival and Library Sources</u>

White House Curator, Rex Scouten (retired)

Carnegie Hall

Libraries -   Columbia University
　　　　　　　LaGuardia Community College (archives)
　　　　　　　Library of Congress
　　　　　　　Lincoln Center Music Library
　　　　　　　New York Public Library - Main Branch
　　　　　　　Yale University School of Music (archives)
　　　　　　　Metro Music Library, Toronto

New-York Historical Society

New York Philharmonic

New York Transit Authority

NW Ayer Incorporated(archives)

The Parkwood Foundation, Oshawa, Canada

The Vanderbilt Estate, Hyde Park, N.Y.

SELECTED BIOGRAPHY

<u>Books</u>

American Historical Society. *Schlegel's German-American Families in the United States, 1916.*

*Baker's Biographical Dictionary of Musicians.* New York: Schirmer Books(Macmillan Publishers Ltd.), 1985.

Bowen, Catherine Drinker. *Anton and Nicolas Rubinstein.* New York: Random House, 1939.

Brown, Henry Collins. *From Alley Pond to Rockefeller Center.* New York: E.P. Dutton and Company, Inc., 1936.

Chapin, Schuyler. *Musical Chairs(A Life in the Arts)*. New York: G.P. Putnam's Sons, 1977.

Closson, Ernest. *History of the Piano*. London: Elck Books Limited, 1944.

Columbia University. *The Columbia Lippincott Gazeteer of the World*, 1964.

*Complete Encyclopedia of Motor Cars 1885-1968*. New York: E.P. Dutton and Company, Inc., 1968. London: George Rainbird Ltd., 1968.

*Contemporary American Biography*. New York: Atlantic Publishing and Engraving Company, 1895.

Corkhill, Thomas. *The Complete Dictionary of Wood*. New York: Stein and Day, 1980.

Cron, Theodore O. and Goldblatt, Burt. *Portrait of Carnegie Hall*. New York: The Macmillan Company, 1966.

Dent, Edward Joseph. *Ferrucio Busoni*. London: Oxford Uni- versity Press, 1933.

Dolge, Alfred. *Pianos and Their Makers*. Covina, California: Covina Publishing Company, 1911.

Drozdowski, Marian Marek. *Ignacy Jan Paderewski*. Warsaw: Interpress, 1981.

Dubal, David. *Reflections From The Keyboard (The World of the Concert Pianist.)* New York: Summit Books(A Division of Simon and Schuster, Inc.), 1984.

Forsee, Aylesa. *Artur Rubinstein: King of the Keyboard*. New York: Thomas Y. Crowell Company, 1969.

Freedland, Michael. *Jerome Kern*. New York: Stein and Day, 1981.

Graffman, Gary. *I Really Should Be Practicing*. New York: Doubleday & Company, Inc., 1981.

Grover, David S. *The Piano: Its Story from Zither to Grand*. London: Robert Hale Limited, 1976.

Hollis, Helen Rice. *The Piano(A Pictorial Account of its Ancestry and Development).* West Vancouver, British Columbia: Douglas David and Charles Limited, 1975.

Hoover, Cynthia Adams. *The Steinways and Their Piano in the Nineteenth Century.* Journal of the American Musical Instruments Society, 1981.

Horowitz, Joseph. *Conversations With Arrau.* New York: Alfred A. Knopf, 1982.

Hubbard, Elbert. *Story of the Steinways.* East Aurora, N.Y.: Roy Crofters, 1911.

Levant, Oscar. *The Unimportance of Being Oscar.* New York: G.P. Putnam's Sons, 1968.

Lochner, Louis P. *Fritz Kreisler.* New York: The Macmillan Company, 1951.

Loesser, Arthur. *Men, Women and Pianos(A Social History).* New York: Simon and Schuster, 1954.

Mach, Elyse. *Great Pianists Speak For Themselves.* New York: Dodd, Mead & Company, 1980.

Maxtone-Graham, John. *The Only Way To Cross.* New York: Collier Books(A Division of Macmillan Publishing Co., Inc.), 1972.

McCombe, Ian. *Piano Handbook.* Newton Abbot, England: David and Charles, 1980.

Mitchell, Jan. *Lüchow's German Cook Book.* Garden City, New York: Doubleday & Co., Inc., 1952.

Nevins, Allan and Commager, Henry Steele. *A Pocket History of the United States.* New York: Washington Square Press, 1960.

*New Encyclopedia of Motorcars 1885 to the Present.* New York: E.P. Dutton & Company, Inc., 1982.

*New Grove Dictionary of Music and Musicians.* London: Macmillan Publishers Ltd., 1980.

Newton, Ivor. *At The Piano: The World of an Accompanist*. London: Hamish Hamilton, 1966.

Edited by Phyllis Hartnoll. *The Oxford Companion to the Theatre.* Oxford University Press, 1983.

Peyser, Ethel. *The House That Music Built*. New York: Robert M. McBride & Co., 1936.

Plaskin, Glenn. *Horowitz - A Biography.* New York: William Morrow & Company, Inc., 1983.

Edited by Oscar James Campbell. *The Reader's Encyclopedia of Shakespeare.* New York: Thomas Y. Crowell Company, 1966.

Rubinstein, Arthur. *My Young Years* and *My Many Years.* New York: Alfred A. Knopf, 1973, 1980.

Schickel, Richard. *The World of Carnegie Hall.* New York: Julian Messner, Inc., 1960.

Scott-Moncrieff, David. *Three-Pointed Star. The Story of Mercedes-Benz.* London: Gentry Books, 1979 revision(original publication date 1955).

Singer, Aaron. *Labor-Management Relations(Steinway and Sons, 1853-1896).* Thesis, 1977.

Social Register
St. Johns, Adela Rogers. *Final Verdict.* Garden City, New York: Doubleday & Company, Inc., 1962.

Steinway & Sons, *Talking About Pianos.* Privately printed, 1982.

Steinway, Theodore E. *People and Pianos: A Century of Service to Music.* Privately printed, 1953.

Steinway, William. *Diary*(April 20, 1861 - November 8, 1896).

Unger-Hamilton, Clive. *Keyboard Instruments.* New York: John Wiley & Sons, 1981.

University of Illinois Press (edited by Frederic Cople Jaher). *The Rich, The Well Born, and The Powerful.* 1973.

Wainwright, David. *The Piano Makers.* London: Hutchinson & Co. (Publishers) Ltd., 1975.

Zamoyski, Adam. *Paderewski.* London: Collins, 1982.

Magazines and Journals

Advertising Age
The American-German Review Magazine
American Heritage
The American-Historical Society
The Atlantic Monthly
Contemporary American Biography
Symphony Magazine(American Symphony Orchestra League)
The Boston Globe
High Fidelity Magazine
Musical America
Music Trades
The New York Times
Town and Country Magazine
The Wall Street Journal
The Washington Post

Also:
Collier's, October 23, 1948.
Scientific American, December 1965.

Documents

Prospectus(August 1, 1995) of the Selmer Company, Inc.: regarding the issue of senior subordinated notes connected to its purchase of Steinway.

U.S. Court of Appeals, Second Circuit, March 3, 1994: Ruling re. A. Michael's Piano, Inc. vs. Federal Trade Commission.

U.S. District Court, Northern District of Illinois, Eastern Division: Report and Recommendation re. Hendricks Music Company vs. Steinway & Sons, April 19, 1988. (Magistrate Joan B. Gottschall)

Objections of Hendricks Music Company to Magistrate Gottschall's Report and Recommendation, April 29, 1988.

## ENDNOTES

Prelude
1. *New York Times,* May 28, 1995.
2. Ibid. International percentage calculated from various articles on piano sales.
3. Selmer Prospectus regarding its purchase of Steinway, p.4.
4. Author's interview with Dana Messina.
5. Letter to author from Gershwin's sister, Frances Godowsky.
6. Author's interview with Sam DeStefano, director of entertainment at Playboy Clubs International at the time described.
7. *New York Times*, June 11, 1986.

Chapter 1
1. Seesen City archives.
2. 1935 letter from Anna Hartmann (Sudevode) Schoch to Steinway & Sons about Henry Engelhard Steinway written in response to a 10 January 1935 request from the company. Her brother, Friedrich Schoch, had been a lacquer varnisher at Steinway & Sons. Seesen City archives.
3. Author's interview with John Steinway.
4. *The Times(London),* December 19, 1850.
5. New-York Historical Society. Also: Aaron Singer, *Labor-Management Relations at Steinway & Sons,* p. 5-6.
6. Ibid.
7. Undated letter, but estimated to have been written in the late 1850s. Steinway Collection, La Guardia Community College.
8. *Music Trades,* October 1953, p. 24.
9. Author's interview with Henry Steinway.
10. Author's interview with John Steinway.
11. *Music Trades,* October 1953, p. 28.
12. Singer, p. 29.
13. Ibid.
14. *Music Trades,* October 1953, p. 25.
15. Ibid., p. 27.
16. Author's interview with Jack Pfeiffer.
17. Ibid.
18. *New York Times,* March 15, 1865.
19. Author's interview with John Steinway.
20. Piano production process based on author's visit to factory.

21. *Music Trades,* October 1953, p. 33.
22. Ibid.
23. Ibid.
24. Ibid., p. 28.
25. *New York Times,* February 8, 1871.
26. Author's interview with John Steinway.
27. *Music Trades,* October 1953, p. 28.

Chapter 2
1. *New York Times,* November 28, 1897.
2. Ibid.
3. William Steinway's *Diary,* Sept. 9, 1878; Oct. 30, 1879; April 1, 1880.
4. *New York Times,* June 17, 1894
5. Oscar Levant, *The Unimportance of Being Oscar,* p. 162.
6. Singer, p. 74.
7. Notice headed *To Manufacturers and Those Seeking Healthful Homes,* issued August 1887 by Steinway & Sons(no exact date given). Steinway Collection, La Guardia Community College.
8. *New York Times,* July 12, 1896.
9. *Diary,* May 27, 1872.
10. Ibid., May 29, 1872.
11. Ibid.
12. Singer, p. 69.
13. Ibid.
14. *Diary,* June 10, 1872.
15. Jan Mitchell, *Lüchow's German Cook Book,* p. 26-27. (The first chapter of the book gives the history of Lüchow's.)
16. *Diary,* December 8, 1867.
17. Catherine Drinker Bowen, *Anton and Nicolas Rubinstein,* p. 226-7.
18. Ibid, p. 239.
19. Arthur Loesser, *Men, Women and Pianos,* p. 515.
20. Bowen, p. 236.
21. Ibid.
22. Ibid.
23. Ibid.
24. Ibid.
25. Loesser, p. 531.
26. Steinway Collection, La Guardia Community College.
27. Loesser, p. 532.

28. Ibid., p. 537.
29. Ibid., p. 535-6.
30. *Diary,* April 23, 1861.
31. Ibid., entries throughout 1861 and 1862.
32. Ibid., Jan. 23, 1862; Apr. 4, 1863.
33. Ibid., Sept. 15, 1875. (*Diary* gives the address only.) The Steinway Collection at La Guardia Community College gives 107 East Fourteenth as a Steinway Hall wareroom address.
34. Ibid., Oct. 12, 1869.
35. Ibid., Dec. 31, 1875.
36. Ibid., Aug. 20, 1876.
37. Ibid., May 20, 1876.
38. *New York Times,* August 18, 1878.
39. *Diary,* Sept. 1876. (Various entries)
40. Ibid., March 10, 1877.
41. Ibid., March 24, 1877.
42. Ibid., March 4, April 15, 1877.
43. Ibid., March 29, 1879.
44. Ibid., Sept. 20, 1879.
45. Ibid., Jan. 12, 1881.
46. *New York Times,* Dec. 11, 1896.

Chapter 3
1. *Diary,* Aug. 11, 1880.
2. Ibid., Dec. 31, 1880.
3. Ibid., Nov. 1, 1880.
4. Author's interview with Ramon Parada.
5. Ibid.
6. Singer, p. 144.
7. Ibid., p. 147.
8. *Diary,* Nov. 15, 1878.
9. Singer, p. 154.
10. Ibid.
11. Ibid., p. 176.
12. *New York Sun,* May 11, 1886.
13. *Diary,* Oct. 23, 1890.
14. *New York Times,* July 12, 1896.
15. Ibid., Jan. 21, 1927.
16. Ibid.
17. *Music Trades,* June 1987, p. 115.

18. Ibid., p. 112.
19. Ibid., p. 115.
20. Author's interview with Frank Mazurco.
21. Ibid.
22. *Music Trades,* August 1987, p. 52.
23. Steinway Collection, La Guardia Community College.
24. Letter to author from Chief Curator, Vanderbilt Mansion (U.S. National Park Service).
25. Author's interview with John Steinway.
26. Louis P. Lochner, *Fritz Kreisler,* p. 27.
27. Ibid., p. 29.
28. David Scott-Moncrieff, *Three-Pointed Star: The Story of Mercedes-Benz,* p. 44.
29. *New York Times,* March 27, 1889.
30. Edward Joseph Dent, *Ferrucio Busoni,* p. 75.
31. *Diary,* Dec. 19, 1891.
32. *New York Times,* June 28, 1939.
33. Ibid., July 11, 1939.
34. Richard Schickel, *The World of Carnegie Hall,* p. 31.
35. Ibid., p. 32.
36. Ibid.
37. Ibid.
38. Ethel Peyser, *The House That Music Built,* p. 54.
39. Loesser, p. 534.
40. Ibid.
41. *Music Trades,* Jan. 22, 1966, p. 97.
42. Schickel, p. 58.
43. Adam Zamoyski, *Paderewski,* p. 65.
44. *New York Times,* Nov. 18, 1891.
45. Schickel, p. 60.
46. *New York Times,* Nov. 20, 1891.
47. Zamoyski, p. 70.
48. American Historical Society, *German-American Families in the United States,* 1916, Vol. I, p. 70.
49. *Diary,* Dec. 26, 1891.
50. David Rogoff, *The Steinway Tunnels,* Electric Railroaders Association, April 1960, p. 3.
51. Ibid., p. 4.
52. *Diary,* Jan. 15, 1893.
53. Ibid., March 1, 1893.
54. Ibid., March 5, 1893.

55. Seesen City archives.
56. *The Great Chicago Piano War,* American Heritage, Oct. 1970, p. 18.
57. Ibid., p. 19.
58. Ibid.
59. Ibid., p. 20.
60. *Diary,* May 2, 1893.
61. *New York Times,* Nov. 24, 1895.
62. Ibid.
63. Ibid.
64. Ibid.
65. Ibid., Oct. 16, 1896.
66. Ibid.
67. Ibid.
68. Ibid., Dec. 1, 1896.
69. Ibid., Nov. 22, 1896.
70. Ibid., Dec. 11, 1896.
71. Ibid., Dec. 1, 1896.
72. The descriptions of the funeral service and interment are from *The New York Times* of Dec. 3, 1896.

Chapter 4
1. *New York Times,* April 11, 1897.
2. Author's interview with Barbara Hamlin, Charles's granddaughter.
3. *New York Times,* April 11, 1897.
4. Ibid.
5. Library of Congress; Music Division, Old Correspondence, L.C. Engel Collection. Junge to Engel, Aug. 24, 1925.
6. Adela Rogers St. Johns, *Final Verdict,* p. 136.
7. Gustav Tetzloff, head technician, Steinway retail department, June 7, 1978 interview for Steinway Project, School of Music's Oral History - American Music, Yale University.
8. Ibid.
9. *Advertising Age,* Aug. 25, 1969, p. 255.
10. Author's interview with Barbara Hamlin.
11. Barbara Hamlin: Steinway Project - Yale University; Oct. 4, 1978 interview.
12. *New York Times,* Nov. 26, 1919.
13. Barbara Hamlin: Steinway Project - Yale University.
14. Ibid.

15. Author's interview with Barbara Hamlin.
16. Ibid.
17. Barbara Hamlin: Steinway Project - Yale University.
18. Author's interview with Sally Steinway (Charles Frederick's daughter-in-law).
19. *Fortune,* Dec. 1934.
20. *New York Times,* May 9, 1978.
21. The origin of the *Instrument of the Immortals* ad is from NW Ayer archives made available to the author.
22. Author's interview with John Birmingham.
23. *New York Times,* Oct. 28, 1925.
24. Ibid., Feb. 28, 1929.
25. *Music Trades,* Jan. 22, 1966.
26. Author's interview with Winston Fitzgerald.
27. Ibid.
28. Author's interview with Sally Steinway.
29. Author's interview with Eleanor Lodge.
30. Author's interview with Henry Steinway.
31. Author's interview with Winston Fitzgerald.
32. Author's interview with Henry Ziegler.
33. Ibid.
34. *New York Times,* Feb. 28, 1957.
35. Letter to author from Greer Garson.
36. Author's interview with Richard Probst.
37. Author's interview with Jack Romann.
38. The description of the Basement is from the author's visit to it.
39. Author's interview with Frederick(Fritz) Steinway.
40. Author's interview with Winston Fitzgerald.

Chapter 5
1. Author's interview with Shirley Bernuth (Maud's daughter).
2. Ibid.
3. Ibid.
4. Ibid.
5. Ibid.
6. Ibid.
7. Alice Jordan(secretary at Steinway for many years), Steinway Project - Yale University, Jan. 28, 1979 interview.
8. Author's interview with Winston Fitzgerald.
9. John Maxtone Graham, *The Only Way To Cross, p. 398-9.*

10. *New York Times,* May 7, 1935.
11. Author's interview with Betty Chapin(Theodore Steinway's daughter).
12. *Music Trades,* Jan. 22, 1966.
13. Author's interview with Richard Gigax.
14. Author's interview with John Steinway.
15. Author's interview with Winston Fitzgerald.
16. *New York Times,* April 22, 1958.
17. Author's interview with Winston Fitzgerald.
18. Alice Jordan, Steinway Project - Yale University.
19. Steinway Collection, La Guardia Community College.
20. Arthur(Artur) Rubinstein, *My Many Years,* p. 513.
21. Ibid., p. 495.
22. Author's interview with Robert Glazebrook.
23. Ibid.
24. Ibid.
25. Ibid.
26. Author's interview with Winston Fitzgerald.
27. Author's interview with Fritz Steinway.
28. Michael Freedland, *Jerome Kern,* p. 131-4.
29. Author's interview with Fritz Steinway.
30. Author's interview with Byron Janis.
31. *Music Trades.* May 1987.
32. *Sensitivity in the New Steinway,* (undated booklet printed by Steinway, probably in the 1930s), Steinway Collection, La Guardia Community College.
33. Author's interview with Jack Pfeiffer.
34. Author's interview with Peter Nero.
35. Author's interview with Jack Romann.
36. Ibid.
37. Ibid.
38. Letter to author from André Previn.
39. Author's interview with Vladimir Ashkenazy.
40. Author's interview with Roger Clemens.
41. Author's interview with Margery Kittredge (Frederick Vietor's daughter)
42. Author's interview with Henry Steinway Ziegler.
43. Ibid.
44. Author's interview with Eleanor Lodge.
45. Author's interview with Henry Steinway Ziegler.
46. Author's interview with Eleanor Lodge.

47. Ibid.
48. Letter to author from archivist, Fordham University Library.
49. Author's interview with Eleanor Lodge.
50. *Music Trades,* Jan. 22, 1966.
51. Parkwood Foundation (McLaughlin's estate was called Parkwood.) Estimate of current value from Toronto, Canada piano dealer Paul Hahn.
52. Author's interview with Max Matthias. (Hamburg)
53. *Music Trades,* Jan. 22, 1966.
54. Ibid.
55. Author's interview with Jack Romann.
56. Author's interview with Paul Murphy, Jr.
57. Author's interview with Rex Scouten.

Chapter 6
1. *Newsday,* May 17, 1979.
2. Steinway Collection, La Guardia Community College.
3. Ivor Newton, *At The Piano,* p. 229-30.
4. NW Ayer archives, Feb. 21, 1951 story.
5. Author's interview with Max Matthias (Hamburg).
6. Author's interview with R. Allen, a longtime employee from before World War II at Steinway-London.
7. Ibid.
8. Ibid.
9. Author's interview with Max Matthias.
10. Ibid.
11. All of Uncle Billie's jokes are from *Steinway News,* Autumn 1960. *Steinway News* was a company newsletter and the entire issue was a tribute to him following his death on Sept. 23, 1960.
12. Author's interview with Leonard Pennario.
13. Author's interview with Ted Kostakis.
14. Author's interview with Betty Chapin.
15. Author's interview with Ruth Loud.
16. Author's interview with Betty Chapin.
17. Ibid.
18. Theodore O. Cron and Burt Goldblatt, *Portrait of Carnegie Hall,* p. 133-4.
19. Author's interview with Betty Chapin.
20. Ibid.
21. Author's interview with Rosalyn Tureck.
22. Author's interview with Betty Chapin.

23. Ibid.
24. Ibid.
25. Author's interview with Fritz Steinway.
26. Author's interview with Betty Chapin.
27. Author's interview with Harry Steinway.
28. Author's interview with Theodore Chapin.
29. Author's interview with Schuyler Chapin.
30. Author's interview with Lydia Cochrane.
31. Author's interview with Betty Chapin.
32. Death certificate, recorded by town clerk in Plymouth, Massachusetts.
33. Author's interview with Gary Graffman.
34. *New York Times,* Oct. 20, 1953.
35. Fritz was in Syracuse Nov. 18-19, 1953. His letter was written Nov. 30, 1953.
36. Fritz was in Spokane Nov. 24, 1953 and wrote his letter Dec. 2, 1953.
37. Author's interview with John Ziegler.
38. Fritz Steinway's Dec. 2, 1953 letter to his father.
39. The letter was written in 1956 but the copy shown the author by Haruki Matsuo, Hiroshi Matsuo's son, only shows the text and not the exact date.
40. Author's interview with Haruki Matsuo.
41. Author's interview with Betty Chapin.
42. For example, Alice Jordan joined Steinway as a secretary in 1948, nine years before Theodore Steinway died; Steinway Project - Yale University.
43. This quote and the following material regarding "Teed" Steinway are from the author's interview with Josephine Steinway.


Chapter 7
1. Author's interview with Henry Steinway.
2. Author's interview with Harry Steinway (Henry's son).
3. Author's interview with Henry Steinway.
4. Ibid.
5. Author's interview with David Rubin.
6. Author's interview with Henry Ziegler.
7. Author's interview with Harry Beall.
8. Author's interview with Jack Pfeiffer.
9. *New York Times,* Dec. 7, 1960.
10 Author's interview with Robert Glazebrook. (London)

11. Author's interview with Vern Edquist.
12. Author's interview with Jack Pfeiffer.
13. *New Yorker,* May 9, 1953.
14. Author's interview with Fritz Steinway.
15. Author's interview with Harry Beall.
16. Ibid.
17. Author's interview with Sally Steinway.
18. Author's interview with Gary Graffman.
19. Author's interview with Franz Mohr.
20. Ibid.
21. Author's interview with Stewart Warkow.
22. Ibid.
23. Ibid
24. Author's interview with John Browning.
25. Author's interview with Peter Nero.
26. *New York Times*, Sept. 21, 1972.
27. Ibid., Sept. 22, 1972.
28. Ibid.
29. Author's interview with Gary Graffman.
30. Author's interview with William Mattlin.
31. Author's interview with Byron Janis.
32. Author's interview with Richard Harrison.
33. Author's interview with John Steinway.
34. Author's interview with Richard Lord.
35. *Music Trades,* October 1973.
36. Author's interview with Knut-Grotrian Steinweg.
37. Ibid.
38. Author's interview with Byron Janis.
39. Steinway Project - Yale University, May 25, 1978 interview.
40. Author's interview with John Steinway.
41. The material in this paragraph comes from Harry Steinway.

Chapter 8
1. Author's interview with Robert Campbell.
2. Author's interview with Henry Ziegler.
3. Author's interview with Robert Campbell.
4. Ibid.
5. Author's interview with Henry Steinway.
6. Ibid.
7. Ibid.

8. Ibid.
9. Author's interview with Henry Ziegler.
10. Author's interview with John Phillips
11. Author's interview with Henry Steinway.
12. Ibid.
13. Author's interview with John Ziegler.
14. Author's interview with Charles Wadsworth.
15. Author's interview with Henry Ziegler.
16. Author's interview with Henry Steinway.
17. Ibid.
18. Ibid.
19. Author's interview with Lydia Cochrane.
20. Ibid.
21. Author's interview with Theodore Chapin.
22. Author's interview with Schuyler and Theodore Chapin.
23. Author's interview with Betty Chapin.
24. Author's interview with Robert Campbell.
25. Author's interview with Henry Steinway.
26. Author's interview with Ed Hendricks.
27. Author's interview with Robert Bull.
28. Author's interview with Robert Glazebrook.
29. Author's interview with Peter Goodrich.
30. Author's interview with Leonard Pennario.
31. This quote and those in the following two paragraphs are from the author's interview with Henry Steinway.
32. Author's interview with Robert Campbell.
33. Author's interview with Robert Bull.
34. Ibid.
35. Ibid.
36. Ibid.
37. Author's interview with Ron Davis.
38. Author's interview with Manny Monti.
39. Ibid.
40. Author's interview with Robert Bull.
41. Author's interview with Ed Hendricks.
42. Ibid.
43. Author's interview with Littlepaige Wemple.
44. Ibid.
45. Author's interview with Robert Bull.
46. Ibid.
47. Author's interview with Harry Steinway.

48. Author's interview with Manny Monti.
49. Author's interview with Robert Bull.
50. Ibid.
51. Author's interview with Harry Steinway.
52. Ibid.
53. Author's interview with Peter Perez.
54. Author's interview with John Phillips.
55. Author's interview with Robert Bull.
56. Author's interview with John Phillips.
57. Author's interview with Peter Perez.
58. Author's interview with Robert Bull.
59. Author's interview with Catherine Bielefeldt.
60. Author's interview with Rosalyn Tureck.
61. Author's interview with Robert Glazebrook.
62. Author's interview with Peter Perez.
63. Ibid.
64. Ibid.
65. Author's interview with Harry Steinway.
66. Ibid.
67. Author's interview with Richard Gigax.
68. Ibid.
69. Author's interview with Harry Steinway.
70. Author's interview with Catherine Bielefeldt.
71. Author's interview with Ed Hendricks.
72. The description of Peter Perez's dismissal is based on the author's interview with him.
73. Author's interview with Richard Gigax.
74. Author's interview with Lloyd Meyer.
75. Author's interview with Ed Hendricks.
76. Author's interview with Henry Steinway.
77. Author's interview with Robert Glazebrook.
78. Ibid.
79. Author's interview with Max Matthias.
80. Author's interview with Lloyd Meyer.
81. Author's interview with Robert Lins.
82. Author's interview with Lloyd Meyer.
83. Author's interview with Richard Probst.
84. Author's interview with Robert Glazebrook.

Chapter 9
1. Author's interview with Harry Steinway.
2. Author's interview with Eric Schwartz.
3. Ibid.
4. Author's interview with Paul Murphy, Jr.
5. Author's interview with Eric Schwartz.
6. Ibid.
7. Author's interview with John Birmingham.
8. Ibid.
9. Ibid.
10. Ibid.
11. Author's interview with Robert Glazebrook.
12. Author's interview with Bruce Stevens.
13. Author's interview with John Birmingham.
14. Author's interview with Robert Birmingham.
15. Author's interview with Bruce Stevens.
16. Ibid.
17. Ibid.
18. Ibid.
19. Author's interview with Joseph Pramberger.
20. Author's interview with Daniel Koenig.
21. Ibid.
22. Ibid.
23. Ibid.
24. The details of the A. Michael's Piano-Steinway disagreement and the cracked soundboard allegations are priimarily from the Mar. 3, 1994 opinion of the United States Court of Appeals, Second Circuit, made available to the author by the Federal Trade Commission's Boston regional office. In addition, the author interviewed J. Michael Yeager.
25. Author's interview with Dana Messina.
26. *Music Trades*, March 1995, p. 184.
27. Author's interview with Robert Glazebrook.
28. Author's interview with Max Matthias.
29. Author's interview with Leonard Pennario.
30. Author's interview with Franz Mohr.
31. Author's interview with Byron Janis.
32. Author's interview with Peter Nero.
33. Author's interview with Robert Glazebrook.
34. Author's interview with Paul Murphy, Jr.
35. Author's interview with Peter Nero.
36. Author's interview with Bella Davidovich.

37. *Music Trades*, Mar. 1995, p. 186.
38. Ibid., Nov. 1994, Inside front cover.
39. United States District Court, Northeastern District of Illinois, Eastern Division: Hendricks Music Company v. Steinway & Sons. Report and Recommendation, April 19, 1988.
40. Ibid.
41. Ibid.
42. Author's interview with Ed Hendricks.
43. Ibid.
44. United States District Court, Northeastern District of Illinois, Eastern Division: Hendricks Music Company v. Steinway & Sons. Report and Recommendation, April 19, 1988.
45. Author's interview with Vladimir Ashkenazy.
46. Author's interview with Bella Davidovich.
47. Author's interview with John Browning.
48. Author's interview with Byron Janis.
49. Author's interview with Peter Nero.
50. Author's interview with John and Robert Birmingham.
51. Selmer Prospectus, p. 15; *Music Trades*, April 1995.
52. *Music Trades*, April 1995.
53. Author's interview with Dana Messina.
54. Selmer Prospectus, p. 4.
55. Author's interview with Dana Messina.
56. Ibid.
57. Ibid.
58. Selmer Prospectus, p. 33-34, 39.
59. *Music Trades*, April 1995.
60. *New York Times*, May 28, 1995.
61. Author's interview with Dana Messina.
62. Selmer Prospectus, p. 41.
63. Ibid., p. 5.
64. Author's interview with Dana Messina.
65. *Music Trades*, Aug. 1995, p. 40.
66. Ibid., April 1995.
67. Author's interview with Dana Messina.
68. Ibid.

# INDEX

**A**
A. Michael's piano, 203, 205
Aberdeen, Countess of, 207
Abram, Jacques, 129
Aeolian American Corporation, 78, 188
Aeolian Company, 78
Alexandra, Princess, 207
Ali, Muhammad, 90
Alma-Tadema, Sir Lawrence, 67
Amateur Comedy Club (of Manhattan), 125, 147, 150, 153
American Piano Company, Inc., 78
American Steel & Wire, 97
Anderson, Marian, 125
Andrews, Julie, 151
Arrau, Claudio, 147, 166, 207
Ashkenazy, Vladimir, 92, 108, 216
Ayer, NW, inc., 80-81, 84-85, 120, 136, 148-149

**B**
Babcock, Alpheus, 26, 28
Babcock, Elisha, 168
Backe, John, 166
Bacon & Raven, 18, 20
Baldwin Piano & Organ Company, 54, 56, 91, 100, 104, 107-108, 115-117, 136, 142-143, 146-148, 150, 184-185, 192, 201, 206, 213, 216-218, 222
Baldwin, Dwight Hamilton, 54-56, 63
Ballon, Ellen, 129
Balogh, Erno, 129
Barenboim, Daniel, 92
Barrymore, Ethel, 129

Bartok, Bela, 107, 151
"Basement, The". *See* Steinway Hall
Basie, Count, 125
Batchelor, Barbara, 83
Batchelor, Bronson, 82-83
Beall, Henry (Harry), 138
Bechstein Piano, 104, 131, 147, 184
Beecham, Sir Thomas, 112
Belmont, August Jr., 69
Berlin, Irving, 81
Berlioz, Hector, 18, 31, 85
Bernstein, Leonard, 107, 148
Bielefeldt, Catherine, 175-176, 179
Bilhuber, Paul, 106
Birmingham, John (Jack), x-xii, 86, 165, 187, 189, 192-202, 204-207, 109-210, 215-219
Birmingham, Mark, 195
Birmingham, Robert, x-xii, 165, 187, 189, 192-202, 204-207, 209-210, 215-219
Blüthner Piano, 104-105
Bolet, Jorge, 107-108, 147
Borge, Victor, 108
Bösendorfer Piano, 27, 100, 104, 108, 144-145, 185, 216
*Boston* Piano, xii, 197, 206-207, 219
Boston Symphony, 115
Brailowsky, Alexander, 129
Brendel, Alfred, 151
British Broadcasting Corporation (BBC), 121, 207
Britten, Benjamin, 107
Broadwood Piano, 120
Browning, John, 92, 144, 216

Brubeck, Dave, 107, 147-148
Brunei, Sultan of, 207
Bull, Robert, 165-166, 168-177, 179-182, 185, 188, 215
Busoni, Ferrucio, 61

C

Camilleri Pianoworks Ltd., 188
Campbell, Robert, 155-158, 160, 164, 168-170, 172, 174-175, 180
Carnegie Hall, xiv, 63-64, 66, 86, 95, 109, 125, 128, 143-144, 202, 210-211
Carter, Rosalyn, 116
Casadesus, Gaby, 129
Casadesus, Robert, 129
Cassebeer, Julia. *See* Steinway, Julia Cassebeer
Cassebeer, Theodore, 137
Cavallaro, Carmen, 92
CBS. *See* Columbia Broadcasting System
CBS/Columbia Group, 158, 165, 174
CBS Musical Instruments, 155-156, 158, 175, 180
Chambers, Charles, 85
Chapln, Elizabeth (Betty) Steinway, 86, 98, 124-128, 132 137, 161-162
Chapin, Henry (Hank), 162
Chapin, Samuel, 162-164, 169
Chapin, Schuyler, 124, 127, 164, 199
Chapin, Thoedore Steinway, 127, 162-164, 169
Chasins, Abram, 129
Cherkassky, Shura, 212
Chesseri, Roy, 206
Chicago Musical Instruments, 168, 181
Chicago Symphony Orchestra, 70, 183
Chickering piano, 188

Chickering & Sons, 22, 42-43, 78
Chickering, Frank, 31, 63, 75
Chickering, George, 75
Chickering Hall, 63-64
Chopin, Frederic, 18, 85, 92, 109
Cincinnati Orchestra, 55
Citicorp, 188
Clemens, Roger, 108
Cleveland, Pres. Grover, 60
Cliburn, Van, 92, 138, 141, 148, 213
Clinton, Pres. Bill, x
Cochrane, Eric, 128
Cochrane, Lydia Steinway, 124, 126-128, 161-162
Columbia Broadcasting System, x-xi, 89, 110-111, 135, 147, 151-152, 155-161, 165-170, 174, 178-180, 182-185, 187-189, 191-193, 196, 199, 204
Columbian Exposition, 68-71
Conn Organ Corporation, 156-157, 175
Cooper, Peter, 21
Cosmopolitan Club, 125, 164
Cristofori, Bartolommeo, 16, 25, 28
Curzon, Clifford, 92, 104, 207

D

Dachauer, Louis, 46, 66
Dachauer, Maria, 46
Daewoo Piano, 185
Daimler, Gottlieb, 60
d'Albert Eugène, 35
Damrosch, Walter, 63
Davidovich, Bella, 213, 216
Davis, Lydia, 135
Davis, Ron, 167, 169-170, 177
Davis, Ruth Gardner. *See* Steinway, Ruth
Decker & Sons, 43
de Majewski, Roman, 98-100, 106, 114, 128, 152, 178
Dickens, Charles, 40

Doheny, Edward, 58
Domingo, Placido, 92
Dorfman, Ania, 129
Duchin, Eddie, 107
Duchin, Peter, 107
Dunn, Harvey, 85

**E**
Eddy, Nelson, 120
Edison, Thomas, 25, 57, 78
Edquist, Vern, 140
Ehret, George, 53-54
Ehrlich, Theodore, 78, 113
Einstein, Albert, 92
Eisenhower, Mamie, 116, 130
Electro Music Company, 157, 191
Elizabeth, Queen Mother, 121
Elphinstone, Lord, 121
Engel, Carl 79
Equitable Life Assurance, 218
Erard Pianos, 104
Eschenbach, Christoph, 141
Eshelby, John, 121

**F**
Fender Guitar, 157-158, 163, 169
Ferrante and Teicher, 107
Fitzgerald, Winston, 88, 92, 102, 137
Flagstad, Kirsten, 107
Foster, Sydney, 129
Francis, Kay, 84
Frick, Henry, 58
Friedberg, Carl, 129
Furlong, John, 153

**G**
Ganz, Rudolf, 129, 143
Garson, Greer, 90-91
Gemeinhardt Flute, 157, 191, 193, 197
Gershwin, George, xiii, 108
Getty, Gordon, 108
Getty, J. Paul, 108
Gibbs, William Francis, 97
Gieseking, Walter, 107

Gigax, Richard (Dick), 99, 142, 177-178, 181
Gilels, Emil, 102
Gillespie, Dizzy, 91
Glazebrook, Michael, 184, 207
Glazebrook, Robert, 104, 166, 176, 182-184, 189, 196, 207-208
Goodrich, Peter, 199
Gorodnitski, Sascha, 129
Gould, Glenn, 92, 108, 139-140
Gould, Jay, 58
Graffman, Gary, 92, 128-129, 141-142
Grainger, Percy, 92
"Great Chicago Piano War", 68, 70-71
Green-Wood Cemetery, 32, 76
Greer, Bernard (Bud), 188-189
Greiner, Alexander (Sascha), 98, 101-106, 137, 140, 211
Greiner, Alexandra, 102
Grotrian, Knut, 24, 151-152
Grotrian piano, 150-152
Grotrian Steinweg: history of, 24, 136, 150; lawsuit against Steinway & Sons, 150-152
Gulbransen Organs, 157, 180, 182
Gunther, Walter, 122-123, 131, 136, 159

**H**
Hambledon, Duchess of, 207
Hambro, Leonard, 129
Hamburg Operations of Steinway. *See* Steinway-Hamburg
Hammond Organ Company, 191
Harewood, Earl of, 207
Harrison, Richard, 108, 147-148
Hart, Judge William, 215
Heath, Edward, 207
Heifetz, Jascha, 27, 89
Henderson, Skitch, 129
Hendricks, Ed, 164-165, 171, 179, 181, 215-216

Hendricks Music Company, 164, 214
Herbert, Bictor, 77
Hess Dame Myra, xi, 90, 92, 102, 104, 121, 126, 128
Hewitt, Mayor Abram, 68, 76
Hofmann, Josef, xi, 80, 84, 86-87, 89, 92, 98, 102, 104, 106, 116, 126
Hoffman, Dustin, 90
Hoffman, Julius, 76
Hollander, Lorin, 147
Horowitz, Sonia, 27
Horowitz, Vladimir, xi, 27, 89, 92, 101, 143, 176, 211
Horowitz, Wanda, 27, 176
Hupfer, Walter, 140
Hupfer, William, 139-140, 143
Humby, Betty, 112
Hurok, Sol, 141

**I**

Ingalls, Quinn & Johnson, 209-210
Integrated Resources, 217-218
Istomin, Eugene, 143
Iturbe, José, 107

**J**

Janis, Byron, 92, 105, 147, 153, 211-212, 216
Jenkins, William, 215
John Elton, 92
John Hancock Mutual Life Insurance, 218
Jonas, Maryla, 92
Judson, Arghur, 141
Judson O'Neil Beall & Steinway (JOBS), 141
Juilliard School of Music, 102, 148
Junge, Henry, 78-79

**K**

Kawai, Koichi, 105-106
Kawai Musical Instrument manufacturing Company, xii, 105, 131-132, 179, 206, 218
Kawai piano, 100, 218
Kawakami, Genichi, 132
Keaton, Diane, 90
Keane, Constance, 129
Kennedy, Pres. John F., 50, 116, 130
Kern, Jerome, 104-105
Kerr, Muriel, 129
Kimball International, 27, 216, 222
Kimball, W.W., 70
Kirkland, Kyle, x, 206, 217-218, 220-221
Kirkland, Messina, 219-221
Kitteredge, Margery Vitor, 109
Kittredge, Susan Cooke, 109
Knabe, William & Co., 64, 78, 104
Knabe piano, 188
Koenig, Daniel, 199-202, 204, 206
Kluge GmbH, 184-185
Kostakis, Ted, 123-124
Koussevitsky, Serge, 115, 147
Kreisler, Fritz, 59-60

**L**

Landowska, Wanda, 140
Lauck, Gerald, 85
Laucht, 19
Lefebvre, Edward, 82-83
Levant, Oscar, 91-92
Lhévinne, Josef, 92
Lhévinne, Rosina, 143
Liberace, 107
Lins, Robert, 185
List, Eugene, 100, 129
Liszt, Franz, xi, 18, 26, 31, 41, 43, 85
Lodge, Eleanor Ziegler, 88-89, 110-111, 156
Lofing, Dan, 205
London Operations of Steinway. *See* Steinway-London

Lord, Geller, Federico, Einstein, Inc., 149-150, 209
Lord, Richard, 149
Loud, Ruth, 124
Lovejoy, Thomas, 139
Lowrey Pianos and Organs Company, 18
Lüchow, August, 40
Lüchow, Restaurant, 40, 99
Lympany, Moura, 129
Lyon & Healy Harps, 104, 157, 179, 191, 193, 197, 214,-215

**M**
McKinley, Pres. William, 75
McLaren, John, 180-181, 188
McLaughlin, R.S., 113
McLean, Evalyn Walsh, 79
Macdonald, Jeanette, 107
Macdowell, Edward, 89, 129
Majewski. *See* de Majewski, Roman
Maczijewski, Siegfried, 159, 184
Mahler, Gustav, 80
Manhattan Life Insurance Company, 138-139
Manning, Selvage & Lee, 209
Mapleson, James Henry, 43
Margaret, Princess, 207
Marquand, Henry G., 57
Mason & Hamlin, 56, 78, 104, 188
Mason & Hamlin piano, 188
Masselos, William, 129
Matsuo, Haruki, 131, 220-221
Matsuo Musical Instruments, 131, 221
Matthias, Max, 183-185, 187, 207-208
Mattlin-Hyde, 146
Mattlin, William, 146
Maybach, William, 60
Mazurko, Frank, 55, 204
Mead, Brian, 149
Mertens, Marie. *See* Steinway, Marie Mertens

Messerschmitt, Joseph, 105
Messina, Dana, x-xi, 206, 217-218, 220-221
Meyer, Lloyd, 146, 165, 178, 181-189, 197
Miller, Mitch, 90
Mills, Sebastian, Bach, 43
Mitropoulos, Dimitri, 129
Mohr, Franz, 143, 211
Monti, Manny, 170
Morton, Pearl, 79
Moseley, Carlos, 135
Muni, Paul, 27
Murphy, Paul Jr., 115, 144, 153, 193, 204

**N**
National Association of Music Manufacturers, 213
Nero, Peter, 107, 144, 212-213
Newman, Paul, 90
Newton, Ivor, 120
New York Philharmonic Orchestra, 47, 63, 70, 88-89, 135, 160, 213
New York Pianomakers' Society, 23
Nixon, Pres. Richard, 116-117
Norlin Corporation, 168
North American Phillips Company, 217
North Beach. *See* under Steinway, William
Northwest Organ, 181
Novaës, Guiomar, 92, 129
Nunns, Robert, 19
Nunns, William, 19, 21
Nunns, William & Company, 19, 21

**O**
Ohlsson, Garrick, 144-145
Ono, Yoko, 191
Ormandy, Eugene, 96-97

## P

Paderewski, Ignacy, xi, xiv, 64-68, 70-71, 78, 81, 86, 98, 102, 104, 151
Paige, Audrey, 139
Paige, Maud Emily Louise Steinway, 49, 69, 94-96, 139
Paige, Raymond, 95, 139
Paley, William, 89, 157, 165-166, 169, 172, 174, 179, 181, 189
Pape, Henri, 28
Parada, Ramon, 50
Pavarotti, Lucien, 107
Pennario, Leonard, 123, 167, 211
Perez, Carroll, 176, 181
Perez, Peter, 165, 173-180, 182, 185-186, 188
Peterson, Oscar, 108
Pfeiffer, Jack, 27, 107, 138
Pfingst, George Bartow, 83
Philbin, Robert, 188
Phillips, John, 158, 172, 174, 188
Piano
    action, 25-26, 106, 145-146, 152, 185
    accelerated action, 110
    art case decoration. See Steinway & Sons
    construction of, xii, 25-32, 152
    Hamburg vs. New York Steinway piano. See Steinway & Sons
    pitch, 96
    quality of. See Steinway & Sons
    regulation of, 50-51
    rim, 27, 29-31, 152, 201-202
    soundboard, 25-26, 29, 106, 110, 152, 202-206
    string layout, 25-26, 28, 184
    Teflon dispute. See Steinway & Sons
Pinza, Ezio, 107
Pirson Piano Co., 21
Playboy Clubs, xiii
Pleyel Piano, 104
Pollini Maurizio, 183
Pons, Lily, 107
Ponselle, Rosa, 107
Poynter, Sir Edward, 57
Pramberger, Joseph, 177, 199-200
Pratt Read Corporation, 184-185
Pressler, Menahem, 129
Previn, Amdré, 107-108
Price, Leontyne, 141
Probst, Richard, 91, 144, 186-187, 199
Pullman, George, 37
Rachmaninoff, Sergei, xi, 18, 86, 89, 92, 104, 108, 126, 140
Ranft, Elizabeth. See Steinway, Elizabeth (Ellie)
Ranft, Richard, 49
Reagan, Pres. Ronald, 51
Reiner, Fritz, 102
Reisenberg, Nadia, 129
Renner, Louis, 159
Renner, Louis GmbH, 159-160, 185
Robert Williams, Inc., 195, 198-199
Robertson, Rae, 129
Rodgers Organ Company, 157, 191, 193, 196-197
Rodgers, Richard, 92
Roessler, Ottilie. See Steinway, Ottilie Roessler
Rogers Drum, 157
Rogers, Earl, 80
Romann, Jack, 91, 108, 148
Roos, Alfred, 45, 47
Roos, George, 47
Roos, Regina. See Steinway, Regina
Roosevelt, Eleanor, xiii
Roosevelt, Pres. Franklin Delano, 97, 115-116
Roosevelt, Pres. Theodore, 78
Rosenthal, Moritz, 59-60
Rosenwald, Julius, 160
Rosenwald, William, 89, 160-161

Rothschild, Lord Nathaniel, 57
Royal Festival Hall (London), 109, 121, 207
Rubicam, Raymond, 85, 148
Rubin, David, 136, 142-145, 148, 179, 186, 199
Rubinstein, Anton, xi, xiv, 40-42, 65-66, 85
Rubinstein, Artur, xi, 89, 91-92, 103-104, 108, 126, 143, 148, 207
Rubinstein, Vera, 40
Rupp, Franz, 129

**S**
Samick Pianos, 100, 185, 206
Sandor, Gyorgy, 129
Scharlau, Barnum, 75
Schein, Harvey, 157, 163
Schimmel Pianos, 54
Schimmel, Wilhelm, 54
Schmitt Music Centers, 215
Schurz, Carl, 46, 76
Schwartz, Eric, 192-193
Scouten, Rex, 116
Selmer Company, x, xii, 217, 219, 222
Serkin, Rudolf, 92, 104, 143, 211, 212
Shearing, George, 107
Sherman Clay & Co., 79, 192-193
Smeterlin, Jan 129
Smith-Corona Typewriters, 97
Smithsonian Institute, 115
Sommer, Adolph, 51-52
Sondheim, Stephen, 107
Spellman, Cardinal, 97
Stanton, Edmund, 63
Steinert, Fred 54
Steinert, M. Company, 54-55, 115, 144, 153, 204
Steinert, Morris, 54
Steinway & Sons, x-xiv, 19-20, 23-25, 32, 38, 44, 48-49, 52, 54-57, 62, 68, 73, 75, 77-78, 80-81, 84, 86, 91-94, 98, 100, 102, 104-108, 110, 112, 114-115, 117, 128, 130, 136, 139-142, 146, 148-156, 160-168, 171, 173-183, 185-189, 191-197, 199, 201-202, 206-207, 210, 213, 217, 219, 222
    advertising, 40, 58-59, 80-81, 84-86, 112, 115-116, 123, 148-150, 179, 187, 208-210, 213
    age of pianos, 21
    art case pianos, 57-58, 79, 113, 116
    awards received, 31, 58-59, 116, 189
    centenary (1953), 128-130
    Civil War, impact of, 23
    cost of pianos, 91, 100, 114, 123, 148, 159, 219
    economic depressions, impact of, 73-74, 93, 110, 112-114, 117
    establishment of, 20
    factories: Fourth Avenue (Manhattan), 22, 32, 36, 38, 40, 51; Long Island City, xi, 30-31, 36-37, 47, 51, 60, 90, 100, 106, 111, 113-114, 119, 124, 130, 132, 138, 153, 155, 163-164, 167, 170, 172, 176-177, 179, 183-184, 186, 192, 199-201, 205, 221 *See also* Steinway-Hamburg
    grand piano, 30-31, 106, 110, 114
    innovations in piano design, 28-29, 31-32, 106
    Korean War recession, 130
    labor disputes, 38-39, 51-52
    London operations. *See* Steinway-London

quality of pianos, x, xii, 31, 50, 107, 136, 148, 169, 184-185, 197, 201
sale to CBS. *See* Chapter 8
sale to Birminghams. *See also* Chapter 9
sale to Selmer. *See* Selmer Company
Teflon, use of, 142, 145-147, 185
upright pianos, 32, 184
World War I, impact of, 113
World War II, impact of, 117, 119-122, 151
Steinway, Albert, 17, 23, 31, 38, 47, 75, 106
Steinway, Anna, 23
Steinway-Berlin, xiii, 78
Steinway, Billie. *See* Steinway, Willliam Richard
Steinway, C.F. Theodor, 17-19, 24, 25, 28-32, 44, 47, 49-51, 61-62, 77, 106-107, 110, 136, 150
Steinway, Charles, 18, 22-24, 61, 75
Steinway, Chales Frederick, 81-82, 84
Steinway, Charles Garland, 88, 141-142, 177
Steinway, Charles Herman, 51-53, 61-62, 64-65, 77-84, 96, 110, 113, 135, 192
Steinway, Daniel, 159
Steinway, Doretta, *See* Ziegler. Doretta Steinway
Steinway, Elizabeth (Ellie), 49, 69
Steinway, Elizabeth (Betty). See Chapin, Elizabeth (Betty)
Steinway, Florence, 82
Steinway Foundation, 210
Steinway, Frederick E. ("Fritz"), 126-127, 130, 137-138, 140-142
Steinway, Frederick Theodore, 61-62, 77, 84-90, 92-93, 98-99, 136

Steinway, George Augustus, 44-47, 49, 61, 77
Steinway Hall : Fourteenth Street, xiv, 39-43, 47, 63-64, 74, 85-86, 99; West 57th Street, 86-87, 90, 98, 105, 109, 111, 114, 120, 123, 125, 127, 138-139, 141, 143, 179-180, 193, 199; "The Basement", 90-92, 104-105, 143, 210-211
Steinway-Hamburg:
advertising, 187
establishment of, xii, 49
factory, xi-xiii, 49, 52-54, 62, 78, 86, 102, 106, 113, 120, 122, 131, 138, 146-147, 150, 153, 159, 164, 166, 172, 185, 219
operations of, 62, 113, 119, 122, 166, 182, 187, 201, 207-208
piano: Steinway Hamburg vs. Steinway New York, 136, 183-184, 186, 216
retail store, xiii, 78, 121, 211
World War II, impact of, 120-121
Steinway, Henry Engelhard, 15-20, 22-24, 32-33, 35, 53, 76, 107, 112, 127, 135, 209, 222; career in Germany, 16-18; childhood, 15; death of, 32; emigration to America, 18; marriage of, 17
Steinway, Heinrich Zacharias. *See* Steinweg, Heinrich Zacharias
Steinway, Henry Jr., 17, 19, 21-22, 24, 28, 35
Steinway, Henry (Harry), 127, 159, 172-173, 177-178, 180, 182, 188, 191-192
Steinway, Henry William Theodore, 62-63

Steinway, Henry Ziegler, xiv, 20-22, 89, 120, 126-128, 132, 133, 135-139, 142, 146, 148, 150-152, 154, 156-161, 164-165, 167-169, 171-180, 182, 187, 189, 191-194, 197, 214-215
Steinway, John Howland, 22, 32, 58, 100, 120, 126, 130, 132, 135-137, 146, 149, 153, 157, 162, 171-172, 179-180, 182, 189, 192-194, 209
Steinway, Josephine, 132-133
Steinway, Julia Cassebeer, 87-90, 98, 129, 137, 160
Steinway, Julia Thiemer, 17, 23, 47
Steinway-London: 65, 77, 104, 122, 164, 172, 189, 211 establishment of, xiii; operations of, 121, 166, 182, 2-7; world War II, 119, 121
Steinway, Lydia. *See* Cochrane, Lydia Steinway
Steinway, Marie (Mrs. William Richard Steinway), 94
Steinway, Marie Louise, 81-84
Steinway, Marie Mertens, 81-83
Steinway, Mary Castle (Cassie), 137
Steinway, Maud Emily Louise. *See* Paige, Maud Emily Louise Steinway
Steinway Musical Properties Inc., 193, 195-196, 197, 199
Steinway, Ottilie Roessler, 61
Steinway, Paula Theoda. *See* von Bernuth, Paula Theoda Steinway
Steinway, Polly, 135
Steinway, Regina Roos, 44-47, 49, 66
Steinway, Ruth Gardner Davis, 94, 97, 124-128, 133, 137, 161, 164
Steinway, Sarah (Sally) Shields, 88, 142
Steinway, Theodor. *See* Steinway, C.F,. Theodor
Steinway, Theodore Alexander ("Sascha"), 133

Steinway, Theodore Davis (Teed), 119, 126, 132-133, 137, 146, 157, 173, 177
Steinway, Theodore Edwin, 49, 61, 69, 77, 87, 93-98, 102, 105-106, 112, 117, 119, 120, 124-128, 130, 132-133, 135, 150, 160, 209
Steinway Village, xiii, 22, 32, 36-37,47, 53, 62
Steinway, Wilhelmina, *See* Vogel, Wilhelmina Steinway
Steinway, William, 17 19-25, 31-33, 35-49, 51-54, 57, 59-63, 66, 68-78, 80, 86-87, 92-94, 107, 110, 116, 135, 155, 160, 189, 213 awards received, 58-59, 81; blue laws views of, 71-73; charitable activities, 37, 74-75; childhood, 17-19; community affairs, involvement in, 35-36, 68, 72, 74-75; death of, 75; early employment in America, 19-20, 75; free silver, views of, 71, 73-74; impresario, role as, 41, 59, 65-68; labor disputes handling of, 23-24, 38-40, 51-52; Long Island-Manhattan tunnels, 53, 68-69; marriages to: (i) Regina Roos, 44-47; (ii) Elizabeth Ranft, 49, 69; North Beach, establishment of, 53-54; physical prowess, 35; politics, role in, 60, 75. *See also* Steinway Village.
Steinway, William Richard ("Uncle Billie"), 49, 61, 63, 69, 93-94, 96, 120, 123-124, 132, 151, 156
Steinway, William Theodore (Bill), 159, 172-174, 177-178, 180, 188, 191
Steinway, Heinrich Engelhard. *See* Steinway, Henry Engelhard.
Steinway & Hunters Point Railroad, 37, 53, 60

Steinweg, Heinrich Zacharias, 15
Stern, Isaac, 90
Stern, Louis, 44-45, 47
Stevens, Bruce, 195-199, 204, 210
Stone, James, 194
Story and Clark Piano Company, 168, 171, 173 181
Story, Hampton, 168
Strauss, Richard, 18, 89, 151
Stravinsky, Igor, 107
Strong, Mayor William L., 75-76
Sun Life Assurance, 218

**T**
Tanglewood Summer Music Festival, 115
Taylor, Arthur, 158, 174
Taylor, Josephine Seitz. *See* Steinway, Josephine
Tchaikovsky, Piotr Ilyich, 64
Teflon, use of. *See* Steinway & Sons
Thiemer, Juliana. *See* Steinway, Juliana Thiemer
Thomas, Theodore, 63, 70
Toscanini, Arturo, 89
Traubel, Helen, 107
Tretbar, Charles, 66
Truman, Pres. Harry 116-117
Truman, Margaret, 117, 132
Tucker, Richard, 107
Tureck, Rosalyn, 92, 109, 126, 176, 207-208
Turner, Ted, 191
Tweed, William "Boss", 36

**U**
Uninsky, Alexander, 129

**V**
Vanderbilt, Frederick, 57
Vietor, Frederick, 106, 109-111
Vogel, Albertina. *See* Ziegler, Albertina Vogel

Vogel, Theodore, 23-24
Vogel, Wilhelmina Steinway, 17, 21, 23, 44, 111
von Bernuth, Louis, 61, 94-95
von Bernuth, Meta, 95
von Bernuth, Paula Theeoda Steinway, 44-46, 49, 61, 94-96
von Bernuth, William Steinway, 95
von Bülow, Hans, 42-43, 65
von Helmholtz, Hermannn, 25
von Holwede, Arthur, 113

**W**
Wadsworth, Charles, 161
Wagner, Richard, xi, 18, 43, 85, 98, 129
Walsh, Frank, 167
Warkow, Stewart, 144
Watts, André, x, 92, 147, 197, 208, 213-214
Weber, Albert, 23, 43-44
Weber Piano Co., 23, 78, 80
Webster, Beveridge, 129
Wemple, Littlepaige, 171-172
White, F. Kingsland, 150
White House, xiii, 79, 115-116, 130 210
White, Stanford, 57
Wilking, Frank, 142
Wilking Music Company, 142
William Nunns & Company. *See* Nunns, William & Company
Williams, Roger, 92
Wilson, Sanford, 200-201
Wolfensohn, James, 144
Woodhull, Victoria, 40
Wornum, Albert, 32
Wulsin, Lucien, 55
Wurlitzer Company, The, 151, 188, 192
Wyeth, N.C., 85
Wyman Thomas, 179-181

## Y

Yamaha Corporation, x-xi, 54, 56, 80, 105, 131-132, 136, 147-148, 150, 180, 197, 213, 215, 217-218, 221
Yamaha piano, xii, 100, 108, 131, 140, 213, 216
Yamaha, Torakusu, 56, 105
Yeager, J. Michael, 203-206
Young, Brigham, 112
Young Chang Pianos, 185
Young, John Orr, 86
Young, Mahonri, 112
Young & Rubicam, 86

## Z

Ziegfield, Dr. Florence, 70
Ziegler, Albert, 112
Ziegler, Albertina Vogel, 111-112
Zielger, Doretta Steinway, 17, 21, 47, 61, 87, 106
Ziegler, Eleanor. *See* Lodge, Eleanor
Ziegler, Eleanor Theodora, 112
Ziegler, Frederick Jacob, 110, 112, 160
Ziegler, Henry L., 61, 106, 110-112, 114
Ziegler, Henry Steinway, 89, 110-111, 136, 156, 158, 160-161
Ziegler, Jacob, 47, 110
Ziegler, John, 110-111, 130, 160